A Half Century of Occupation

A Half Century of Occupation

Israel, Palestine, and the
World's Most Intractable Conflict

GERSHON SHAFIR

UNIVERSITY OF CALIFORNIA PRESS

University of California Press, one of the most
distinguished university presses in the United
States, enriches lives around the world by
advancing scholarship in the humanities, social
sciences, and natural sciences. Its activities are
supported by the UC Press Foundation and by
philanthropic contributions from individuals
and institutions. For more information, visit
www.ucpress.edu.

University of California Press
Oakland, California

© 2017 by Gershon Shafir

Library of Congress Cataloging-in-Publication Data

Names: Shafir, Gershon, author.
Title: A half century of occupation : Israel,
    Palestine, and the world's most intractable
    conflict / Gershon Shafir.
Description: Oakland, California : University of
    California Press, [2017] | Includes bibliographical
    references and index.
Identifiers: LCCN 2016046910 | ISBN 9780520293502
    (cloth : alk. paper) | ISBN 9780520966734 (eBook)
Subjects: LCSH: Arab-Israeli conflict—1993- —
    Peace. | Diplomatic negotiations in international
    disputes. | Security, International—Economic
    aspects—Israel. | Security, International—
    Economic aspects—Palestine. | Israel—Foreign
    relations—Palestine. | Palestine—Foreign
    relations—Israel.
Classification: LCC DS119.76 .S526 2017 |
    DDC 956.9405—dc23
LC record available at
    https://lccn.loc.gov/2016046910

25 24 23 22 21 20 19 18 17
10 9 8 7 6 5 4 3 2 1

To Anya, Zev, and Anyu

CONTENTS

ILLUSTRATIONS

AIPAC	American Israel Public Affairs Committee
ANC	African National Congress
BCM	Black Consciousness Movement
BDS	Boycott, Divest, Sanction
DOP	Declaration of Principles
HCJ	High Court of Justice
ICAHD	Israeli Committee against House Demolitions
ICJ	International Court of Justice
ICRC	International Committee of the Red Cross
IDF	Israeli Defense Forces
IHL	international humanitarian law
JA	Jewish Agency
JNF	Jewish National Fund
LSM	Labor Settlement Movement
MK	Umkhonto we Sizwe (Spear of the Nation)
NGO	nongovernmental organization
NP	National Party
OPT	Occupied Palestinian Territories

PAC   Pan African Congress
PCATI   Public Committee Against Torture in Israel
PLO   Palestinian Liberation Organization
PNA   Palestinian National Authority
UNCCP   United Nations Conciliation Commission for Palestine
UNHCR   United Nations High Commission for Refugees
UNRWA   United Nations Refugee Welfare Agency
UNSCOP   United Nations Special Committee on Palestine
WZO   World Zionist Organization

Introduction

In 1851, the British historian Sir Edward Creasy coined the term *decisive battle*, a battle that "may give an impulse which will sway the fortunes of successive generations of mankind."[1] The 1967 War was such a battle, and though Israelis commonly call it the Six-Day War while Arabs call it *al Naksa* (the setback), it is in fact one of thirteen wars fought (up to the writing of this book) by Israel and the Palestinians and their Arab neighbors—one battle in a long war.

After the 1948 War—the War of Independence for Israelis and *al Nakba* (the disaster) for Palestinians—the defeated Arab states identified the need to modernize their societies and militaries in advance of the next round of battles with Israel. Following the 1956 War, they highlighted the active military and imperialist intervention of the United Kingdom and France on behalf of Israel as the cause of their setbacks. The Arab side kept alive the expectation of a next and decisive round in which they could destroy Israel by pressing the claim that in a fair and square war they would prevail. The auspicious circumstances for the showdown seemed to have come together in the spring of 1967 as both revolutionary and moderate Arab regimes cooperated and amassed their troops, Egypt closed down the access to the Red Sea for Israeli shipping, and Israel was fighting alone. The Arab publics had the impression that the hour of decision was at hand and that Israel would finally be defeated. As summarized by the political scientist Ian Lustick, "The June War was fought amidst high-hopes bordering on exaltation in the

Arab world and real trepidation among ordinary Israelis. These emotions, the lopsided outcome of the war, and the absence of any direct outside involvement on Israel's side combined to make the Six-Day War a turning point in the Arab–Israeli conflict." [2]

At 6:30 pm (16:30 GMT) on June 10, 1967, the last gun fell silent. The war—lasting only six brief days—was over, but it had radically altered the dynamic of the Middle East. That evening Israel was in control of Egypt's massive Sinai Peninsula and the buffer zone of Syria's Golan Heights. Most significantly, with the seizure of the Gaza Strip from Egypt and the West Bank and East Jerusalem from Jordan, the 1967 War had now brought all of what was Mandatory Palestine under Israeli rule, while joining the nineteen-year-old state of Israel with the homeland of Jewish antiquity. It also brought together the Palestinian citizens of Israel and the Palestinians in the OPT, who were placed under Israeli military government. Linguistically, the transition was seamless, as Hebrew does not dedicate separate words to conquest and occupation, using the word *kibush* for both. In every other way, the changeover was and remains troubled.

The "War of the Seventh Day," as Israeli peace activist Uri Avneri was to call it in 1968, the war over setting the proper relationship between the pre- and post-1967 territories (and thereby between Israelis and Palestinians), had begun. The seventh day, however, has lasted a half century and has no end in sight. And during those fifty years, Avneri's war has been repeatedly transformed from a metaphor into a stone-throwing, stabbing, and shooting war. The war over the occupation, as part of a larger struggle to shape Israeli and Palestinian futures, is still being played out, incurring ever-deeper bitterness and greater losses that make a peaceful resolution more and more difficult to achieve. They have not foreclosed, however, the option of compromise, territorial partition, and a diplomatic resolution.

As the recognition set in that the destruction of Israel was an impossible goal, pan-Arab unity was shattered. Egypt and Syria launched the 1973 War not to dismantle Israel but to recover their own territories lost in the 1967 War, and there emerged clear signs of a turn to diplomatic solutions among Egyptian, Jordanian, and Palestinian elites. When Egypt signed the first Arab peace treaty with Israel in March 1979 in return for full Israeli withdrawal from the Sinai, it found itself shunned in the Arab world. In September 1993, Israel and the Palestinian Liberation Organization (PLO) signed a mutual recognition agreement in Oslo and launched a negotiated peace process. Israel soon afterward signed a peace accord with Jordan. Though the agreements with the two Arab neighboring states led only to a "cold peace" between the countries, they are still in effect today. In contrast, the over twenty-year-long negotiations between Israel and the PLO have yielded only limited results and collapsed in April 2014. Why is the path toward peaceful Israeli-Palestinian relations still blocked?

In this book, I offer three extended reflections on crucial aspects of the War of the Seventh Day that, taken together, help us unpack its dynamics and highlight its major turning points while also pondering its possible outcomes. I chose to structure the book not chronologically—which would have required of me to cover the terrain evenly but thinly—but rather as a set of three essays, each of which seeks to answer a distinct question. This organization allows me to highlight and explore in greater depth those aspects of the tangled web of the occupation that I consider unique and pivotal and to provide a carefully crafted response to each question by combining several perspectives. My three guiding questions are as follows.

ONE

What Is the Occupation?

My task in the first essay—to *describe* the occupation—is complicated by both the occupation's growing complexity and efforts to deny its very existence. The occupation of the West Bank, East Jerusalem, and Gaza (since 2005, from its outer perimeter) by Israeli armed forces remains a *legal category* and an *everyday experience* for the Palestinian populations of these territories, making them an occupied population. *Palestinian resistance,* an understandable desire to overthrow foreign occupation and gain self-determination, is as much a part of the occupation as the two components just listed. The fourth facet of the occupation—on top of the legal framework, the everyday experience of the occupied Palestinians, and their resistance—is the ongoing *colonization* of the OPT, the occupation's driving force and possibly its most distinct hallmark. Since each of these four facets provides a distinct perspective on the occupation, I will explore all of them in order, as well as their interaction, to understand how the occupation has become what it is.

The construction of settlements in the West Bank entails the separation, by law and by force, of the land itself from the people living on it. Beyond the Palestinians' defiance of the occupation, it is the Israeli settlement project—indeed, the desire to accommodate the latter in the face of the former—that accounts for the current motley and heterogeneous character of the occupation. Today, Israel's occupation is—above all—a geographical *mosaic* of distinct forms of domination. The complexity and repeated adjustments of the tools of occupation have helped the occupation authorities overcome crises and have played a key role in its persistence. But, as I will emphasize, these same tools and their repeated reengineering have also produced a patchwork of legal inconsistencies and competing interests that weaken the occupation's hold and leave it vulnerable to challenge.

TWO

Why Has This Occupation Lasted So Long?
My goal in the second essay is to provide a *historical overview* of the occupation from the perspective of the social sciences. Its focus is the confluence of factors that facilitate Israel's continued control of and tightening grip over the OPT, despite the noxious character of the occupation, Palestinian resistance, Israeli domestic dissent, and international opprobrium.

I will review the colonization in the OPT following the 1967 War and compare it to settler colonialism as Israel's state-building strategy prior to 1948. Continuities abound, including the use of old and still available institutions to support the occupation, as well as the prestige and resources settlers enjoy. The West Bank, however, though the site of the sacred geography of Jewish antiquity, is also the most densely inhabited area of Palestine. Consequently, the old practices and patterns of settlement have by and large proved ineffective there.

The reinvention of settlement required the rearticulation of customary nationalist aspirations in more radical—religious—terms, bringing about more radical forms of Palestinian legitimation and resistance in response. In this essay I highlight the vanguard role played by the religious nationalist communities of the respective societies—Gush Emunim (the Bloc of the Faithful) in Israel and Hamas among Palestinians—in providing, for Israelis, religious legitimation of settlement and of the opposition to territorial compromise and, for Palestinians, religious legitimation of attacks aimed at Jewish civilians within Israel. I also examine how each group has obstructed the diplomatic process that began in Oslo.

Yet neither Gush Emunim nor Hamas has been able to transform its respective society in its image, and both face considerable opposition from moderate parties ready to compromise with their counterparts. Each movement is also divided internally. Furthermore, Gush Emunim represents only a small segment of Israeli society, while Hamas is a true mass movement that has shown signs of pragmatism over the years, to the extent of considering a long-term truce with Israel. It remains unclear how effective Gush Emunim and Hamas would be in blocking a potential partition of Palestine into two states.

The Israeli occupation of the OPT is not just a two-sided or domestic issue. A great deal depends, as it always has in the Middle East, on international forces. I will conclude the essay with an analysis of the reasons for the absence of effective external countervailing forces. In fact, the two most important external factors, US foreign policy and international humanitarian law, instead of inhibiting the occupation, have enabled its continuation. As long as Israel is able to defy the United States and the international legal community, it will be able to move more settlers into the OPT and will have no incentive to negotiate the end of the occupation. However, US policy toward Israel—currently viewed as a "special relationship"—has undergone change over the years and remains open to new directions.

THREE

How Has the Occupation Transformed the Israeli-Palestinian Conflict?

In the third essay I will ask, *What now?* To start with, I will examine the tail end of the Israeli-Palestinian diplomatic effort—the 2008 Annapolis negotiations between Ehud Olmert and Mahmoud Abbas—since its terms will tell us how far the parties have managed to narrow their differences. Then I will tackle the "big question": Is Israeli colonization irreversible? Has the implantation of Israeli settlers closed off the possibility of the territorial partition of the West Bank and East Jerusalem, so that, as many now believe, the creation of one state for both Israelis and Palestinians has become the only nonviolent alternative to continued conflict?

Mine is not a philosophical discussion of the merits and demerits of these political outcomes, but rather a much more modestly conceived feasibility study from the perspective of the social sciences. I will offer analyses that evaluate the likelihood of the two- and one-state solutions.

As part of the first feasibility study, I will examine the percentage of land taken up by Israeli settlements and their layout, the demographic ratio of Israeli Jews to Palestinians in the OPT, the composition of the settler population and the rate of its growth, the settlements' contribution to Israeli security, and the settlers' economic ties to their places of residence. I will then calculate the number of settler families that would need to be moved and the extent of territorial exchange that would be required and feasible in return for the annexation of several settlement blocs to Israel, as well as the estimated cost of this option, as part of a mutually agreed-upon territorial partition.

The second feasibility study will assess both versions of the one-state solution: a binational state and the multinational civic polity of "one person, one vote." Binationalism was originally a Jewish idea of the Mandatory period that the Palestinians rejected, and I will ask what we can learn from its failure and will consider the likelihood of its success now that Palestinians have adopted it. I will then follow in the footsteps of scholars who have studied the conditions—from institutional architecture, to relative group sizes, to shared values and notions of justice—that potentially enable transitions from conflict to a stable multinational state. I will also inquire what we can learn for the Israel-Palestine case from contemporary sectarian and nationalist tensions and violent outbreaks in both the Middle East and Europe.

The conclusion of these feasibility studies is that a two-state resolution through territorial partition, though elusive, is not out of the question. At the same time, I suggest that while those who favor having Israelis and Palestinians share a single civil state have offered a lofty idea, they have not yet created, and very possibly cannot create, a credible outline of stages leading toward such a novel political entity. Palestinians and Israelis cannot be pacified though the invention of new institutions alone, nor can such institutions procure the mutual trust that would be needed for their construction in the first place.

I will conclude the essay with an overview of the just over ten-year-old Palestinian civil society movement Boycott, Divest, Sanction (BDS), which alarms and dismays Israeli governments. Since BDS was inspired by the antiapartheid movement of South Africa and the postapartheid society created to replace it, I will compare it to Nelson Mandela's African National Congress and Israel itself to South Africa to assess the usefulness of this model for the resolution of the Israeli-Palestinian conflict.

This brief overview of the questions I raise and my answers in each of the three essays highlights just how tragic the conflict has been and continues to be but also offers clues that the occupation, along with the colonization project that drives it, is riven with paradoxes, legal inconsistencies, and conflicting interests that weaken its structure. The religious vanguards of the two populations are not in control of their societies or unmovable in their commitment to continue the conflict until their demands are met in full. Finally, the territorial partition of Palestine still appears feasible at a price that would not be destructive of Israeli society or lead to an unviable Palestinian state. A fine-grained analysis reveals a measure of light among the dark clouds. The state of affairs at present and in the foreseeable future is tragic but not hopeless.

A fiftieth anniversary carries special significance in Judaism. It is a *jubilee*, a holy year following seven cycles of seven years. It is ushered in with a blow of the trumpet on Yom Kippur, and it imposes special obligations on the faithful. As laid down in Leviticus 25:10: "You shall make the fiftieth year holy, and proclaim liberty throughout the land to all its inhabitants [*lekol yoshveya*]. It shall be a jubilee to you; and each of you shall return to his own property, and each of you shall return to his family. That fiftieth year shall be a jubilee to you." The jubilee is the year in which social harmony is restored through the reinstatement of the status quo ante: in addition to the freeing of slaves and the return of indebted hereditary land to its owners or heirs, later rabbinical authorities required the cancellation of all monetary debts. The land was to lie fallow, but by God's special grace prior harvests would be plentiful, and the people would dwell in the land safely. Like all biblical texts, the Leviticus passage was given different interpretations and later refinements. It has been suggested, for example, that only Hebrew slaves were to be emancipated. But on this point the text is clear enough: all of the inhabitants of the land of Israel should be the beneficiaries of the jubilee year. The book of Leviticus does not exempt Jews from their jubilee year obligations toward non-Jewish inhabitants of the land.

Our times and experiences are remote from both the Hebrew Bible and the many generations of its interpreters and reinterpreters, but the restorative spirit of the jubilee remains as inspirational as ever. Tragically, most of those religious Zionists who seek to live by scriptural commandments as a living text are the first to ignore admonitions and commandments that inconveniently interfere with their devotion to colonizing the Palestinian lands occupied fifty years ago, and they continue ignoring the claims of Palestinian inhabitants to a measure of restorative justice. Secular Israeli Jews who carry out their own colonization plans—and enable and underwrite all forms of settlement, or ignore and deny its consequences—would benefit equally from deliberating their own role in light of this moral legacy. On the jubilee of the 1967 War and of the Israeli occupation of the West Bank, East Jerusalem, and Gaza, Leviticus provides an impetus to reconsider the path taken so that all the people of Israel/Palestine may dwell in the land safely.

What Is the Occupation?

Military occupation is a rare phenomenon in today's world. In recent US memory, Iraq was occupied, but the US military left in 2011, eight years after the invasion of Iraq. An ongoing, decades-long occupation is even rarer. We are, in short, not accustomed to the term and its practical and political significance. Its importance and the high stakes associated with its use are made amply clear by the Democratic Party's refusal to include the term in its 2016 presidential election platform when describing Israel's presence in the West Bank. The Republicans, realizing that they could not simply bypass the term, went even further in declaring, "We reject the false notion that Israel is an occupier."[1] Prime Minister Netanyahu and his government ministers have been particularly vociferous in their denunciations of the term. Not surprisingly, in a May 2016 survey of the Israeli Democracy Institute, as many as 72 percent of Jewish Israelis answered that Israel does not occupy the Palestinian territories outside the Green Line (Israel's pre-1967 boundary with the West Bank).[2] Apparently not satisfied, even with these results, the deputy minister of defense from the religious Zionist Jewish Home Party called on educators to teach their students that "there is no occupation."[3] I reject these clumsy attempts to define out of existence what we can plainly see.

My task in this essay is to unpack the term *occupation* by recovering the phenomenon's often-obscured features and highlighting the reasons for its persistence.

The occupation of the West Bank, East Jerusalem, and Gaza (since 2005 from its outer perimeter)—the Occupied Palestinian Territories (OPT)—by Israeli armed forces remains a *legal category* and an *everyday experience* for the Palestinian populations of these territories, making them an occupied population. Like other occupied peoples, the Palestinian population give the impression of obeying the Israeli military government while also avoiding compliance as much as possible. The denial of national freedom and the indignities of everyday life under occupation inevitably lead to *resistance*, which comes in many forms. Nonviolent forms of resistance allow more democratic organization, mobilize greater worldwide sympathy, and leave less of a legacy of fear and bitterness among their opponents than violent ones, especially when the violence does not discriminate between combatants and civilians. The First Intifada (1987–93), mostly nonviolent, the Second Intifada (2000–2005), in which violence was pervasive, and the *al-habbah al-sha'biyya* (the youth outburst; a series of violent confrontations characterized by the near-daily individual knife attacks that started in September 2015) have themselves shaped the occupation. It was resistance that initially led to the diplomatic process, the Oslo negotiations between Israel and Palestinian leadership in 1993. Resistance to occupation, therefore, is an integral and unavoidable part of the occupation.

The fourth facet of the occupation, added to the legal framework, the everyday experience of the occupied Palestinians, and their resistance, is the ongoing *colonization* of the OPT, the occupation's driving force and possibly its most distinct hallmark. Examination of each of these four facets provides a distinct perspective on the occupation. The interaction of these four aspects makes the occupation what it is and affords us as complete a picture as possible of its characteristics.

Israel's post–1967 dilemma was captured as soon as the hostilities were over in a folksy metaphor provided by Prime Minister Levi Eshkol. The trouble, he suggested was that "we won the war and received a nice dowry of territory, but the dowry came with a bride whom we don't like": that is, Israel wanted the just-conquered territory but without its sizable Palestinian population.[4] Eshkol's attempted quip makes abundantly clear that the territory and its population can be separated only in wishful thinking: not only is the land taken in 1967 occupied, but so is the population residing on it. Palestinians in the West Bank, Gaza, and East Jerusalem (as well as the Druze on the Golan) are an occupied people.

Israel was then, and is now, caught on the horns of the classic colonial dilemma: the extension of its sovereignty to the OPT would confer citizenship on, or at least provide the choice of citizenship to, its Palestinian population and thus would diminish the Jewish majority of Israel, but withdrawal would mark the abandonment of its territorial aspirations. This conundrum has landed all Israeli governments to date in an endless interregnum that encourages a focus on land while discounting the land's population. Israeli governments have dealt with this challenge by manipulating the international legal framework and, in general, miring the country in ever-deeper denial of the causes for the untenable situation wrought by continued occupation and the resistance it generates.

We commonly think of denial as a defense mechanism used to shield our inner selves from painful knowledge. In her massive study of Ottoman and Turkish approaches toward centuries of violence aimed at Armenians and the ultimate genocide committed against them, Fatma Müge Göçek distinguishes three components of denial: (1) silence—censoring oneself; (2) secrecy—concealing information from others; and (3) subversion—corrupting the truth.[5] "Denial," as observed by Eva Illouz, "is . . . not a lack of knowledge, but a complex form of knowledge." A measure of deliberateness lurks at the bottom of every denial, whether one denies the health consequences of smoking or the psychological consequences of sexual abuse. What we choose not to recognize remains an open secret (a combination of silence and secrecy). Living with such open secrets promotes numbness and

What Is the Occupation?

indifference among the bystanders and, simultaneously, avoidance of witnesses and human rights organizations—"the eyes that see."[6]

There is an even deeper layer to denial—*denialism*, the subversion of truth. Mark Hoofnagle, author of the environmentalist Denialism Blog, explains that denialism is a system of employing "rhetorical tactics to give the appearance of argument or legitimate debate, when in actuality there is none,"[7] in an attempt to support a viewpoint against overwhelming evidence to the contrary. The practitioners of denialism, including climate change and Holocaust deniers, go beyond individual denial, fabricating, to use Illouz's term, a "pact of ignorance." Denialism is both more deliberate and collective than mere denial and, consequently, fosters a politics of denial. It expresses not just an inability but a refusal to recognize the responsibility for causal chains of actions. The practice of denialism frequently displaces guilt from the perpetrators of wrongdoing onto the victims.

Occupations are riven by many smaller and bigger denials but ultimately they are the story of a people denied. Keeping a people under occupation means subjecting them to rule by foreigners and denying them political freedom and free expression of national identity. Nowhere is this clearer than in the unique manipulation and combination of the three types of legal protection that are available to occupied Palestinians in today's world. These are citizenship, human rights, and humanitarianism, none of which is fully available in the OPT.

In nation-states, people access rights through citizenship. Citizenship—civil, political, social, and cultural—offers the most unassailable protection available because it is both defined as a right and granted by a state, the only framework with effective enforcement capabilities. A second layer of protection in the post–Second World War era is human rights. Many human rights overlap with, though they are not fully identical to, citizenship rights. While citizenship rights are anchored in political membership, human rights are bestowed on people, not by virtue of membership in a state but because of their humanity. Human rights remain a weaker branch of the international legal order. Human rights are more fragile than citizenship rights, lack a political dimension, and have a more ambiguous and disputed scope. Notwithstanding their global reach, the practical enforcement of human rights is fragmented. Human rights abuses are monitored by NGOs and the UN (and its relevant councils), bodies that have only reporting authority, not the power to enforce. Human rights are significant because they apply to and are invoked by populations who cannot call on citizenship to claim rights and, consequently, need an alternative regime of rights.

Finally, there is a third layer, not of rights, but of humanitarian protections. This layer's most detailed component is international humanitarian law (IHL), also referred to as the law of armed conflict, particularly its subcategory of the law of belligerent occupation. IHL is a testament to humanitarian reformers' good intentions in the face of humanity's failure to abolish war. Humanitarian protections remain an expression of a limited ambition to make war less terrible once hostilities have begun. Under IHL, belligerent occupation is a temporary status of suspended sovereignty, which requires the occupying force to ensure the welfare of the occupied population while permitting steps to ensure the security of its own forces. There are two central documents of IHL: the Hague Regulation of 1907 and the 1949 Geneva Conventions relative to the Protection of Civilian Persons in Times of War (in particular the Fourth Convention, which regulates occupations). Compliance with IHL is monitored by the rapporteurs of international organizations: the UN and its Human Rights Council, the International Committee of the Red Cross (ICRC), and the International Court of Justice (ICJ). None of these agencies possesses enforcement capabilities.

As part of my analysis of the legal side of the occupation, I will examine all three layers of rights and protections in Sections I to III of this essay. I will devote most of my attention to IHL because it is the controlling legal authority in the OPT. In Sections IV through VI, I will survey the everyday experi-

What Is the Occupation?

ence of life of Palestinian under occupation, with particular attention to the most prevalent and intrusive forms of control in the Israeli occupation tool kit. In Sections VII and VIII, I will move on to consider Palestinian resistance to the occupation and, in particular, the First Intifada and the diplomatic process it launched, as well as the Second Intifada and the changes in the mechanisms of occupation instituted in response. Sections VIII through X will include a detailed examination of the colonization project, demonstrating its many and sometimes conflicting aspects across different geographical territories and different populations, and exploring the manifold mechanisms of land seizure and the widespread illegality that upholds the transfer of land into the hands of the Israeli government and from it to settlers. Section XI will bring together the arguments and observations of the previous sections.

I

While most Palestinian became refugees during the 1948 War—the War of Independence to Israelis and the Nakba (catastrophe) to Palestinians—about 125,000 were able to remain in Israel and another 35,000 were added as part of a territorial arrangement with Jordan. They received Israeli citizenship rights as individuals—though these remain significantly less robust than those of their Jewish counterparts. In contrast, Palestinians of Gaza and the West Bank who came under Israeli occupation in the wake of the 1967 War do not have citizenship rights. Citizenship was were never made available to them. Of course extending Israeli citizenship to occupied Palestinians cannot be viewed only as a matter of Israeli generosity, an expression of second thoughts about the feasibility of a state founded on *jus sanguinis,* or descent through blood lineage. It must be equally examined from the perspective of its potential recipients. A more general question, as to whether occupiers can enhance the liberty of people they have conquered, casts an even darker shadow on this query. Israel has not tested this proposition even in the few cases in which it was willing to provide rights to residents in the territories occupied in 1967, since these rights always fell short of citizenship.

In three cases Israel has extended rights that resemble but do not amount to full citizenship. Under prime ministers Golda Meir and Shimon Peres, Israel permitted Palestinians in the West Bank to conduct municipal elections. In 1972, elections were held under the constraining Jordanian franchise, but in 1976 Israel enfranchised women and tripled the electoral roster. The first local elections returned the traditional elites, but in 1976 PLO-sponsored nationalist candidates took power. The golem had risen on its master: the mayors of Nablus, Hebron, and the other towns led protests and demonstrations and won several concessions. Subsequently, they banded together under a National Guidance Committee and expanded their demands. By the early 1980s, Israel had deported several mayors and dismissed the rest, replacing them with military officers.[8] Clearly, the experiment of placing democracy in the service of the occupation had failed, as local empowerment was overshadowed by dissatisfaction with continued national disenfranchisement. Democratization from above was not an effective option for a long-term occupying regime.

Two zones of the occupied territories—the Golan Heights and East Jerusalem—were annexed by Israel and potentially could have been made the sites of Israeli citizenship as a means of eliciting loyalty from their residents. But their residents—the roughly 20,000 Druze and 66,000 Palestinian residents of East Jerusalem and villages annexed to it (a number that by 2015 had risen to 300,200)—were not given automatic citizenship. After all, Israel did not wish to increase the size of its Palestinian Arab population. Rather, it extended to these non-Jewish populations only the status of permanent residence. Palestinian permanent residents are eligible to participate in Jerusalem's municipal elections as voters and candidates, though very few choose to exercise this right because it could amount to legitimizing Israel's occupation and the annexation of their villages and neighborhoods. The Pales-

What Is the Occupation?

tinians of East Jerusalem and the Druze of the Golan can convert their permanent resident status into citizenship—in a process that takes about two years—upon the fulfillment of several conditions: (1) they cannot be citizens of another country, (2) they must have a working knowledge of Hebrew, and (3) they must be willing to take an oath of allegiance to the state of Israel. Most do not wish to travel this route, and only about 10 percent of East Jerusalem Palestinians or Golan Druze have chosen to do so. In these cases, their most common justification for acquiring citizenship is to avoid the possibility of having their reentry refused.

Ironically, by making only permanent residency status available to Palestinians, the invader furnished the erstwhile residents with rights commonly provided to immigrants. But this irony had tragic consequences for Palestinian permanent residents. Palestinians living in Jerusalem, who possess only a locally valid "Jerusalem residence," are in danger of losing their legal right to reside in their home city if they move out of town, for example, to marry someone from another West Bank town or to study abroad for a higher degree. Permanent Jerusalem residents must be able to bring documentary evidence from their employer, school, or health care provider that their "center of life" remains Jerusalem. Between 1967 and 2015, 14,416 Palestinians from East Jerusalem had their residency revoked, and even today approximately another 25,000 Palestinians who have never been able to get residency in the first place because they cannot prove that Jerusalem is the material center of their life reside in their birth city illegally. Though East Jerusalem's Palestinian villages and neighborhoods fall under Israeli jurisdiction, most of their residents have in effect been neglected, receiving only a fraction of the municipal services enjoyed by their Jewish neighbors. The residents of Kfar 'Aqab, Shu'afat, and part of the Qalandia refugee camps fared even worse when the Separation Wall disconnected them from East Jerusalem, leaving them to languish in a no-man's-land without services or police protection. In stark contrast to the Palestinians' situation, Jewish residents of East and West Jerusalem are citizens of Israel and are the beneficiaries of the full range of municipal services; they would not lose their ability to return to and live in Jerusalem if they switched their "center of life" temporarily elsewhere. This disparity in legal rights is a direct reflection of the 1970s demographic plan to limit the percentage of Arabs within the municipal boundaries of unified Jerusalem to 28.8 percent.[9] Even though by 2015 this percentage had risen to 36.8 percent, there has been no attempt to revisit their legal situation with the intent to reduce tensions in the city.[10]

Israel created an irregular and arbitrary legal regime in the Syrian Golan Heights and East Jerusalem, the two territories it annexed. It placed these areas under Israeli sovereignty without extending citizenship to their inhabitants. Residents instead received a status that is inferior to citizenship. Even this limited option does not exist for the rest of the occupied Palestinians (in the West Bank and Gaza). Their status in the eyes of the Israeli state is forever temporary. All Israel desires of Palestinians is acquiescence to the occupation; in the opinion of the late Israeli sociologist Baruch Kimmerling, Israel displays virtually no ambition to create a common identity or even, at a minimum, a civic value system that would legitimize its presence. In the absence of citizenship, Palestinians in the OPT are a superfluous people, orphans of the international order, whose denial of political rights leaves them in legal limbo.[11]

II

How effective and deep are Palestinians' human rights under Israeli occupation? Rulings of the Israeli Supreme Court sitting as a court of first instance, that is, a High Court of Justice (HCJ), offer us a window into this subject.

I will start my examination with two judgments rendered by the HCJ in 2002. The first concerns an order issued by the West Bank military commander in April 2002 during Operation Defensive Shield. This military action involved the temporary reoccupation of West Bank cities in response to weeks of the worst loss of Israeli civilian lives within the Green Line in the Second Intifada. During the operation the military arrested around six thousand Palestinian suspects and, given the difficulty of processing such large numbers, ordered that they might be detained for up to eighteen days without being interrogated, meeting legal counsel, or appearing before a military judge. The court struck down the order, arguing that arresting people who were not suspects "just for the purpose of an investigation" violated the balance between security needs and human rights.[12] Significantly, this restraining ruling was issued at the height of the intifada. Yet it was fairly narrowly focused on strengthening procedural constraints on the military, and especially ensuring access to legal counsel and the courts.

This decision, however, represents more of an exception than the rule. An analysis of the HCJ's rulings on petitions by Palestinian residents of the OPT by legal scholar David Kretzmer makes abundantly clear that the duty to uphold human rights "has more often been part of the Court's rhetoric than of its actual decision-making."[13] I find it particularly telling that in spite of intermittent judicial decisions to uphold a measure of human rights, the military occupation is, overall, a "carceral enterprise." This term was coined by Lisa Hajjar, who studied the military court system in the OPT. Within the OPT, the percentage of incarcerated Palestinians is high by any measure. During the 1980s, an average of 4,500 Palestinians were in custody in any given day; meanwhile, during the First Intifada, 20,000 to 25,000 Palestinians were arrested per year, producing the highest per capita incarceration rate in the world. In the course of the occupation, according to Uri Savir (general manager of the Israeli Ministry of Foreign Affairs and a negotiator of the Oslo Declaration of Principles), "Almost every third Palestinian in the territories had at some time or another been imprisoned or detained."[14]

A second HCJ ruling that focused explicitly on the question of competing legal protections was the Ajuri case. The ruling, written by Chief Justice Aharon Barak, rejected the appeals of three West Bank residents against the area's military commander, who had ordered them to be relocated to Gaza for two years. The decision was based on Article 78 of the Fourth Geneva Convention, which allows the occupying power to move someone from his or her residence if it deems this necessary for security reasons. An order of the military commander under this article, the court concluded, "does not constitute a violation of human rights." By the doctrine of *lex specialis*, according to which law governing a specific subject overrides law governing general matters, articles of IHL that cover specifics are to be prioritized over human rights even if they conflict with more general articles of the convention. It is a matter of principle according to the HCJ that "the extent of permitted restrictions on human rights is determined . . . by humanitarian law contained in the law concerning armed conflict."[15] The most sweeping Israeli interpretation of this perspective, offered by Yoram Dinstein, the former dean of Tel Aviv Law School, is that "the special law of belligerent occupation trumps the general law of human rights."[16] Palestinians of the OPT, consequently, enjoy only limited rights under international human rights conventions, since being occupied takes precedence over their humanity.

The Israeli position on the applicability of human rights in the OPT is summed up in a 2004 report of the UN general secretary as follows:

> Israel denies that the International Covenant on Civil and Political Rights and the International Covenant on Economic, Social and Cultural Rights, both of which it has signed, are applicable to the occupied Palestinian territory. It asserts that humanitarian law is the protection granted in a conflict situation such as the one in the West Bank and Gaza Strip, whereas human rights treaties were intended for the protection of citizens from their own Government in times of peace.[17]

The advisory opinion of the Hague ICJ regarding the Israeli Separation Wall asserts, in contrast, that human rights and humanitarian law should be in concord. In line with a growing corpus of international jurisprudence, the ICJ sees the two branches of international law as converging. Consequently, in 1998 it reached the conclusion that human rights conventions remain in effect in times of war, even when a state exercises its jurisdiction on foreign territory, and that human rights should be concurrently available alongside IHL. Given Israel's effective military control of the OPT, its long duration, and its "ambiguous attitude towards their future status," human rights conventions apply to the OPT's population.[18] Israel's position on the limited applicability of human rights in the OPT is not shared by international jurists or courts.

Even if Israel wanted to, it would have been hampered in administering Palestinian human rights effectively. Since occupation is a function of conflict, Kretzmer observed, domestic courts cannot maintain a position of evenhandedness when adjudicating disputes between Israel's military authorities and the residents of the OPT.[19] Deference to the military government extends from the military courts in the OPT all the way to the Supreme Court in Jerusalem. Though military judges seek to uphold the ideal of judicial impartiality, they are cognizant of their role within the larger military system as one of "restoring order by punishing those who resist."[20] Even during the tenure of Chief Justice Barak—who was appointed to his post on the heels of the Knesset's adoption of the Human Dignity and Freedom Law (the closest thing Israel has to a Bill of Rights) and who took on a uniquely activist role—the affirmation of human rights was "generally conspicuous by its absence" in the rulings that touched on the OPT. The HCJ stated that, while applying IHL, it would adopt "the interpretation that is the least invasive of state sovereignty."[21] When Peace Now—an Israel mass movement that promotes a two-state solution—challenged the legality of Israel's settlement policy in 1991, the HCJ held no hearings on the merits of the case and rejected the appeal on the grounds that it was not justiciable.[22]

The HCJ appears to have taken an active interest in applying human rights considerations to only three areas: (1) the occasional, but inconsistent, balancing of security considerations and human rights, (2) procedural matters, and (3) the protection of private Palestinian property. The result is a legal interregnum that reduces legal constraints to the minimum that the legal and executive branches can agree upon. Human rights remain an abridged promise in the OPT, their application limited by deference to the military government and state sovereignty.

III

I turn now to the controlling international legal framework in the OPT—international humanitarian law. While occupied Palestinians possess no citizenship rights and only vestiges of human rights, IHL provides the best, and frequently the only, protection they enjoy. Though the law of belligerent occupation has a long history and is the best-codified part of humanitarianism (another area is refugee protection), Israel adopted from early on a mixed—in fact, contradictory—attitude to its obligations to the occupied Palestinian residents as mandated by IHL. A telegram sent by the Ministry of Foreign Affairs in March 1968 to Yitzhak Rabin, then ambassador in Washington, explained that "explicit recognition on our part of the applicability of the Geneva Conventions would highlight serious problems under the convention in regard to house demolitions, expulsions, settlement, and more." [23] Instead of using the term *occupied territories*, Michael Comay, the foreign minister's policy adviser, recommended the expression *territories under Israeli control* and later *administered territories*, the term that was ultimately adopted by Israel under its Labor Party government. But unlike great powers that violate international norms unreservedly and use their Security Council veto to bend the international community to their will, Israel has always paid attention to appearances and sought to maintain a meticulous cover of legality. Notwithstanding the list of violations already enumerated in the telegram, the policy put forth was "to try to prevent clear violations of the Geneva Conventions without getting into the question of the conventions' applicability." [24]

I suggest that it is time to replace the Israeli assertion of being "the only democracy in the Middle East" with the claim of being the "most legalistic country in the Middle East." This is not particularly surprising. After all, the Yishuv (the Jewish community in Mandatory Palestine) has been the long-term beneficiary of international legal bodies and frameworks. From the League of Nations' incorporation of the Balfour Declaration into the British Mandate for Palestine, through the UN General Assembly's November 1947 resolution to partition Mandatory Palestine into Jewish and Arab states, to the rejection of claims of Israeli aggression in Security Council Resolution 242 (which concluded the 1967 War), it has been a favored party and wishes to remain so in the future.

Israel's legal doctrine with regard to the OPT is a three-article framework. I shall call it the Shamgar Doctrine, after the government's legal counsel (*yoetz mishpati*) Meir Shamgar, who put it into effect in the years immediately following the 1967 War.[25] It is an elaborate form of legal denialism. Its first plank is that Israeli control of the OPT territories does not constitute an occupation because what became the OPT passed from British Mandatory rule to Egypt and Jordan when they seized control during the 1948 Arab-Israeli War. Egypt and Jordan, it is argued, did not have bona fide sovereignty over these areas before Israel conquered them, so those countries should themselves be considered occupiers and cannot be construed as countries whose sovereign rights deserve protection as High Contracting Parties to the Geneva Conventions. Gaza and the West Bank, by this interpretation, are not occupied but "disputed" territories. Israel never called the West Bank an occupied territory but an "administered territory," until even that designation was replaced by the biblical geographical names of Judea and Samaria.

The audacity of this claim is breathtaking on two levels. The 1967 War completed what had begun in the 1948 War. In the 1948 War, the land designated by the UN partition resolution for the Arab State in Palestine was divided between three parties: Jordan (with the largest chunk), Israel (with a midsized portion), and Egypt (with the smallest share). Following the war, Israel annexed the territories it conquered and would have been aghast at the suggestion that the Galilee, originally allocated to the Arab State, was not under Israeli sovereignty. In 1967, Israel became the sole occupier of the whole of Palestine by conquering the rest from the two countries with which it had shared the project of dismembering Palestine. Even so, according to the Shamgar Doctrine, the Fourth Geneva Convention is inapplicable to the OPT because the Egyptian conquest of Gaza and the Jordanian annexation of the West Bank in April 1950 should not be recognized.

On top of arguing that what is good for the goose is not good for the gander, Israel put forward another circular argument. The second article of the Shamgar Doctrine holds that only sovereign states, and not stateless people, have ownership of their land. The UN General Assembly recognized the Arabs of Palestine as a nation in 1947, but when they failed to create their state in 1948—a rejection from which Israel benefited territorially—Shamgar held that Palestinians should no longer be able to do so. From 1948 on, Palestinians were to remain a stateless people who therefore could not be a party to the Geneva Conventions. The Shamgar Doctrine writes the Palestinian people out of the history of Palestine.

Though these articles are clear cases of special pleading, they also pose a broad challenge to the international legal framework put in place following the Second World War. The aspects of the new normative order that are relevant to our discussion are spelled out in Eyal Benvenisti's authoritative *The International Law of Occupation:* "Over the years the changing attitudes about sovereignty and about entitlement to sovereignty also modified the law on occupation, as the principles of self-determination, democracy, and human rights pierced the veil of national sovereignty." [26] The Fourth Geneva Convention was one of three foundational legal documents adopted over a period of nine months in 1948-49. The other two were the Convention on the Prevention and Punishment of the Crime of Genocide and the Universal Declaration of Human Rights. These documents cannot be easily separated from one another. In particular, a Jewish-majority state born out of the ashes of the Holocaust and the Second World War is ill-placed to reject the legal legacies of that war that were intended to prevent the repetition of its horrors. Israel's claim that the West Bank, East Jerusalem, and Gaza are not occupied, consequently, ignores the clear trend of international law to affirm the rights of peoples and individuals with growing vigor.

The third article of the Shamgar Doctrine is that even though Israel holds that the Convention is not binding on the state, it agreed to voluntarily abide by what it views as the Convention's "humanitarian provisions." However, the ICRC holds that *all* of the Convention's provisions are humanitarian. While tugs-of-war between legal interpretations (particularly in the area of international law) are common, what singles out the Shamgar Doctrine is not just the lopsided nature of the disagreement—pitting one country against the rest of the world—but what it reveals to us about the only context in which the Israeli position makes sense. Israel's fixation with land and concomitant denial of the rights of the people residing on it freeze history at the moment before the successful post–Second World War decolonization movement that led to the tidal wave of independence in Asia and Africa. Rewinding history to the era of the old imperial and colonial regimes denies both self-determination and human rights to the Palestinians, leaving in place only one remaining set of protections, humanitarianism. The Shamgar Doctrine places Israel on the opposite side of the principles of democracy and self-determination, as well as of human rights and international humanitarian law conventions, and on the same side as colonialism and settler colonialism. The Shamgar Doctrine is a throwback, colonialism under a new name.

Relevant international organizations, such as the UN, the ICRC, and the ICJ, as well as all states, view Israel as a belligerent occupier of the part of Palestine it conquered in the 1967 War. The ICJ, for example, concluded that regardless of the prior status of a territory that, through war, has changed hands between two High Contracting Parties to the Geneva Convention, it falls under the Geneva Convention's purview. In particular, the Israeli rejection of Article 49 of the Fourth Geneva Convention is frowned upon. This article reads, "Individual or mass forcible transfers, as well as deportations of protected persons from occupied territory to the territory of the Occupying Power or to that of any other country, occupied or not, are prohibited, regardless of their motive." The Israeli interpretation is that this clause, adopted in reaction to Nazi Germany's population transfer policies, does not apply in the OPT, since unlike Nazi Germany during World War II Israel does not compel its population to settle. Consequently, colonization by Israeli citizens on occupied land is legitimate. By this upside-down logic, the Geneva Convention would be protecting the occupying power and not the occupied population.

Furthermore, as much as Article 49 might be a reaction to Second World War practices, it lays down a general principle: it prohibits the expansion of a state's sovereign territory through the settlement of its population in the territory of another state with the intention of annexing it. Article 49 puts an end to settler colonialism. Many countries were formed by colonization, and in this respect Israel is not different from Australia, Argentina, the United States, or South Africa (more on this topic in the second essay). What makes Israel unique is that it is a belated, nineteenth-century settler colony and even more that it carries on the colonization by which it was formed into the late twentieth and early twenty-first centuries. The continuation of the practice of colonization is the main, though not the single, reason that makes the clash between Israelis and Palestinians the world's most intransigent conflict.

Unlike the government, the Israeli judicial system recognizes the state's obligations under IHL. However, the Israeli legislative and executive branches at different times accept, reject, or simply ignore the applicability of IHL. Shortly after the 1967 War, the HCJ decided that it would review peti-

tions from the OPT, and over the years it has come to adjudicate these petitions on the basis of Israeli administrative law, the British Defense Emergency Regulations of 1945, and IHL. The HCJ accepts the applicability of the
Hague Regulation as international customary law, a standing it denies to the
Fourth Geneva Convention. And while rejecting the Geneva Convention as a
whole, the HCJ applies the Convention selectively. Significantly, the HCJ
views the Palestinian residents of the OPT as "protected persons," as is
required by both the Hague and Geneva laws.

Where citizenship is absent and human rights are few, humanitarianism
will matter, but how much? Conversely, what happens when most humanitarian protections are lost as well? I suggest that two tests provide some support for the conclusion that humanitarian protections in the OPT remain the
strongest strand of legal protection and may make a difference (mostly *in*
extremis). The first is the "expulsion test," and the second the "shadow of the
court" test.

One widely shared opinion voiced, among others, by Saree Makdisi in
his *Palestine Inside Out* is that the ultimate goal of the Israeli occupation is to
precipitate major demographic shifts, possibly culminating in the expulsion
of occupied Palestinians to give Israel undisputed control of the territory it
wishes to acquire.[27] In contrast, scholars who approach the occupation from
a legal perspective make the difficult but necessary distinction between the
harshness of military occupation, which, though affording no input from
the occupied population into its institutions and practices, enjoys a legal
basis for its rule, and the even harsher reality of domination by brute force
alone. As Hajjar reasons, "Because the Israeli state has committed itself to
legality . . . , it has opened itself to being judged and criticized by standards
of law." [28]

Recycling evocative terms used in very different contexts, the scholar of
international relations Jim Ron holds that as long as Palestinians live under
Israeli occupation in what he calls a "ghetto," they are protected under

Israel's generalized human rights and other international commitments. Following his argument, Palestinians and Arabs of bordering enemy states who live on the margins or outside Israeli occupation, on the "frontier"—for example, in southern Lebanon—lose most of their humanitarian protections and become potential subjects of massive destruction, displacement, and expulsion.[29] Israel's "disengagement" from Gaza in 2005—the withdrawal of the Israeli army and the dismantlement of all Israeli settlements there—is a case in point. The withdrawal transformed Gaza from a ghetto into a "frontier," and the three destructive wars between Israel and Hamas (in 2008–9, 2102, and 2014) hit Gaza particularly hard, leaving in their wake highly disproportionate casualty ratios between the two sides and a particularly high percentage of Palestinian civilian casualties. The distinction between frontier and ghetto might provide limited comfort for those living under occupation, but Hajjar and Ron remind us that even when the rule of law is deficient we should not ignore altogether the role of the law as a shield.

In addition, what Kretzmer called "settlements in the Court's shadow,"[30] namely out-of-court settlements of disputes on Palestinian rights, show higher success of Palestinian petitioners than actual decisions do and thus suggest that the court's restraining influence can be greater than we could glean from its rulings. The former prime minister and minister of defense Yitzhak Rabin famously justified the signing of the Oslo DOP by arguing that the protocol's transfer of powers to Arafat meant he now had a partner who would "deal with Gaza without the problems of the High Court of Justice, without the problems of B'Tselem [the Israeli Information Center for Human Rights in the Occupied Territories], and without the problems of all kinds of sensitive souls."[31] It is not particularly difficult to find examples of the court's restraining influence both in its rulings and in their anticipation. The Israeli decision to legalize "moderate physical pressure" (or "torture lite"; for a detailed discussion see Section V) and the subsequent HCJ ruling to abolish it took place, by happenstance, on

the eves of the First and Second Intifadas, respectively. During the First Intifada, though resistance was only non- or semiviolent, sixteen Palestinians
were reported to have died from punitive beatings at the time of or shortly
after arrest by Israeli forces; at least eight others died in detention centers.
During the Second Intifada, in spite of its abundant violence, no Palestinian
detainees died. Shortly after the court's reversal of the policy of "torture
lite," forty-three legislators proposed a law permitting the use of "physical
pressure" against terror suspects, but it never passed the Knesset. Even
against the backdrop of the waves of suicide bombings against Israeli civilians, the HCJ's recent decision and the attorney general's legal opinion for its
implementation had a restraining impact.[32]

Rulings of the HCJ that limit the powers of the military and government
invariably lead to calls by members of Prime Minister Netanyahu's Likud
Party and the religious Zionist Jewish Home Party to constrain the HCJ's
authority, as well as to institutional reforms that would allow the politicization of the choice of its new members. The attempts to cut back on the court's
authority demonstrate that the shadow of the court is real, the only remaining legacy of the so-called "enlightened occupation" period (see Section IV
of this essay). At the same time, attempts to curtail the court's authority
confirm that legal autonomy is becoming endangered the longer the occupation continues, and we cannot rule out the possibility of the collapse of judicial review even if the appearance of legalism is unlikely to disappear. Two
chief justices, Dorit Beinish in 2011 and Miriam Naor in 2015, have expressed
apprehensions about the repeated efforts of Likud and Jewish Home Party
leaders to reduce the authority of Israel's legal system over an ever-growing
range of issues.[33] A hobbled court will be even less willing to apply the protections of IHL to the occupied Palestinian population. We need to keep
reexamining whether the court's shadow survives.

The occupation from the legal perspective, then, is created by twisting
together different strands of legal rights and protections: (1) citizenship

manqué for Palestinians of East Jerusalem and the Druze of the Golan Heights, (2) human rights that are available (in a limited edition) to all Palestinians in procedural and concrete matters but are never codified as principle, and, the rest of the time, (3) humanitarian protections and the vestiges of humanitarianism. This legal ambiguity is not only an essential aspect of Israel's continued occupation but a *necessary precondition* for the occupation. Indeed, Israel must allow for the applicability of the Hague Regulation and the Fourth Geneva Convention in practice because IHL provides the only available international legitimacy to continued Israeli military presence across the Green Line. As much as Israeli governments champion occupation denialism, they remain dependent on the continued legal definition of the West Bank as occupied territory.

I V

Occupation is an international legal concept and is commonly treated as such. It is also an everyday Palestinian experience. I now turn from the legal perspective to an examination of how the occupier's obligation to protect the occupied population has been put into effect, as well as used to benefit the occupiers, and how it is experienced from the perspective of those who are occupied.

A half-century-long occupation has its own history, including reorganizations adopted in response to Palestinian resistance, and its practices and institutions add up to a distinct form of government and domination. The occupation regime has two distinct phases, divided in roughly equal halves by the Oslo DOP. The first phase lasted from June 1967 to September 1993, and the second from 1993 onward. Sections IV and V will examine the early period, and Section VI will take us to the second phase, the post-Oslo years.

The first stage of occupation policy was personally designed by Defense Minister Moshe Dayan and, though its practices were tightened repeatedly,

What Is the Occupation?

remained in effect until the outbreak of the First Intifada in December 1987. Dayan's goal was to create a so-called temporary, moral, and nonexistent occupation,[34] though I would qualify this description by suggesting that it was made to appear *normal* for Palestinians while remaining *invisible* to Jews and the rest of the world. To this date, Israeli and foreign scholars regularly edit and publish volumes on contemporary Israel that avoid any mention of the occupation of noncitizen Palestinians who live under Israeli rule.

This "illusory" occupation regime was half-seriously, half-jestingly labeled by Israelis an *enlightened occupation*. Although Israel, as the occupying power, is required under IHL to assume the obligation of protecting Palestinians, it has attempted instead to make the occupation benefit Israelis. Before the First Intifada, the Israeli regime also strove to keep the costs of occupation down so as to have a cheap occupation and not impose the burden on Israeli taxpayers.

The three main elements of the illusory "enlightened occupation" were (1) an "indirect method of rule" that kept in place Palestinian local administrators under the military government, though the military government had the actual responsibility over the lives of occupied Palestinians; (2) the integration of the OPT's economy with the Israeli economy; and (3) the formal subjugation of the military government of the OPT to the jurisdiction of the HCJ. Of these three elements, only the third survives in its original form today; the other two have been revised, retooled, and in some cases abandoned.

After rapidly ruling out plans to reach a political agreement with the Palestinian urban elite of the West Bank and, consequently, rejecting some of the classic colonial forms of ruling over satellite states or protectorates, Israel settled on a combination of what is best termed indirect rule and military rule.[35] Its purpose was to shield the military administration, the General Security Services (GSS, the Shabak or the Shin Bet), and the Israeli police from the gaze of its subjects, as well as to reduce friction between the new rulers and their subjects. To allow the local population to conduct its life with minimum interference or involvement, Jordanian institutions and the vast majority of their incumbents (mayors, qadis, civil servants, and teachers) were left in their old posts. These people also continued drawing salaries from Jordan, which enabled Jordan to maintain a measure of local influence in anticipation and hope of a time when it would be able to recover control over the territories lost to Israel in 1967. Atop the local authorities, the now sovereign authority was vested in the military, which ruled through a hierarchy of military governors. To carry out its obligations toward the civilian population, a committee of the directors-general of the main ministries was assembled and placed under the coordinator of Israeli government operations in the OPT, himself an officer subordinate to the minister of defense. As long as the military administration was able to operate through the Palestinian functionaries, it propagated the illusion that the military occupiers remained "invisible."

By foregrounding the economic sphere, Israel sought to normalize the relationship of occupier and occupied. This approach was a direct continuation of the expectation formed during the Yishuv that the economic benefits of the modern Jewish economy would also benefit the land's native Arabs and diminish their aspiration for political independence. Israel adopted an "open bridges" policy to allow a continuation of the economic ties between the two banks of the Jordan River. Just one year into the occupation, the Israeli Ministry of Defense already published its first English-language report on its administration, subtitled *A Record of Progress,* and thereafter published annual reports piling on the positive numbers that resulted from modernizing the Palestinian economy. The years 1967-73 indeed witnessed a rapid rise in the Palestinian standard of living, due in equal part to the higher wages paid within the Green Line and remittances from the Gulf States. However, the Israeli economy's lost decade after the 1973 War and the collapse of the oil-driven boom in the Gulf in the 1980s reversed that rise.[36]

The attachment of the Palestinians to the Israeli economy benefited individual Palestinians but did little to modernize the Palestinian economy, since Israel not only failed to encourage the development of Palestinian industry but refused licenses for the construction of locally owned factories whose wares would compete with Israeli manufactured goods. The OPT's rate of growth, consequently, correlated closely not with the Israeli economy but with the regional rate and placed West Bank and Gaza's GNP only marginally higher than the GNPs of comparably endowed Syria and Jordan two decades after the occupation. In Geoffrey Aronson's summation, the "economic foundation for Palestinian participation in the status quo did not produce normalization."[37]

The greatest impetus for the improvement of the Palestinian standard of living was the opening of the Israeli labor market, which led to the employment of as much as 39.2 percent of the Palestinian labor force within the Green Line by 1987. Palestinian employees are congregated in the low-paying agricultural and construction sectors. Though required to pay full social insurance taxes, they receive only a portion of the benefits accruing to their Israeli counterparts. A portion of their revenues finances the military government, making Palestinian laborers pay an occupation premium to the Israeli authorities. Recognizing the moderating influence of employment, Israel continues to issue work permits to Palestinian laborers to date, though the Israeli state adjusts their ebb and flow according to the level of Palestinian resistance over the years.

While the economic policy—even as it was beset by contradictions—held the promise of flexibility and prosperity, there was no such openness in either the educational or the political spheres. Until the First Intifada, according to Major General Shlomo Gazit, Israel's coordinator of Israeli government operations in the territories, Palestinians in the OPT were under a total prohibition of political organization. Even the acts of displaying Palestinian flags and singing nationalist songs were strictly forbidden and severely punished.[38] Military censorship of all reading material led to the banning of some 1,700 books, and its logic was so convoluted that even Shakespeare's

Merchant of Venice was forbidden in the OPT. Israel pursued a single-minded and heavy-handed policy to prevent any and all expression of Palestinian national identity or cultural heritage in the schools. Local newspapers were instructed by the military censor to replace the word *Palestinian*—one with potential political significance—with *Arab*, viewed as a more general cultural identity. It encouraged identification with extended family or religion—for example, through the licensing of mosque construction. To thwart secular nationalism, the military government encouraged what it expected to be an apolitical, quietist fundamentalism. For example, it allowed the Palestinian branch of the Muslim Brotherhood to take possession of religious endowments (waqf), leading to the flourishing of this traditional practice, which was already in decline in other parts of the Middle East. Finally, it allowed Hamas, which grew out of the local chapter of the Brotherhood, to expand its social services in Gaza.

The enlightened occupation, such as it was, at most postponed the day of reckoning and was unsustainable. Already from its beginning, behind its facade of normalcy lurked a repressive apparatus.

V

Though Israelis were happy to convince themselves that their tactic of controlling the OPT by pulling the strings from behind was effective, they also maintained a large measure of direct and frequently violent military control that was experienced by occupied Palestinians as part of their daily life. Avraham Shalom, a past head of Israel's Shin Bet, and one of Adolf Eichmann's captors, who was in office up to the outbreak of the First Intifada, summed up the everyday experience of occupied Palestinians with these words: "We've become cruel. To ourselves as well, but mainly to the occupied population." The army, he added, had become "a brutal occupation force, similar to the Germans in World War II" in its treatment not of Jews but of the conquered peoples.[39]

Heeding Shalom's observation, I will delve into the role played by violence in Israel's tool kit of domination. State violence is as extreme as it is exceptional in the everyday experience of most people living in a rulebound democracy. Thus, as Ariella Azoulay and Adi Ophir point out, violence by the Israeli state is commonly viewed and discussed merely as a military instrument used intermittently in response to upsurges of Palestinian hostility and as the expression of the security needs of an otherwise peaceful Israeli society—or at least one entitled to defend its armed forces and civilians.[40] From this view, violence is confined to the following events: the two intifadas; General Sharon's clearing operations in the Gaza refugee camps starting in December 1970; Operation Defensive Shield during the Second Intifada; the three military operations, indeed wars, between Israel and Gaza in the past decade; and the measures to suppress *al-habbah al-sha'biyya* knife attacks since October 2015. "Military violence is [thus] dissociated from the ongoing operation of the apparatus of domination"[41]—that is, from the military rule and government of the OPT.

Under occupation, however, violence is more accurately described as occurring on a continuum that runs the gamut from coercive state action to suppression and war. The former almost invariably leads to resistance and thus is the precursor to and cause of the latter. The occupation therefore is best understood as ongoing, day-in and day-out coercion, and its injuries include material, psychological, social, and bodily harm. The coercive techniques of the institutions of occupation deployed to enforce submission produce the occasional eruptions of "military operations" and wars. Violence is omnipresent and found in all facets of the occupation; consequently, the most intense and bloody suppression of uprisings and wars cannot be considered in isolation from the occupation regime as an everyday experience.

I will survey five of the prominent technologies in the Israeli domination matrix—the permit system, administrative detention, deportation, house demolitions, and torture—and explore each in turn. Of course, these only-too-visible aspects of the occupation have worked against its more "enlightened" aspirations.

Occupied Palestinians were required to apply for ID cards and permits to travel, to work, to relocate, to study abroad, to rezone land, and to open a business; later, specialized personnel had to apply for authorization to move about under curfew. The Shin Bet holds the ultimate authority for the approval of permits. As pointed out by Yael Berda, who has conducted the most thorough study of the permit system, frequently there is a tug-of-war between the Shin Bet's representative and the coordinator of Israeli government operations in the territories, with the former being risk-averse and the latter being fearful of the adverse economic consequences of a restrictive use of permits.[42]

The Shin Bet has been able to use the permit system as a tool of control in an additional way. By handing out permits as favors to "good" (that is, moderate or apolitical) Arabs, the Shin Bet has been able to build up a network of collaborators. In 1994, the executive director of B'Tselem Yitzhak Be'er and Saleh 'Abdel-Jawad estimated that between 40,000 and 120,000 individuals—who make up some 1 to 4 percent of the Palestinian population—were turned into collaborators through a combination of incentives, threats, and extortion.[43] The information provided by collaborators led to interrogations, persecutions, and even expulsions, undermining bonds of solidarity among Palestinians and dividing the occupied population against itself. During the intifadas, and later during the wars of Gaza, hundreds of suspected collaborators were executed, some by neighbors but mostly by Hamas.

Administrative detention under the occupation involves the detention of people deemed dangerous without due process for multiples of six months, and without allowing the detainee to mount a proper defense. While it is not without precedents elsewhere and is commonly viewed as a last resort, the widespread use of administrative detention by Israel is sobering. Thousands of occupied Palestinians have been held under military governors' detention orders:

1,261 in 1970; as many as 1,794 in November 1989, during the First Intifada; and 466 in the month of July 2014. Since the beginning of the *al-habbah al-sha'biyya* or youth outburst—the knife attacks that have sporadically taken place mostly in Jerusalem and Hebron since October 2015——the new charge of incitement, including Facebook postings in support of resistance, has led to administrative detentions as well.

From 1967 to 1992, Israel deported 1,522 Palestinian residents of the OPT, mostly to Jordan and Lebanon. The largest single group deportation took place during the forty-eight hours of December 16–17, 1992. In response to the killing of six Israeli soldiers and border policemen during the month, the Rabin government swiftly arrested 415 individuals accused of affiliation with Hamas or Islamic Jihad and deported them with the last-minute consent of the HCJ for either one or two years. Like other deportees, the members of this large group were neither charged, tried, nor convicted but merely processed through administrative channels. The arrests were carried out hastily, and sixteen deportees were allowed to return after it was determined that they had been included in the group by mistake.[44] This policy was subsequently suspended, but since 2002 Israel has again deported residents of the West Bank to Gaza, though only in small numbers.

The demolition of the houses of the families of suicide bombers, bombing planners, and even perpetrators of failed stabbing attacks is a form of collective punishment because it renders homeless relatives, including the elderly, women, and children who have not been charged with complicity. The legal basis for demolition or sealing houses is the British Defense Emergency Regulations of 1945, charting a direct line from British colonial to equivalent Israeli occupation practices. Statistics compiled by the Israeli Committee against House Demolitions (ICAHD) for the period between 1983, when punitive demolitions were first undertaken, until 2009 show that altogether 1,522 houses were demolished. The peak periods were in the height of the two intifadas. According to the ICAHD, during the Second Intifada

628 Palestinian residences (mostly single-dwelling houses) were demolished, leaving over seven thousand homeless, on the average twelve individuals in each instance. Several studies by Israeli researchers and military officers reached the conclusion that this practice carries no deterrent effect. On the contrary, they reported a rise in attacks following the policy's implementation. In 2005, the government adopted the recommendations of a military committee chaired by Major General Shani to end house demolitions. In 2014, in response to the *al-habbah al-sha'biyya*, the government authorized the resumption of the practice on a smaller scale following the abduction and killing of three yeshiva students at the Gush Etzion junction in the OPT, without ever providing a new rationale. Punishment, it appears, is now sufficient cause, even when it is not a deterrent.[45]

What stands out from the dry statistics of ICAHD is that houses are demolished not only as punishment but for many reasons: for example, to facilitate control during military operations or for lack of a permit. Demolitions justified by military need and unspecified reasons were at their highest at the beginning of the occupation; between 1967 and 1969 altogether 7,554 houses were demolished. This number includes the Moroccan (Mughrabi) Quarter of East Jerusalem, which was cleared out to make room for an esplanade in front of the Western Wall. All told, of the 24,132 demolished houses between 1967 and 2009, only 6 percent were destroyed for punitive reasons, placing this technique of domination within the larger context of policies aimed at reducing the geographic hold of Palestinians in Palestine.[46] This conclusion is clearly borne out by continued demolitions in the past two decades in Area C, where the majority of settlers reside and which remains under Israeli military and civilian authority. Israel allows practically no new Palestinian construction in this area and is systematically using demolitions, often repeatedly, not just of houses but also of tents, shacks of corrugated metal, makeshift homes, and even the caves of impoverished Bedouin tribes to remove Palestinian residents.

What Is the Occupation?

Nothing exposes the brutal and all-encompassing nature of the occupation as clearly as its penetration into the physical bodies of the occupied. The Israeli government had repeatedly denied the allegations, as it did in response to the London *Times*'s claim, on June 19, 1977, that "Israeli interrogators routinely ill-treat and often torture Arab prisoners." A decade later, a commission, headed by former chief justice Moshe Landau (who had presided over the Eichmann trial) concluded that in denying the use of torture "the Shin Bet lied for sixteen years." The Landau Commission's preferred option was to confront the dilemma openly and, by justifying the exceptional use of force against terror suspects under the "necessity" defense, make permissible the use of "moderate physical pressure." Though the commission qualified the level of physical pressure by specifying that it should "never reach the level of physical torture or maltreatment . . . which deprives [the suspect] of his human dignity." [47] This restraint was not adhered to. Its recommendation, in fact, made Israel the only democracy to officially approve practices deemed illegal by the Convention against Torture and Other Cruel, Inhuman or Degrading Treatment or Punishment, to which it is a signatory. During the First Intifada, the monitoring ministerial committee approved the use of "enhanced physical pressure." This included forceful shaking, excessive tightening of cuffs, sleep deprivation, the contorted "Frog Crouch," and the "Shabak Position," as well as combinations of these methods. B'Tselem estimated that some 85 percent of the 1,000 to 1,500 prisoners interrogated each year by the Shin Bet were tortured during their investigation,[48] and during the First Intifada twenty-four Palestinians were reported to have died after punitive beatings during their arrests or while in detention centers. Justice Landau himself admitted to feeling betrayed by the Shin Bet's practice of regularly exceeding the constraints his commission sought to impose, but by making Israel the only democracy to legalize torture he set this odious practice on a slippery slope.

On September 9, 1999, the HCJ, in an opinion written by Chief Justice Aharon Barak, forbade the Shin Bet from using physical pressure against

Palestinians it suspected of terrorism. This was a powerful symbolic ruling, but it eliminated neither the ill treatment of detainees during the predetention period (when the suspects are in the hands of the military or the police) nor forms of "moderate physical pressure" not on the Landau Commission's list. It also allowed the infliction of "sleep deprivation" when it was not an end in itself but a side effect of the interrogation. The HCJ and the government's legal counsel retained the ex post facto "necessity" defense for the use of physical pressure in the case of "ticking bombs." [49] Hajjar, one of the most astute observers of the torture debates in Israel and the United States, aptly captures the meaning of the HCJ ruling: "A qualified victory in this struggle was achieved in September 1999, when the Israeli High Court finally rendered a decision against the commonplace use of state-sanctioned 'pressure' tactics, although this decision does not go so far as to close the window of opportunity for continuing torture." [50]

An adverse outcome in the aftermath of the decision to reverse part of the Landau Commission's recommendations has been the HCJ's unwillingness to hear subsequent petitions of terror suspects concerning incidents of torture. The Public Committee Against Torture in Israel (PCATI) submitted 124 petitions requesting permission for detainees to meet with their lawyers during the course of the interrogation, but the court accepted none. In 2002, the Shin Bet acknowledged that since the HCJ's 1999 ruling ninety Palestinian terror suspects had been defined as "ticking bombs" and subjected to "physical pressure," though PCATI believes that the actual number might be higher. The state prosecutor referred complaints to the Shin Bet itself for investigation, and the latter found none in which physical pressure was deemed unnecessary. Finally, though the guidelines from the government's legal counsel defined the applicability of the "necessity" defense very narrowly, he granted his approval *ex post facto* to every single case in which physical pressure was used.[51] Today, the Shin Bet receives information extracted through torture from the police forces of the Palestine Authority.

In late 2015, "exceptional measures of interrogation" were approved against Jewish terror suspects for the first time, to gather evidence on their suspected involvement in the firebombing of a Palestinian house in Douma that led to the death of three of its inhabitants.[52] The use of torture against Jewish suspects was exceptional, though the group that the suspects belonged to was also exceptional—an underground organization seeking to replace the state of Israel with a *halachic* state. This new state would be based not on secular legislation but on Jewish law. Though Israel has cut back since 1999, it continues to engage in various forms of torture.

V I

The first and second intifadas, and since September 2015 the *habbah al-sha'biyya*, are hardly the sum total of Palestinian resistance to Israeli occupation. Early attempts by the various factions of the Palestinian Liberation Organization (PLO)—the umbrella body of Palestinian resistance movements—to establish bases of support in the West Bank and wage popularly supported guerilla warfare of Maoist inspiration against Israel did not bear fruit. But in Gaza the presence of PLO units and the sympathetic attitude of Nasser produced a sustained series of shootings and the planting of land mines. It took the Israeli military some three years of heavy-handed suppression, implemented and frequently initiated by General Ariel Sharon, the head of the Southern Command, to achieve a desired level of "pacification."

By the late 1970s and early 1980s, the most active and violent resistance had moved to the West Bank. The political context for this wave of resistance was the expansion of the Labor Party's limited colonization into an ambitious plan to settle throughout the West Bank by the first Likud government under Prime Minister Menachem Begin. Israel now replaced the mayors who had supported the PLO with the collaborationist Village Leagues. The combination of colonization and the suppression of local leadership, however, led to the opposite results in the late 1970s—the first widespread Palestinian opposition to Israeli occupation. The Israeli reaction included collective punishments by closing down the West Bank universities for months at a time, foremost among them Birzeit University near Ramallah, and censoring East Jerusalem newspapers and banning their circulation in the rest of the OPT. Massive demonstrations were put down with firepower, and the Israeli disclaimers that its troops shot above the heads of the protesters was belied by the large number of Palestinian casualties. The military government was replaced by the Civil Administration in 1981, ostensibly to allow Palestinians autonomous rule, but the new body is actually a department of the Central Command of the Israeli military and is staffed by military appointees. By the early 1980s, all civilian affairs were centrally managed.[53] This more direct method of Israeli rule reduced the buffer between the military government and the occupied population, and the period of "enlightened occupation" came to an end.

The First Intifada was the first in a historic wave of democratic movements and revolutions that sprang up toward the end of the Cold War and hastened the demise of authoritarian regimes and the communist bloc. These movements and the First Intifada are strikingly similar in their relatively nonviolent character and their organizational structure, particularly the leading role played by existing and emerging civil society institutions. As the goal of the Intifada was to cut off Palestinian relations with the Israeli state through a variety of methods—including a tax strike, a boycott of Israeli-produced goods, and disengagement from the Civil Administration—Palestinians were limited to their meager resources and forced to depend on each other for mutual assistance. During the five or six years of the First Intifada, a network of neighborhood committees provided the backbone of the movement, filling in the institutional gap, acting as the proto-state Palestinians lacked. These committees were frequently the representative organs of the politically less represented groups, the younger and poorer sectors of Palestinian society, which worked with recently formed women's organiza-

What Is the Occupation?

tions and the older labor unions. Israeli repression was frequently indiscriminate and further united Palestinian society. When businesses were ordered by the demonstrators to close, soldiers raided them and ordered their owners to reopen so they could reap taxes. Such repression led to closer ties between the Palestinian middle class and the protesters. The intifada transformed rapidly from a series of spontaneous and local acts of confrontation to an organized uprising with a distinct dynamic and leadership structure. An emergent Unified National Command coordinated the local and neighborhood bodies, setting the tone and directing the stages and forms of resistance through its periodic communiqués.

As a mass movement controlled not by small clandestine ideological bodies but by civil society committees and institutions, the resistance movement was able to place limits on the extent of the violence deployed. Demonstrations and protests were accompanied by barricade construction, tire burning, and stone throwing to prevent the entry of Israeli patrols but not by the use of knives or firearms. As the intifada dragged on, Israeli reactions escalated to include mass imprisonments, deportations, and beatings of stone throwers, and the incidence of Palestinian violent acts also increased sharply. Violence was perpetrated by lone individuals and by the Islamicist Hamas, whose influence was growing throughout the intifada.

The intifada made a low-cost and low-casualty occupation impossible and strained the resources of the Israeli state. The resurrection of the idea that Israel should draw its boundary at the Green Line—a border that had disappeared from the consciousness of most Israelis and that seriously challenged the argument that holding the OPT was essential for Israel's security—was even more significant. The realization by Prime Minister Rabin of the Labor Party that it was no longer possible to return to the regime of "enlightened occupation," or to reinstate control through the Civil Administration's all-intrusive permit regime, or to suppress the intifada violently, led him to the negotiating table.[54] Concurrently, Yasser Arafat's Fatah—the largest

Palestinian resistance movement—was on the outs with the Arab world because of its support for Saddam Hussein's conquest of Kuwait. This "hurting stalemate"—a situation in which the status quo is no longer tenable, there is unwillingness to endure the pain required by further escalation, and there are alternative outcomes—led both sides to make a dramatic turn to diplomacy that would result in the Oslo DOP in September 1993.[55]

The Oslo process (I will focus here only on the administrative changes it wrought and will offer a thorough discussion of its context and significance in my second essay) created an interim and then an elected Palestinian National Authority (PNA) and led to the division of the West Bank (and initially Gaza) into three areas. The Palestinian cities of Jericho, Qalqilya, Ramallah, Bethlehem, Jenin, Nablus, Tulkarm, and part of Hebron, as well as the cities of the Gaza Strip, were declared "Area A" and placed under the security and civilian authority of the PNA. Four hundred forty villages and their surrounding land in the West Bank were designated "Area B" and placed under Palestinian civilian and Israeli security authority. The rest—that is, 60 percent the West Bank and all the Israeli settlements— are now "Area C," which was left under Israeli security and civilian control (see map 1). The suppression of Palestinian violent resistance to Israel was now outsourced to the PNA. As a consequence of "Oslo" (as the negotiating process was called in short), a new indirect method of Israeli rule was put into place. Though an elected national-level Palestinian authority was created, the occupation persists even in Area A, as the Israeli military controls ingress and egress to each city and enclave and, since the peak of the second intifada's violence, conducts raids into the cities of Area A as well.

The Oslo peace process put an end to the intifada but was undermined by continued violence by both sides' extremists and did not lead to a permanent political compromise. In September 2000, a US-sponsored round of peace talks at Camp David to reach a final agreement failed. An already volatile situation was further inflamed by a provocative visit of Ariel Sharon, accom-

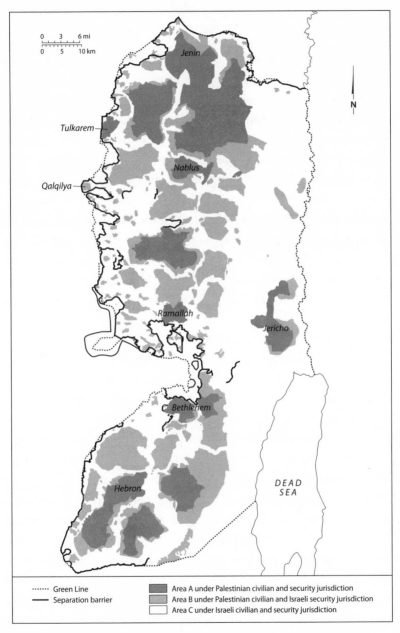

Map 1. Areas A, B, and C and the Separation Wall. Used by permission of B'Tselem. Based on "The West Bank: Settlements and the Separation Barrier, November 2014," www.btselem.org/download/201411_btselem_map_of_wb_eng.pdf.

panied by hundreds of security forces, to Temple Mount and by a disproportionate use of live ammunition in response to ensuing Palestinian stone
throwing. By the time of the Second Intifada, it was no longer possible to
generate a nonviolent, community-driven uprising akin to the First Intifada.
The West Bank was subdivided into small enclaves as part of the establishment of Areas A, B, and C. The fragmentation of Areas A and B into land cells
without territorial contiguity prevented Palestinian civil society activists
from mobilizing large groups across the OPT. As observed by the peace studies scholars Marwan Darweish and Andrew Rigby, Palestinians became dis-
illusioned with the PNA but no longer had a unified political organization to
lead their struggle. Under these conditions, their resort to violence was
unsurprising.[56] Throughout the cycle of attack and retaliation, violence
intensified as both sides escalated their tactics. Several incidents of particular brutality, including the killing of children, raised public outrage and
made attempts to restrain violence all but impossible. The Islamic groups of
Hamas and Islamic Jihad engaged in suicide bombings against Israeli civilians; secular Palestinian organizations, such as the al-Aqsa Martyrs Brigade
(an offshoot of Fatah), later followed with additional suicide bombing
attacks. Israel, on its part, resorted to the targeted assassination of Hamas
leaders and operatives. Israeli soldiers conducted extensive searches for suspected terrorists and in the process took control of private Palestinian residences and offices for surveillance and staging areas. Villages and whole
towns were placed under siege for extended periods of time.

Peaks of resistance witnessed Palestinians putting at risk or sacrificing
their bodies, from stone throwers facing off against heavily armed military
forces to suicide bombers engaged in a complex calculus of pain, resistance,
redemption, and revenge. Bader Araj, who interviewed close family members and friends of several dozen suicide bombers (as well as senior leaders of
Hamas, Fatah, and other Palestinian organizations) and examined the wills
that the bombers left behind, distinguishes three main motivations of such

bombers: (1) religion—inspiration by deep religious feelings to give one's life for the sake of other Muslims and Islam; (2) nationalism—an aspiration to play a role in liberating one's homeland and sometimes to undermine the peace process, itself viewed as counterproductive and a disgrace; and (3) vengeance—the wish to avenge Israeli soldiers' killing of relatives, friends, and other members of Hamas or other organizations behind earlier bombings. Most bombers had mixed motivations. Surprisingly, some had no nationalist motives, but in many cases, even if other motivations were present, revenge played a major role. A measure of religious casuistry was also involved. Suicide is forbidden by all religions, but suicide as martyrdom in the service of a larger national or religious cause has been reinterpreted as a justification for this forbidden act.

Araj dismisses explanations that focus on psychological characteristics that propel individuals to become suicide bombers. In his research, suicide bombers showed no signs of social maladjustment. Most were employed and close to their families. Indeed, to carry out their murderous attacks they had to be part of and rely on elaborate social networks of bomb makers, spotters, drivers, and the like. Socioeconomic considerations also seem to have played only a minor role in motivating them: fewer than one-third came from refugee camps or were from refugee families living outside camps, those commonly thought to be the lowest socioeconomic class of Palestinian society. The financial support their families received, either from Palestinian organizations or from Saddam Hussein's Iraq, was usually small, akin to welfare payments. The death of one of the family's main breadwinners and the demolition of the family home by the Israeli military following the attack rendered subsequent financial help meaningless.[57] Emile Durkheim, the French Jewish sociologist who made his name by studying the topic of suicide, categorized types of suicide as egoistic, anomic, fatalistic, and altruistic. This last type was carried out in the service of tight-knit social groups, whose members' degree of both social integration and regulation was "too high." Such acts, mostly motivated by a search for revenge, were pressed into the service of Palestinian resistance and became a hallmark of the Second Intifada.

In the Second Intifada, 1,137 Israelis were killed and 8,341 Israelis were wounded, most of them in suicide bombings. From the beginning of the Second Intifada until early 2005, 78 percent of those killed and 68 percent of those wounded were civilians. The number of Palestinians killed in both the West Bank and Gaza reached 3,135. Of these, 181 Palestinians were killed in targeted assassinations and another 288 were collateral victims. Zaki Shalom, researcher in national security studies, and the military historian and journalist Yoaz Hendel argue that the Second Intifada broke down the distinction between strategic threats from Israel's neighboring states and their militaries that put Israel's existence at risk and tactical threats to individual lives from terrorist organizations. Now both war and terror were perceived as strategic threats.[58] I would suggest that it was not the blurring of existential and individual threats that defined the nature of the Second Intifada to Israelis but another of its features. Suicide bombings, targeting civilians, were not confined to the OPT but took place on both sides of the Green Line. This radical innovation signaled that Palestinian resistance was not aimed just against the occupation or settlers but against all Israelis. The Second Intifada blurred the borders that the First Intifada had marked off between Israelis and Palestinians. The Israeli peace camp became discredited and most Israelis (since it longer mattered whether one was a settler in the OPT or not) united against the threat of Palestinian terror attacks on civilians. Both intifadas radicalized their respective sides and were turning points in the character of Israeli occupation.

VII

Towards the end of the era of "enlightened occupation" direct control of Palestinian everyday life grew considerably. The central characteristic of the new, post-First Intifada, occupation regime, as pointed out by Neve Gordon and outlined in detail by Ariel Handel, was separation from Palestinians in a "them there and us here" approach. Its first measures preceded the Oslo Accords and were part and parcel of the reestablishment of the Green Line during the First Gulf War. Reluctantly, but more forcefully, additional measures were adopted in response to the first wave of suicide bombings in Israeli cities after 1994 and again in the wake of the al-Aqsa Intifada.

Though the new separation emerged piecemeal in response to regional and local security concerns, it could be turned into an orderly regime only when the PNA was established and headquartered in Ramallah within the OPT. The First Intifada demonstrated to Israel that both the "enlightened occupation" and the more direct technologies of control by the Civil Administration (introduced around 1981) lost their effectiveness against intense Palestinian resistance. The Oslo Accords allowed Israel to resort to a new and better-camouflaged indirect control. As part of the new separatist regime, some powers of the Israeli military administration were transferred to the newly created PNA, and in this fashion Israel's responsibility for the everyday life of the Palestinians of the West Bank and Gaza was reduced. Though the direction that PNA-Israeli relations would take was not settled at the time of the Oslo Accords, the PNA's survival and continued cooperation with Israel in the face of the failing peace process transformed the PNA into another authority in a chain of indirect rule.

The new technologies of Israeli domination are founded on control of people's movements, and their most visible manifestation is the checkpoint. The West Bank is peppered with permanent manned checkpoints built of concrete as well as mobile "flying checkpoints," consisting of an armored vehicle or several jeeps and a squad of soldiers that are temporarily placed at various locations. In January 2006, for example, there were 58 manned and 471 unmanned checkpoints. These checkpoints divided the West Bank, according to the UN Office for the Coordination of Humanitarian Affairs, into 101 land cells, most of which were detached from their neighboring cells.[59] From each cell vehicular transportation is frequently allowed into just one other cell. Where passage is permitted, as in East Jerusalem and the Jordan Valley, it is frequently available only for local residents. These restrictions are complemented by other obstacles, such as a low fence along Road 317 in Mt. Hebron or a deep canal surrounding most of the city of Jericho. Areas around the circumference of settlements, outposts, and military camps, as well as some roads, are designated as restricted military areas, further restricting the territory open to Palestinians.

And, of course, there is the mammoth Separation Wall. About 70 percent of its planned 450 miles have been completed as of 2014, and about 85 percent of its route is within the West Bank proper. For most of its length, the barrier consists of a sensor-equipped intrusion detection fence (with a dual set of dirt paths to detect footprints), a patrol road, a ditch, a pyramid-shaped stack of six coils of barbed wire on the eastern side of the structure, and barbed wire on the western side, extending to an average width of sixty-five yards. In Palestinian towns and neighborhoods, it becomes a concrete wall eight meters (twenty-six feet) high.[60] Ariel Handel suggests that we flip our image of the West Bank as an aggregate of "gated" colonies and replace it with the picture of a "single, contiguous gated [Jewish settler] community gating, in turn, Palestinian 'islands' within it." [61]

Movement control is complemented by an "uncertainty principle." The number and location of checkpoints are varied by the Israeli military on the basis of operational intelligence, sometimes with great frequency. An Israeli women's human rights organization—Machsom (that is, Checkpoint) Watch—which monitors the conduct of soldiers and policemen, concluded that the reasons for prohibiting an individual's passage through a checkpoint "are so numerous, and the use made of them so changeable, that uncertainty becomes the ultimate system of control within the framework of the certainty of the occupation." [62] The role of checkpoints during and following the Second Intifada, therefore, is to enhance security not only by controlling and channeling movement but by freezing everyday life. Unlike the regime of the "enlightened occupation," which required the whole population to pass through offices of the military (and later civilian) government where registration, identification, and acceptable information were exchanged for permits, arbitrariness has become the new rule.

Since most checkpoints are improvised manned roadblocks, they lack computers or operational diaries. There Palestinian would-be-passers show a variety of documents, uncertain which may be deemed sufficient, and seek to convince the soldiers manning the roadblock that they have a good reason to pass. They do not know the changing regulations at a given checkpoint, for example, that at any given time only women over forty and boys under sixteen are let through, or that only residents of Nablus can cross but not necessarily return. Here is how Handel sums up their experience: "Passing through [checkpoints] resembles more a piece of theater than an administrative act." [63] Those whose passage is denied are neither detained nor investigated, and there is no follow-up to their exchange with the soldiers; they "simply return to their point of origin." Thus checkpoints, instead of serving their ostensible purpose of facilitating safe movement, act as barriers to movement by shrinking Palestinian space.

The control of Palestinians' movements appropriates both space and time. It not only wastes the time of individual Palestinians and makes it impossible for them to estimate traveling time but also destroys the stability of time and space. Checkpoints, walls, ditches, and inconsistent regulations upend the taken-for-granted building blocks of everyday life and render uncertain the calculations used to plan it. Under occupation, as Marx put it in a different context, "All that is solid melts into air." Handel compares the experience of the occupied people to a "geography of disaster": they have to navigate circumstances that commonly prevail after a natural disaster, but in the West Bank such circumstances are manmade.[64]

The first half of the half-century occupation, from June 1967 to September 1993, featured "internal" control effected through the presence of Israeli troops all throughout Gaza and the West Bank, whereas the post-Oslo era, from September 1993 to the present, features "external" domination. The first stage involved control of both land and the occupied population's everyday life; the second has given up on managing the population's everyday life and is concentrated on controlling its movements. The method of control from the outside is nowhere better illustrated than in Gaza. In 2005, Israel dismantled its colonies—the seventeen settlements known as the Katif Bloc—within the Gaza Strip and withdrew both its settlers and its soldiers. But then, it placed Gaza under a blockade. This started when Gaza came under Hamas control as the result of the 2006 elections, and the measures of control were tightened following the June 2007 Battle of Gaza in which Hamas expelled Fatah officials and took full control of Gaza. The blockade of land, air, and sea access to the Gaza Strip gives Israel direct control over the goods allowed to enter. The extent of the control is attested by a draft document prepared for Israel's coordinator of government activities in the territories, which calculated the minimum number of calories needed to prevent malnutrition and thus avoid a humanitarian crisis as a result of the blockade. While the report of the Palmer Commission appointed by the secretary-general of the UN reached the conclusion that a naval blockade is permissible under conditions of active hostilities, another report, by the Goldstone Commission set up by the UN Human Rights Council, concluded that the blockade as a whole constitutes collective punishment against the inhabitants of Gaza and, as such, is illegal.[65]

The spatial arrangement between Jews and Palestinians as separation *tout court* is only half of the story. In large parts of the West Bank, Jewish settlements are interspersed with Palestinian towns and villages. Jews and Palestinians are not arrayed along a border but intermixed on a *frontier*. A frontier opens with the arrival of an intrusive society engaged in competition

What Is the Occupation?

and conflict with the society it found already in place (as we learned from the white-Native American encounter in North America). Its outcome—the closing of the Israeli/Palestinian frontier and the form that closing will take—still looms in the future.

VIII

Israeli journalist Bradley Burston pithily observed, "It is the settlement enterprise which runs the occupation." [66] Similarly, Birzeit University professors Rema Hammami and Salim Tamari argue that "occupation has always been Israel's means rather than its end," which has been territorial expansion.[67] This conclusion is inescapable and brings me to the fourth—the last, and most illuminating—perspective from which to comprehend the occupation.

The centrality of the "settlement enterprise" within the occupation is partially obscured by the use of the multivalent and anodyne term *settlement*, a word that among other meanings denotes the ending of a dispute or the calming of a contestation. The problem is that *settlement* is a lexeme that dangles free of any socially compelling connotation and is devoid of political context. It is not, however, the universal term of choice to describe the Israeli undertaking in the OPT. The French prefer the term *colonisation*, taken from their own historical vocabulary, where it was used synonymously with the English expression of "planting colonies." The term *colonization* has the advantage of announcing clearly the undertaking's historical meaning and placing it in a comparative framework. In addition, the term restores the distinct political aim of the project—forming a new society by changing the ownership and control of a territory through the partial replacement of its population. Restoring this concept will also account for the bitterness surrounding the settlement enterprise.

The term *colonization* was, in fact, the term of choice for many of the early Zionists as well. In the 1880s, the settlers of the First Aliya (wave of Zionist immigration to Palestine between 1882 and 1903) named their form of settlement *moshava*, the Hebrew equivalent of colony. Arthur Ruppin, head of the World Zionist Organization's Jaffa office, titled his 1926 book *The Agricultural Colonization of the Zionist Organization in Palestine*, and Ze'ev Jabotinsky not only used the term in his famed 1923 article "[On] The Iron Wall" but sought to dispel any confusion about its meaning and significance as follows: "Colonization carries its own explanation, the only possible explanation, unalterable and clear as daylight to every Jew and every Arab with his wits about him." [68] Let us then not be shy in restoring this word to its proper place and using it side by side with *settlement* to remind us what is at stake.

Not only is the term *settlement* misleading, but so is the plural term *Israeli settlements*, which agglomerates and flattens their diversity. Israeli settlements are not cast in a single mold, nor did their evolution follow a master plan (see map 2). For Israelis "settlements" are like snow for Inuits; different types are designated by distinct Hebrew words.

It was the self-designated Labor Settlement Movement (LSM, in Hebrew *hahityashvut haovedet*)—the broad conglomeration of socialist parties and institutions that ruled Israel through the Labor Party until 1977—that became the champion of colonization during the Second Aliya (1904-14). After the 1967 War, the LSM would champion colonization in the OPT but, like a sorcerer's apprentice, would lose control of the process to other apprentices-in-waiting. These new colonizers dreamt up even more ambitious projects by spreading to areas that earlier waves had not envisioned for settlement, thereby radicalizing the colonization enterprise. Consequently, as pointed out by Eyal Weizman, who has studied the architecture and political space created by the Israeli occupation, "The 'authorship' of this project was diffused . . . among a multiplicity of agents and organizations and embodied more contradictions than a set of coherent strategies." [69] A proper understanding of the colonization project requires that we place it within a complex interplay of three components: settlement, land seizure, and planning. I will examine each of these components in turn.

What Is the Occupation?

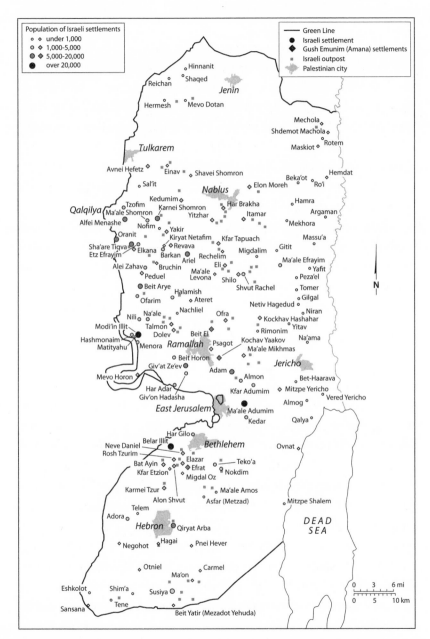

Map 2. Israeli settlements in the West Bank. Used by permission of B'Tselem. Based on "The West Bank: Settlements and the Separation Barrier, November 2014," www.btselem. org/download/201411_btselem_map_of_wb_eng.pdf.

There have been at least five types of colonies built in successive waves, each creating its distinct frontier. I will distinguish between military, religious, secular suburban, Orthodox suburban, and outpost (*ma'achaz*) frontiers. These waves of colonization were sometimes undertaken to counteract the purpose of previous waves. The preference for some of these settlements over others is the basis of much of the political discussion within Israel, and these distinctions matter a great deal when the potential outlines of Israeli-Palestinian territorial accords are debated. In addition, there is a sixth type: Israel has built a ring of new Jewish towns around East Jerusalem.

At the conclusion of the 1967 War, Israel contemplated full territorial withdrawal in return for a peace accord on its borders with Egypt and Syria but, as shown by Avi Raz, it never considered withdrawing from all of the West Bank or from any part of East Jerusalem.[70] Shortly after the war, Minister of Labor Yigal Allon proposed Israel's first settlement plan to the cabinet. Allon's intention was to turn the part of the West Bank farthest from Israel (the rift of the Jordan Valley and the Judea Desert) into a buffer zone between Israel and Jordan, while also cutting the rest of the West Bank into two separate zones by creating a wide east-west corridor from the Jordan Valley to Jerusalem (see map 2). Along the rift, an "eastern column" of agricultural settlements (named *he'achzut*)—themselves a security barrier—was to be constructed. Fittingly, the first colonists were soldiers of the Nachal, a special settlement brigade tasked with creating an agricultural and residential infrastructure in areas that were relatively inhospitable. The normal course of affairs was to turn Nachal's colonized areas into civilian settlements, renamed *yishuv*, within a few years. The Allon Plan would have annexed to Israel about 35 percent of the West Bank but only a small portion of its Palestinian population. Indeed, besides being a military border, this was the plan's deeper rationale: the annexation of a sizable territory with as few Palestinians as possible, following the model of prestate settlement.

As with Rabelais's Gargantua, appetite came with the eating: neither Allon nor his Labor Party (under prime ministers Eshkol, Golda Meir, and Rabin) could abide by their own self-imposed territorial restrictions for long. At first, yielding to grassroots pressure, they permitted the illegal, supposedly "temporary" establishment of two settlements outside the Jordan Valley. Kfar Etzion (halfway between Jerusalem and Hebron), one of a handful of Jewish settlements conquered by the Jordanian Arab Legion in 1948, and the Jewish quarter of Hebron, depopulated in a 1929 attack by their Arab neighbors, occupied a special place in Israel's frontier memory and could plausibly be explained as being "resettled." Not only was Eshkol willing to cooperate with the children of Kfar Etzion's original settlers, but Allon used the religious Zionist rabbi Moshe Levinger's settlement group to lay claim to Hebron. Eshkol, a onetime director of the Jewish Agency's Settlement Department, as the Israeli journalist Gershom Gorenberg reports, "personally directed settlement in occupied territory." [71]

The willingness of LSM leaders to commission religious settlers had two significant consequences. First, the restoration of the phantom limbs of pre-1948 settlement empowered religious Zionist settlers who sought the prestige and authority that came with colonization in Israel. Second, ex post facto incorporation of unplanned sites into Allon's settlement map opened the door to a series of piecemeal decisions that gradually expanded the range of settlements without overtly changing the settlement policy.

By September 1973, on the eve of the planned 1973 general elections and, unknowingly, of a new Arab-Israeli war, the Labor Party adopted for its electoral platform a more sprawling settlement plan. The Galili Protocol included the construction of (1) the city of Yamit in northern Sinai, (2) the city of Katzrin on the Golan Heights, and (3) the regional urban center of Ma'ale Efraim in the Jordan Valley, as well as a triangle of settlements in western Samaria, across from Kfar Saba, to be anchored by the town of Ariel. A mere six years after the 1967 War, the Labor Party was no longer bound by the Allon Plan, and in its final two years in power it expanded settlement more rapidly than at any other time since 1967. Even so, on the eve of losing power to the Likud in 1977, its settlements remained a rump project, consisting of about 4,400 settlers in thirty-one settlements. The reason was simple. The Jordan Valley was chosen for colonization because it had only a small Palestinian population, but it was far from Israel's heartland, and it was hot and inhospitable. By the mid-1970s the Labor Party had already had its day on the frontier.[72] But determined colonists-to-be only had to break down the Labor Party's rotten door to expand colonization beyond its geographical restrictions.

A second, and more radical, colonization wave commenced with the formation of Gush Emunim (Bloc of the Faithful) following Israel's initial setbacks in the 1973 War. Its leadership cadre arose from the retroactively authorized grassroots religious Zionist settlements that had started in Kfar Etzion and Hebron. The movement began with a series of protest activities aimed at halting Israeli withdrawals on the Egyptian and Syrian fronts. Gush Emunim demanded that policies restricting settlement locations to the "military frontier" be lifted and that unbridled settlement be allowed on all fronts—with special emphasis on Samaria, the northern half of the West Bank. Replacing *yishuv* (settlement), the term used by the LSM, with *hit-nachalut* (religious patrimony), a term that recalled Joshua's conquest of Canaan, Gush Emunim highlighted its religious aims. Its settlers were what I will call "legacy settlers," in that, unlike the settlers before 1948, they sought to reclaim lands that they regarded as their legacy from biblical times. Gush Emunim is best viewed not only as a religious Zionist movement but as a messianic one, seeking to release the radical potential of Judaism in the service of fulfilling the biblical promise to the possession of the Holy Land.

These far-reaching goals were accompanied by new and militant stratagems. Yearly marches of thirty to forty thousand participants across Samaria,

What Is the Occupation?

frequent street demonstrations, and, most significantly, repeated attempts to occupy unauthorized sites by force in the face of evacuations by the military placed Gush Emunim on the margins of Israeli democracy but at the heart of Israeli politics. During Rabin's first tenure as prime minister (1974–77), only three Gush Emunim settlements were set up, one inside a military camp, another as a so-called work camp, and yet another as an "archaeological excavation," and all three were designated temporary. Rabin was the most forceful opponent of messianic settlement, going so far as to accuse it of being "comparable to cancer." [73] But the end of the Labor era and the formation of Menachem Begin's Likud government opened the sluice gate to the overflowing energies of Gush Emunim. The Likud—not having an independent settlement policy, and having only an insignificant settlement movement of its own—used Gush Emunim during this period as its major settlement force. Gush Emunim, on its part, also failed to create a mass movement of settlers. Its messianic appeal remained limited to the religious Zionist segment of the Jewish population. The man- and woman-power reserves of Gush Emunim were quickly exhausted, without having made a demographic dent in the Palestinian majority on the West Bank. By 1981, about 16,200 Jewish settlers resided in sixty-eight settlements in the West Bank. What mattered, however, was not the number of colonies or the numbers by which they augmented the settler population but their layout. The new colonies constituted a second, "central" column, a roughly north-south line of settlements parallel to the first column of settlements that run along the Jordan River. This central column of settlements was perched on the mountainous heights of the northern West Bank (see map 2). Its small colonies were scattered amid hundreds of Palestinian towns and villages in the mostly densely populated area of the West Bank. By breaking up Palestinian contiguity, Gush Emunim colonies cast aside the demographic calculus of the LSM and sought to undermine the very possibility of future territorial partition.

Gush Emunim, a social movement, soon evolved into two stable and powerful institutions. Amana, its settlement, or logistics, branch, builds colonies and maintains them. It taxes the settlers and uses the proceeds for new ventures, sometimes in defiance of Israeli governments. The second institution is the Council of Judea, Samaria, and Gaza (Mo'etzet Yesha, or Yesha Council), an umbrella organization of the heads of local and regional councils and towns built in the OPT. The council is under the continued influence of the religious Zionist settlers and serves as the settlers' lobbying body. With the institutionalization of their colonization drive, Gush Emunim settlers lost a great deal of their messianic zeal and instead of being labeled *mitnachalim* (legacy settlers) now prefer to be called *mithyashvim* (settlers): that is, they have adopted the designation used by the LSM and the secular settlers in the OPT.

Colonization by the Likud came into its own only during the second Begin government. In 1981, it set up a new, parallel Settlement Division within the World Zionist Organization, headed by Mattetyahu Drobles. Drobles laid the groundwork for settling tens of thousands of Jews in the West Bank. He projected that in thirty years, that is by 2010, 1.3 million Jews would be living alongside 1.8 million Arabs in the West Bank.[74] In fact, he greatly underestimated the projected population of Arabs while grossly inflating that of Jews, and the target figure of 1.3 million Jewish settlers has not been met to this day, but this has not been for lack of trying.

The Drobles Plan transformed Israeli colonization for the third time. A rising standard of living in Israel and the accompanying *embourgeoisement* of large segments of the society gave rise in the late 1970s to urban sprawl, that is, to the movement of people from the aging Tel Aviv metropolitan area to smaller townships, and from two- or three-room condominium apartments to private homes with gardens. It was this process of urban sprawl and suburbanization that the Likud government redirected, by its grand settlement plan, toward the West Bank. By harnessing the individual self-interest of an emerging economic liberalism to the colonization project, the Likud turned traditional patterns of settlement upside down, replacing small rural settlements with town-size urban settlements and cooperative pioneering with capitalist ventures. The major reason for the lower housing prices in the West Bank was absurdly low land prices: the government charged construction companies only 5 percent of the value of the land, while in nearby areas on the Israeli side of the border they were obliged to pay 80 percent. The Likud governments of Begin and Shamir subsidized the settlements in myriad ways and authorized private companies to build them. Israelis, even if they held moderate political opinions, moved to these newly constructed "quality of life" settlements because of their affordability and, sometimes, even luxury. A massive road construction scheme placed the residents of the new towns within short commuting distances of the center of the country, and, given their regular access to Israel, they did not come to view themselves as settlers. They are connected to the Israeli transportation grid by twenty-nine highways, while other, smaller settlements are linked up with the highways via bypass roads, most of which were built after 1993. The three hundred miles of these highways have sizable margins that required the removal of adjacent Palestinian houses, orchards, and fields.[75] The large towns constitute a third, "western" column of colonies, organized in five "settlement blocs," which are less invasive into the OPT, territorially speaking, since they lie adjacent to the Green Line. While the wave of Likud colonization has mobilized the largest portion of Jewish population, its destination is a "near abroad."

The potential hidden in the suburban frontier was manifested again when planners recruited another—the least likely—Jewish population to settle in the West Bank. The *haredim*, ultra-Orthodox, are pious, but unlike the religious Zionists who rallied behind Gush Emunim's messianic frontier they are indifferent or even hostile to Zionism. For them, Zionism is human hubris in defiance of God's design for the Jewish people, and the attachment of the religious Zionists to land more than to the Torah is viewed as nothing short of pagan. The *haredim*, however, with their large families and limited modern educational skills, are, besides citizen Palestinians, also the poorest stratum of Israel's population. Priced out of the housing market in the center of the country and unwanted as neighbors because of their close-knit communities, they saw the West Bank as a haven that combined segregated existence and affordable housing. At first, *haredim* moved into a few smaller communities; then two cities were built for them. Modi'in Illit, with a population of 63,187 in 2014, and Beitar Illit, with a population of 46,874, are the largest of the only four Jewish cities in the West Bank (see map 2).The *haredim*—who are a quarter of the settler population—account for roughly one-half of the settler population's annual growth. Most of them are young families with numerous children, and the population of their cities grows by over 10 percent annually. Overall, their suburban cities make up another, distinctly *haredi* suburban frontier, the least ideological of the many settlement frontiers.

The potential of both the secular and the religious suburban colonies to absorb new settlers and extend without interruption became obvious after 1993. In spite of the violence of the post-Oslo years, settlement continued apace and took place mostly in suburbia. The number of Jewish settlers doubled from roughly one hundred thousand to two hundred thousand during the years of the Oslo negotiations and continued even as the Second Intifada was raging on. Further growth, this time mostly in the *haredi* cities, brought the total number of West Bank colonists to 268,400 by 2006.

Finally, we turn to the newest crop of colonies: the so-called illegal outpost of squatters (*ma'achaz*). After the Oslo process began, Israel pledged to build no new settlements, but starting in 1995 a new settlement wave—the pirate outposts, apparently undertaken spontaneously by settlers without government authorization—commenced. In fact, the big wave of outpost construction was between 1998 and 2002, particularly in the spring of 1999

What Is the Occupation?

after the call of Ariel Sharon, foreign minister at the time, "to run and grab the hills" (see map 2). "The goal," as explained by political scientist Moriel Ram and historian Mark LeVine, "was to replace the suburban culture of the established settlements with a renewed frontier ethos that would make it impossible to adopt any territorial compromise."[76] Outposts are erected by small groups with the active help of a nearby established settlement, the local or regional council, and Amana. Most outposts have a makeshift character—a hastily prepared road, temporary housing of various sorts, trailers, huts, tents, a generator, and a large water tank, soon to be followed by small permanent edifices for a synagogue and kindergarten.

Their founders are mostly second-generation religious settlers but also an assortment of adventure seekers and even delinquent youth looking for new beginnings. Many of the outposts' members are transient, and the "hilltop youth" are known for their hippie-like appearance: untucked, soiled T-shirt, freely dangling *tzizith* (fringed or tasseled religious garment), and soup bowl–size yarmulke. Some residents wish to "return to nature" and have agricultural pursuits from raising sheep and bees to growing fruit. Others are focused on religious learning, and many of their members are idle, as the main collective goal is to keep the outpost manned.

While this description suggests that the outposts were erected haphazardly, they commonly are located in between other settlements. This layout connects the outposts, creating strategic links in a broader settlement plan. Within a few years more than one hundred such settlements have proliferated. Their settlers soon become beneficiaries of government-provided services, electrical lines, and paved roads. These government-provided benefits indicate that being "unauthorized" does not mean that state authorities view these colonies as any less legal than those established by government decree. In the novel *The Hilltop*, by Israeli author Assaf Gavron, one of the settlers explains his outpost's status to a supportive American millionaire, Sheldon Mamelstein:

Ma'aleh Hermesh C cannot be illegal because, according to Defense Ministry records, the outpost was evacuated years ago. . . . But we do have an approved agricultural farm, which the military protects. . . . The Settlement Department of the Jewish Agency arranged for the establishment of the agricultural farm, which doesn't require government permits. Through the Civil Administration, we also secured a generator, and the army took care of the water supply. Most of the trailers were provided by the Housing Ministry, via the Amidar public housing company. Fortunately for us, the right hand has no clue what the left one is doing.[77]

In the telling explanation of Moshe Ya'alon, then minister for strategic affairs, "All the outposts were authorized, and it's only the planning that remains incomplete." In other words, land was allocated to some of the outposts, but their residents moved in before the planning process was completed. Why not wait? The planning of these colonies could not be completed, since from the mid-1990s onward Israel has not authorized the construction of new settlements. There is a game of chicken going on: some outposts are retroactively approved as new neighborhoods of older settlements (to keep up appearances), a handful are removed, and most stay put.

The use of the term *settlements* obscures the existence of another group of colonies: the Jewish neighborhoods built in East Jerusalem following its annexation to Israel. Just eighteen days after the 1967 War, Israel vastly expanded West Jerusalem's municipal boundaries, adding to its thirty-eight square kilometers not only East Jerusalem's six square kilometers but another sixty-four square kilometers. Most of present-day Jerusalem, which includes twenty-eight Palestinian villages, laid out in a gerrymandered configuration that includes as few Palestinians as possible, was part of the West Bank. Not satisfied with the legal hold provided by the government's decision, the Knesset passed, in July 1980, the "Basic Law: Jerusalem," which declares the united city as Israel's capital to further entrench its annexation.

What Is the Occupation?

As far back as 1967, Israel began construction in East Jerusalem, expanding the Talpiot neighborhood into a no-man's-land enclave, which until then was controlled by the UN. The Ramat Eshkol, Giv'at Hamivtar, Ma'alot Dafna, Sanhedriya Murchevet, and French Hill residential neighborhoods were to connect the campus of Hebrew University on Mount Scopus (a community that, until 1967, was a stand-alone Israeli enclave surrounded by Jordanian territory), to West Jerusalem (see map 3). To expedite the construction of these "seam" (*bariach*) neighborhods, planning procedures were bypassed and part of the land was expropriated from Palestinian owners. By 1972, Israeli construction moved on to a new and more ambitious phase: the building of the ring neighborhoods of Ramot, Gilo, and Neve Yaakov at a further remove, to detach East Jerusalem from the West Bank. Three more neighborhoods (Pisgat Ze'ev in 1985 and Ramat Shlomo and Har Homa in the mid-1990s) were added to bring the number of new neighborhoods in East Jerusalem to a dozen. By 1993, the size of the Jewish population in East Jerusalem matched that of the Palestinians. By mid-2016, however, the share of the 207,100 Jews who lived in the seam and ring towns had declined to 39 percent of East Jerusalem's population because of the higher Palestinian birth rate.

East Jerusalem is of additional interest because it adds a unique twist to the overall settlement project: a process of settling in the midst of a dense urban Palestinian population. As part of settlement in East Jerusalem, starting as far back as April 1968, Israel expropriated twenty-nine acres not on the outskirts but in what was the Jewish Quarter of the Old City. This was another area that fell to the Jordanian Arab Legion in 1948 and thus could conceivably be another phantom limb to be regrown in order to reestablish Jewish presence in the Old City.

Such "restoration," however, was a matter not of reversing history but of rewriting it. To facilitate repossession, Israeli governments recognized the property rights of Jews in any part of the West Bank and East Jerusalem from before the 1948 War. Palestinian ownership rights of houses in West Jerusalem

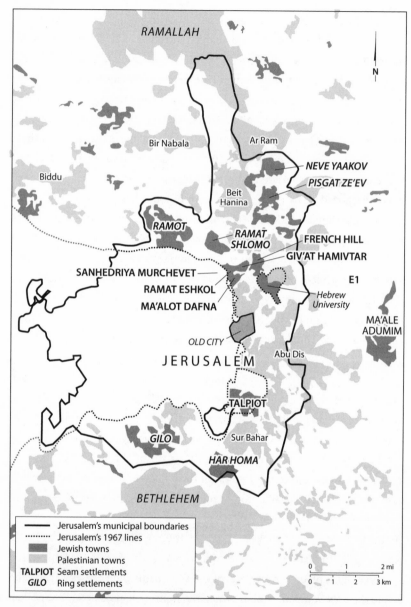

Map 3. Greater Jerusalem and its seam and ring towns. Used by permission of Shaul Arieli. Based on "United Jerusalem, 2012," www.shaularieli.com/image/users/77951/ftp/my_files/maps/hesderim_mediniim/map37.gif?id=10118319.

received no corresponding legal standing. Jewish property rights were only the beginning rather than the end of mixed settlement. The part of the Old City that was expropriated included all of the Jewish Quarter, although only a small portion of its houses were Jewish owned in 1948 (since none of the quarters had a religiously homogeneous population). The new Jewish Quarter was built by the Company for the Reconstruction and Development of the Jewish Quarter, which was placed directly under the Prime Minister's Office and the Inter-Ministerial Committee for Jerusalem Affairs. It took a decade, well-documented harassment of Palestinian residents, and a change in the compensation law to complete the transfer of the quarter into the hands of its new owners.

The construction of the seam and ring neighborhoods and of the Jewish Quarter had the support of all Israeli governments and was a centrally planned "wholesale" project. Additionally, Jewish settlers established several retail urban settlement projects in the other parts of East Jerusalem. Starting in the 1980s, settler nongovernmental organizations (NGOs) commenced claiming and sometimes purchasing houses within the Muslim Quarter as well, and, in 1987 the then minister of housing Ariel Sharon occupied a property in the Muslim Quarter. About seventy religious Jewish families now live in the Muslim and Christian Quarters, their homes marked by Israeli flags.

A similar house-by-house battle takes place in the even older part of Jerusalem, which once was the Jebusite city of Zion and is now the Palestinian village of Silwan, just outside the Old City wall. Since 1997, the Elad NGO, in an unprecedented move received the concession from the Israel Nature and Park Authority to manage the City of David National Park in Silwan and to fund local archaeological excavations of the Antiquities Authority. Elad, run by and for religious settlers, is now involved with the administration of almost all the major archaeological sites in East Jerusalem. The archaeological park serves to facilitate Elad's entry into adjacent houses inhabited by Palestinians. Following this trend, the Ateret Kohanim (Priestly Crown) NGO has laid claim through the Custodian for Absentee

Property to the neighborhood of Batan al-Hawa in the middle of Silwan, where houses owned by Jews from Yemen once stood. The Custodian transferred ownership of the area to the NGO without a tender that would have potentially allowed their Palestinian residents—many of them refugees of the 1948 War—to buy their homes at below-market prices. The Jewish National Fund, for its part, has provided settlers with protected tenants' agreements. As of 2014, there were about five hundred Jewish settlers among the village's twenty thousand residents. Though both Elad and Ateret Kohamim claim to have either purchased the houses from Palestinian owners or paid them to leave voluntarily before eviction orders were to be executed, all instances of the replacement of Palestinian tenants with Jewish ones have been carried out under heavy police protection. The Custodian files are classified, and, as a rule, Israeli courts also keep secret the identities of the land purchasers on behalf of the settler NGOs to protect them from retaliation. The best-known example of such settlement in the heart of a large urban Arab population is the Jewish community in Hebron's Old City. There about eight hundred Jews, protected by hundreds of soldiers, live amid some twenty thousand Palestinian residents whose movements are severely curtailed and whose shops have been boarded up.

As of 2016, the number of Jewish settlers in military, religious, secular suburban, *haredi* suburban, and outpost colonies in the West Bank as well as the ring and seam towns of East Jerusalem reached 612,258, and 207,100 of these lived in a dozen newly built Jerusalem neighborhoods. By mid-2016, according to the Civilian Administration, 405,158 Jewish settlers lived in 126 officially recognized settlements and over one hundred illegal outposts.

I X

The military, messianic, secular, and *haredi* suburban settlements and outposts within the boundaries of their local and regional councils collectively possess half of the West Bank's landmass (not even counting East Jerusalem).

How has land been made available for such a massive project of colonization in an area densely populated by Palestinians? It is time to turn from the topic of colonization to Israel's *land seizure* mechanisms, every bit as complex, diverse, and self-contradictory as those of colonization, and sometimes on the margin and frequently over the edge of criminality. Hunger for land brought out the most ruthless practices, marking the moral boundaries of colonialism, and highlighting the gaps between colonial and legal practices.

The counterpoint to the remarkable diversity and occasional chaos of the Israeli colonization project is the stringent Israeli planning process for settlements and new housing. The construction of any new settlement until the Oslo DOP was be preceded by a political decision and today, the construction of new housing units or neighborhoods is subject to similarly stringent conditions. Between 1970 and 1996, the Joint Settlement Committee of the Israeli Government and the World Zionist Organization, a body that represents world Jewry, approved or denied settlement requests. Since 1996, decisions also have had to receive the approval of the Israeli minister of defense and government.[78] As a second step, the Custodian for Government and Abandoned Property in Judea and Samaria, which is a department in the Civil Administration, must allocate the land itself. Now planning can begin within the Supreme Planning Council of Judea and Samaria, also housed in the Civilian Administration in Beth El and composed of Israeli experts and military lawyers. All this must happen prior to construction. Six distinct deliberative phases take place before the approval of an outline plan: planning authorization, review prior to unveiling for public comment, initial publication, review of objections, review prior to authorization, and authorization. Subsequently the Local Planning and Construction Committee, which is a branch of the local authority—either the regional council or the settlement—has to fill in the details of the outline plan before construction can begin. Upon completion of the planning stages, but before construction may begin, tenders are issued for construction in urban sites, whereas in rural settlements land is transferred to the settlement directly by the World Zionist Organization. Contractors need both a land development permit from the minister of defense and a construction permit from the local authority.

Altogether there are some ten planning steps for each colony or housing unit, and since there is frequently public opposition on part of local Palestinian residents, Israeli NGOs, or both at many of these stages, the mistaken impression is often created that many more housing units, neighborhoods, or settlements are being built than in fact is the case. Since all stages of planning must receive prior authorization from the minister of defense, who at times has used his authority to stop the issuing of politically sensitive tenders, many colonization projects are stuck in the planning pipeline, some for decades. Though the clamor against new settlement construction visits international opprobrium on Israel, ironically, the dual tracks of orderly planning and chaotic construction serve to project the impression that the colonization project is more massive than it is.

While the planning of settlements aims at the dispersal of Jews throughout the West Bank, similar mechanisms are employed to concentrate Palestinian construction within narrow confines. Israel has transferred all planning authority from Jordanian bodies to its own military government. Thus the Samaria Regional Planning Scheme of 1945, which zoned the entirety of the West Bank as agricultural land, is used to limit new Palestinian construction to areas already built up. This scheme is employed to deny practically all requests for rezoning and building permits on agricultural land. It also allows the Israeli government to condemn and demolish unauthorized houses. The Jerusalem Regional Planning Scheme from 1942 is used to similar effect.[79]

X

Land requisition and expropriation were, from the start, part of a large, almost industrial-scale project; hence, the related legal tools are best termed *mechanisms of seizure.* To enable land requisition very early on after the conquest of the West Bank, the Israeli military laid the foundations for assuming all authority over land. As far back as June 18, 1967, Military Order No. 25 required the military's approval of all property and land transactions.[80] Order No. 59 authorized the military to take possession of properties belonging to Jordan, an enemy state, and manage them. On January 1, 1969, Order No. 291 froze Jordanian land registration, stopping the process that had begun under the Mandatory authorities, leaving two-thirds of the land unregistered. It did so on the grounds of wishing to protect the rights of the Jordanian government and landowners who took refuge in Jordan during the 1967 War. In fact, far from doing so, the military threw open all unregistered land to Israeli confiscation.[81]

The Israeli government applies and supports four major mechanisms for land seizure, which enable the transfer of West Bank land into Israeli hands: (1) the declaration of land as abandoned property, (2) the expropriation of land for public need, (3) the requisition of land for "essential and urgent military needs," and, most far-reaching of all, (4) the declaration of coveted areas as "state land." In contrast to the colonization waves, which followed a distinct sequence (though now they overlap with each other), land requisition takes a scattershot approach, following parallel tracks to reach the same aim. For example, the settlement of Shilo was established in 1985 on a swath of land acquired through the combination of military requisition, declaration as state land, and seizure for public need.[82] All these legal schemes have a single goal, to make land available by any and all means for colonization.

Israel used the first scheme, the declaration of land as abandoned property, to seize Palestinian land very soon after the end of the 1967 War. Property belonging to owners who had left the West Bank before, during, or after the 1967 War fell into this category, and their land's management was entrusted to the Custodian for Abandoned Property. This mechanism yielded about 430,000 *dunams* (a land measure unit of one thousand square meters) and eleven thousand buildings to the inventory available for colonization.

Israel created this stock in three ways. First, it forbade the return of refugees to the West Bank, thereby forestalling the restitution of their land. Second, it unified the Custodian for Abandoned Property (whose ostensible aim is the protection of unclaimed property on behalf of their owners) with the Custodian for Government Property (which administers public land on behalf of the government). Through this merger, Israel placed government interests above the trustee role of the Custodian. Third, whenever it was discovered through judicial proceedings that land had not, in fact, been abandoned and that the owner still resided in the West Bank, the transfer of the land by the Custodian to colonizing bodies was determined to be irreversible if it had been done "in good faith," [83] giving an altogether unsavory meaning to the expression.

A second mechanism for acquiring Palestinian land for Jewish colonization is its expropriation for "public need." This procedure has been used less extensively, yielding only around 100,000 *dunams*, mostly because it raises the awkward question of just which public's benefit is being served when West Bank Palestinian land is being expropriated. The measure has mostly served to construct roads that bypass Palestinian villages and connect settlements to one another and to Israel. In one location, however, private land expropriation for public need has played a major colonizing role: the twelve new Jewish neighborhoods built in East Jerusalem were constructed mostly on expropriated land that serves Jews only, though the government claimed that it was for the benefit of Jews and Arabs alike.[84]

The third land seizure mechanism adopted by Israel is the use of privately owned Palestinian land for military needs under authority granted to military commanders. Under IHL, private land can be only temporarily requisitioned, but this process was used to establish Qiryat Arba, Efrat, Har Gilo, and another ten settlements. In some cases, the settlements were initially constructed as a Nachal *he'achzut*, a military protosettlement later turned over to civilians.[85] In 1979, however, this mechanism came under serious legal challenge in what appeared to throw the whole colonization drive into a major crisis. In the famed 1979 *Elon Moreh* case, the HCJ rejected the use of military requisition of private Palestinian land for the purpose of settlement building. This was an exceptional ruling, but it was made under unusual circumstances. The court heard the appeal shortly after the signing of the Israeli-Egyptian peace treaty, which reduced the authority of single-minded security justifications for governmental decisions. In addition, the government's majority decision to settle Gush Emunim's Elon Moreh nucleus was challenged in court by several of its own members and retired officers on the grounds that there was no military justification for its construction. When the HCJ sided with the applicants, it seemed that a legal Rubicon had been crossed and colonization would have to be seriously curtailed.

The effect of the *Elon Moreh* decision, however, remained limited. Without skipping a beat, the new Likud government adopted and expanded a new and even more sweeping mechanism of land acquisition: the declaration of West Bank land as "state land." [86] While before 1979 only about 47,000 *dunam*s had been requisitioned for ostensibly military purposes and another 600,000 *dunam*s had been classified by the British Mandate and Jordan as state land, after the *Elon Moreh* decision 913,000 *dunam*s were declared as state land between 1980 and 1984. State land, under the authority of the Custodian for State Property, "comprises 75 percent of the settlements' municipal area and 66 percent of their built-up area." [87] This mechanism was then used to transfer into Israeli hands over a quarter of the West Bank.

As part of this new legal strategy of land acquisition, Israel set the legal-administrative clock back to Ottoman times. Under the 1858 Ottoman Land Code, agricultural land reverted to the state if (1) it had not been under cultivation for three consecutive years, (2) it had not been cultivated for a decade and thus was under no ownership rights secured by the cultivator (*makhlul*), or (3) it lay far from a village (*mawat*). The Israeli interpretation of Ottoman precedent opted for particularly harsh tests of cultivation and, in fact, disregarded both Ottoman practice and, subsequent, less onerous Mandatory rulings. In an additional Orwellian twist, when Palestinian owners were denied access to their plots that were confiscated for military needs, the absence of cultivation could now serve as justification for land seizures.[88]

There is a Military Appeals Committee that adjudicates appeals of the Custodian's decision to declare a plot as "state land." This quasi-judicial body is appointed by and dependent upon the very military that issues the land seizure orders. The Appeals Committee is also exempt from following rules of evidence. Its decisions only have the power of recommendation to the regional military commander who makes the final decisions, and are not subject to appeal.[89] Finally, the Custodian is in the habit of allocating to settlement construction "survey land" whose ownership has not been finalized.[90]

The multifaceted Israeli land seizure approach is characterized by haste, confusion, corruption, and illegality. In 2004, bowing to US pressure, Prime Minister Sharon commissioned Talia Sasson, from the Ministry of Justice, to investigate the legal status of the recently established outposts. About the same time, he also tasked Brigadier General Baruch Spiegel to prepare a database to chart the outer construction line of existing settlements so that a settlement freeze he had committed to could take place. Sasson implicated the full range of authorities—military and civilian—in breaking the law and pointed to the Civil Administration of the OPT as the hub of illegality. The purported goal of the Civil Administration under international humanitarian law is to ensure the well-being of the "protected" Palestinian population. In fact, it has become the main body enabling the colonization process and ensuring settlers' access to government resources, in tandem with other bodies. Sasson's conclusions concerning the outposts in the West Bank were sweeping:

> The violation of the law became institutionalized. We face not a felon or a group of felons violating the law. The big picture is a bold violation of laws by certain state authorities, public authorities, regional councils in Judea,

What Is the Occupation?

Samaria, and Gaza and settlers, while falsely presenting an organized legal system. . . . The establishment of unauthorized outposts violates standard procedure, good governing rules, and [constitutes] an especially bold and ongoing violation of law.[91]

It would be misleading to conclude from the Sasson Report that only unauthorized settlements, the so-called outposts, benefited from lax legal enforcement. Spiegel's database reveals the broader picture. Even authorized settlements have profited from widespread illegality, since the overall framework of Israeli colonization in the West Bank teeters on the verge of the wrongful and unlawful. One commentator explained the implications of the humdrum database thus: "Everyone is talking about the 107 [illegal] outposts, but that is small change. The really big picture is the older settlements, the 'legal' ones. The construction there has been ongoing for years in blatant violation of the law and the regulations of proper governance."[92]

Spiegel's database uncovered that between thirty and fifty-one settlements were constructed in part on officially seized land and in part on privately owned Palestinian land that lay outside the settlement's jurisdiction.[93] A sample survey of the state comptroller in 2000–2003 found at least fourteen cases of illegal construction on Palestinian private land financed by the Housing Ministry. "Illegal construction," as reported by B'Tselem, the Israeli information center for human rights in the OPT, "encompasses enormous swaths of land. It spans, for example, almost all the built-up area in each of the settlements Itamar, Beit-El, Chemdat, Yitav, Ofra, and all the southern neighborhoods of Modi'in Illit."[94] Building violations were classified a criminal offense in the West Bank (as they are in Israel) only in 2007, but no settlers have been prosecuted for engaging in such unlawful activities even after that date. The Civil Administration has ordered demolitions in only 3 percent of building violation cases it has investigated.[95] In contrast, when the Bil'in Village Council petitioned the HCJ to stop the construction of apartments in Modi'in Illit on land owned by its residents, the Court rejected the petition because the reversal of the construction would have constituted a "disproportionate sanction" against the purchasers. Outright theft of privately owned Palestinian land and construction of new colonies on it, as well as reliance on forged purchase contracts, are so widespread that large parts of land east of the Green Line have become the "Wild West Bank." When it comes to land seizure, planning, and colonization, the Israeli state acts as a traditional colonial power underwriting the plunder of the native population. Together, the four components of the occupation—IHL, everyday life, repression and resistance, and colonization—make it a colonial framework for the post–World War II era.

X I

As the legal historian Lauren Benton has observed, European empires from the fifteenth century on were constituted by two simple legal principles, both derived from settler-colonial practices. On the one hand, they sought to export their legal framework to protect their citizens who colonized the imperial territory and to expand the domain of European cultural mission. On the other hand, they resisted the complete annexation of their imperial territories and the assumption of full sovereignty, since that would have extended citizenship to all inhabitants. Wherever colonists arrived, so did European law, but that law could not be generalized. This contradiction created a layered imperial sovereignty, among them estuary-centered entities with uncertain control of hinterlands, legal piracy, military colonies, enclaves connected by corridors surrounded by areas outside of imperial control, areas under martial law, states of exception, anomalous legal zones—a diversity that raised significant legal issues and threatened to undermine imperial sovereignty. Not only has "the whole of the imperial world represented a zone of legal anomaly vis-à-vis the metropole," [96] but colonization made the application of an international legal regime impossible. Sovereignty in colonies, therefore, remained incomplete, elastic, and

What Is the Occupation?

open. The colonies' denial of equality to the indigenous population also meant that their status remained unsettled, or contested. The absence of citizenship signals the difference between a state and the colonial parts of an empire.

In spite of the geographical and historical differences between early modern European and contemporary Israeli colonization, Benton's observations serve as a fitting framework for a summary account of the tangled web of half a century of Israeli occupation. The Israeli occupation has evolved in the crucible of this paradox: the attempt to annex territory without its Palestinian residents, who consequently remain a legal anomaly. Just three weeks into the occupation, the Knesset gave Israeli courts concurrent jurisdiction with its military courts to ensure that Israeli citizens would not be subject to the military and emergency laws used to rule over occupied Palestinians. Subsequently, Israeli settlements were incorporated according to and placed under Israeli municipal law. Jewish settlers, as well as all other Israelis and all Jews (namely people who fall under the Law of Return) for the duration of their stay in the OPT, and the territory of their settlements are subject to Israeli legal frameworks. In contrast, for occupied Palestinians the Israeli military serves as both the legislative and the executive authority. Wherever they are arrested, Palestinians are subject to Jordanian law and the orders of military governors. The limits placed on occupied Palestinians' human rights and their limited protection through IHL, which is applied selectively as put forth in the Shamgar Doctrine, demonstrate Israel's unwillingness to move beyond the colonial era. Withholding citizenship from occupied Palestinians colors Israel as a colonial empire builder.

At the same time, Israel is unable to annex the vast majority of the OPT because it does not wish to make the Palestinians into its citizens. At the opening of the Knesset's winter 2015 session, Stav Shaffir, the fiery Knesset member from the Zionist Camp Party, goaded Prime Minister Netanyahu and his allies from the religious Zionist Jewish Home Party to carry out their promises. Netanyahu has been prime minister close to a decade, she argued, and then inquired, "Who's preventing you from annexing the territories? Who's stopping you from rebuilding [the settlements in Gaza]? Annex the territories! Why aren't you doing it?" [97] Though IHL has not been an effective barrier to colonization in the WB, it shares the UN's legal norm of "territorial integrity." Thus IHL presents an ultimate barrier to the annexation of the West Bank, or parts of it, by Israel. As demonstrated by Mark Zacher, since the Second World War the norm of territorial integrity has held up remarkably well and there have been few challenges to it and no cases of internationally sanctioned territorial expansion.[98] Israel's own annexations of East Jerusalem and the Golan Heights, not surprisingly, have not been internationally recognized.

Let me use Benton's framework to answer the question "What is the Occupation?" I will do so by assessing the current structure and layout of the occupation. Much of Israeli legal discourse and institutional practice has been deployed with the intention of denying Palestinian rights and offering an alternative denialist framework of ostensible rights—running the gamut from the "enlightened occupation," through the establishment of the Civil Administration, to the establishment of Areas A, B, and C. But the occupation regime has been challenged by many acts of resistance as well as two intifadas. Israel's adjustments to Palestinian resistance and its desire to shield its colonies have led to the creation of the uneven imperial geographies outlined by Benton. The OPT today are like multiple subdivisions, each with its distinct legal status. This geographical mosaic is the result of the continued occupation tempered by Israeli concessions, as partial and contingent as they are, to Palestinian resistance.

The Oslo Accords divide the West Bank into three zones. Area A encompasses eight large Palestinian cities that enjoy full Palestinian civilian and security control and make up 18 percent of the West Bank. Area B includes 440 Palestinian villages and their surrounding areas, under Palestinian civil and Israeli military control, encompassing 22 percent of the West Bank. Some of the towns and villages in these areas, such as Nablus, can be accessed only by passage through permanent checkpoints, while others can be accessed through side roads open only to Palestinians (but not the main roads, which are available only to settlers). Between 165 and 190 checkpoints control movement within Areas A and B; many of these areas are noncontiguous "islands" separated by portions of Area C. Area C is the only area with territorial contiguity. It includes the areas within settler local and regional council boundaries, is under full Israeli civilian and security control, and makes up a full 60 percent of the West Bank (see map 1). Area C also includes 297,000 Palestinians in 532 communities and villages.[99] The land belonging to some of the villagers in Area C is found in Areas A and B, and their access to it is restricted through multiple checkpoints. The PNA provides health and educational services to the remaining Palestinian population in Area C, while the construction and maintenance of their infrastructure are Israel's responsibility. Thirty-eight Palestinian communities of Area C are within areas declared firing zones by the Israel Defense Forces and are subject to periodic evacuations. Some closed-off enclaves in Area C—for example, in the Jordan Valley—can be entered only by their residents. Further, a special arrangement places 20 percent of the Arab city of Hebron, Area H2 within Area C, under full Israeli control.

The completed part of the Separation Wall runs in large part through the OPT and has created a series of geographical anomalies of its own. The Seam Zone (*marchav hatefer*)—the area between the Green Line and the Wall itself—is home to over fifty-seven thousand Palestinians. Another one hundred thousand Palestinians live east of their land, which is located west of the Wall. Residents needing access to their fields require special permits from the Civil Administration. On the occasion of the Separation Wall's construction, Kfar 'Aqab, Shu'afat, and part of the Qalandia refugee camps were separated from Jerusalem, to which they had belonged since the annexation of East Jerusalem to Israel. There is even a single family's enclave, the Ammar family's house, trapped between the colony of Elkana and the Separation Wall; it has its own special gate in the Wall.

Finally, there is the Gaza Strip, from which Israel withdrew its settlers and military in August 2005, making this area the least occupied among the Palestinian territories. The Israeli state attorney holds that, following the termination of its military government, Israel no longer carries any responsibility under IHL toward Gaza's residents. In August 2014, Israel declared the Gaza Strip to be enemy territory, further eliminating any responsibility for damages incurred by Gaza residents as a consequence of Israeli military actions and operations. Though Gaza has no colonists or settlers, Israel still maintains "effective control" over the Strip, the defining characteristic of belligerent occupation. At the same time, any sweeping view of continued Israeli occupation is mitigated by the fact that Gaza has two borders. Egypt controls the Rafah land crossing and, except for the short period of the Muslim Brotherhood's rule, has maintained its own harsh border controls and has restricted the entry and exit of individual Palestinians and goods. Further, it has destroyed hundreds of tunnels built by Gazans to deliver goods from the Sinai into the Strip. Nevertheless, even a brief survey of Israel's effective control over Gaza demonstrates just how intrusive its presence is.

Since the takeover of Gaza by Hamas in 2008, Israel has imposed a blockade of supplies to Gaza. It has constructed a Separation Wall between Israel and Gaza, and it enforces a no-go buffer zone on the Gazan side of the Wall. Israel maintains direct control over all six of Gaza's land crossings that border on Israel, as well as its airspace and seacoast, and prevents the construction of a deep seaport in Gaza. Israel opens some of the land crossings to allow in hundreds of trucks each day with goods it deems nonmilitary that supply the amount of calories Israel has calculated to be sufficient per person. The Hamas government of Gaza has not been able to rebuild the houses, factories, and power stations that were destroyed in the three wars with Israel, since Israel controls the entry of construction materials. Most unusually, Israel maintains Gaza's population registry to control the entry and departure of its residents, in effect retaining the governmental authority to determine who is and who is not a lawful resident of Gaza. Finally, Gaza remains dependent upon Israel's supply of the majority of its water, electricity, and telecommunications and still uses the Israeli shekel as its legal tender. Gaza, in short, remains occupied, but from the outside. The UN, most governments, the ICRC, and human rights NGOs still view Gaza as having remained under Israeli occupation.

A second facet of the unevenness of the occupation is highlighted by the multiplicity, the spontaneity, and even the chaotic and wild nature of post-1967 Israeli colonization. The resistance of the occupied Palestinians and the disapproving international legal context did not allow for the kind of planned and organized settlement construction that Israel had undertaken within the Green Line in its early years. The distinctiveness of military, religious, even messianic, and suburban colonization drives introduces an element of internal conflict into the project of colonization: each variety of settlement occupies a different region, appeals to a different constituency, and has a different political agenda attached to it. From among one of these drives (the messianic one), in the past decade or so, an even more radical fringe has arisen. Some of its prominent leaders now envision the construction of a Third Temple on the Haram as-Sharif or Temple Mount, in the Old City of Jerusalem.

The Labor Party views the large settlement blocs along the Green Line as the area that it, the Likud, and the religious Zionists agree to annex to Israel, but this search for consensus also highlights the profound internal Israeli disagreement concerning the future of the rest of the West Bank. Over one hundred squatter outposts have not been authorized by the Israeli government and are illegal even by Israeli standards. The early-established colonies, for example those in Gush Etzion, are concerned that the outposts and their settlers' vigilante attacks on neighboring Palestinian villages may place their existence in danger as well. The mixed-colonization settlements—those in the midst of a dense urban Palestinian population, as in Hebron, Jerusalem's Old City, and Silwan—are hotbeds of intercommunal violence and require massive and expensive protection. The recent knife attacks in Hebron and Greater, or "united," Jerusalem have led to calls to abandon some of its Arab neighborhoods by shrinking the city's municipal boundaries.

The half-century-long occupation is legitimated through a *sui generis* Israeli interpretation of IHL that allows the colonization of the OPT. Its denialism, the attempt to create an alternative legal framework where there is none, aims to keep the international community out and the Palestinians down. Under the legal umbrella of occupation, Israel has been engaging in an intensive colonization project to extend its pre-1948 state-building project and unite the new with the ancient Jewish homeland. But what appears to be fifty years of solid accomplishments of sustained colonization is an opportunistic project that uses now one method of land acquisition and now another, establishes now one type of settlement and now another, settles one group in one part of the West Bank and another in a different part. Each segment— the Allon Plan settlers on the security frontier, those in search of a suburban lifestyle, religious Zionist and messianic groups, *haredim*—settled on its own terms and in areas of its own choice. "Settlement" carries within its structure all the diverse and conflicting interests of Israeli society and in many respects remains a hollow undertaking. The mosaic-like geography, the legal contortions, the administrative maze, even the blatant illegality of a considerable part of settlement construction all demonstrate that Israeli colonization is not a single or single-minded project and is vulnerable to challenges and pressures.

The Palestinian territory occupied by Israel in the 1967 War that is available for colonization has shrunk over the past half century. Israel has withdrawn from Gaza, and the ceding of the civilian authority in Areas A and B to the PNA, as well as the construction of the Separation Wall as a stand-in for a potential border, shows us both the contradictions within and the limits to Israel's colonization project. These withdrawals and redeployments are responses to checks on the colonization project and indicate the shrinking of Israeli territorial ambitions. The settlement enterprise's complexity and contradictions, which have served it well at times, also leave the project vulnerable to change. The colonies' prospects, depending as much on Palestinian resistance as on Israeli potentials and intentions, and on international interests, are far from certain, and their future is yet to be written.

Why Has the Occupation Lasted This Long?

Why does Israel hold the contemporary world record of belligerent occupation, having occupied the West Bank, East Jerusalem, and the Golan Heights for more than a half century? How is Israel able to keep control and tighten its hold on the Occupied Palestinian Territories (OPT)—and still oversee access to Gaza—despite the noxious character of the occupation, increased Palestinian resistance, Israeli domestic dissent, and international opprobrium? In this essay I will offer a historical perspective—not a straightforward or detailed history but one filtered through the perspective of the social sciences—in search of both larger patterns and social turns that prolong the occupation and enable the occupier.

My proposition is that the occupation is dragged out by the Israeli desire to continue its state building by colonizing and subsequently annexing parts of the OPT. The dynamic of this process is made manifest by Israel's preference for colonization over of peacemaking, and even security, at each point when the possibility of the diplomatic resolution of either the Israeli-Arab or the Israeli-Palestinian conflict has arisen. The driving force behind this preference is the ambition *to continue* Israel's history of state building through settlement into the OPT. I will focus on the role and ethos of colonization in Israeli state building in sections I and II. Colonization undertaken by the Israeli right wing, the Likud, and the religious Zionist Jewish Home Party, however, is not the simple extension of past practices. It requires the radicalization of the new colonization's legitimation, an ongoing attempt to replace both secular Zionism and the post-1967 "land for peace" formula with religious legitimacy. Among Palestinians a similar, and in part reactive, religious legitimation has taken place and stands in opposition to the Oslo process's promise of compromise. It is against the background of the Oslo approach that we can most fruitfully examine how the Israeli and Palestinian religious vanguards have set back the negotiations.

Religious turns are a global trend nourished by local aspirations and grievances. However, in the case of the Israeli-Palestinian conflict, the respective Judaic and Islamic radicalizations fed on one another, each encouraging the further radicalization of its counterpart. Any symmetry between the religious legitimations, nonetheless, does not extend to the prolongation of the occupation, which is due to the Israeli ambition to hold on to the OPT. Palestinians, on their part, would like nothing more than to see the occupation in the rearview mirror. These religious changes, however, have gone a long way toward solidifying Israeli and Palestinian positions by replacing the nationalist assertion of claims with exclusivist territory-based religious discourses, making compromise all the more difficult. These vanguards exert considerable influence, but they have not been able to remake their respective societies in their own image, and they have encountered considerable opposition to their religiously claimed mandates to claim all of Palestine for themselves.

In Sections III through V, I will chart the domestic changes experienced by Israeli society, and in Sections VI and VII I will turn my attention to the changes Palestinian society has undergone, transformations that sustain both the occupation and the struggle against it. In each society religious nationalist movements and parties—Gush Emunim (Bloc of the Faithful) and Hamas (Islamic Resistance Movement), respectively—have taken on the role of vanguards, seeking to provide a model for the rest of society. They have rearticulated and radicalized, in religious terms, earlier nationalist aspirations; they also serve as conduits for socioeconomic aspirations.

In Sections VIII and IX of this essay, I will broaden my perspective to examine the role played by the occupation's direct and indirect international enablers. The two most important external factors, US foreign policy and international humanitarian law, instead of inhibiting the occupation, have enabled its continuation. The Israeli-Palestinian conflict plays out, as it has since the penetration of the great powers into the Middle East in the late Ottoman years as a global conflict. The post–First World War system of Mandates was a last-ditch attempt to reward victorious countries with territorial assets and to maintain the old imperial order over non-European possessions; it provided the legal framework and, when necessary, the muscle to implement the Zionist program. In contrast, international humanitarian law (IHL) is the distillation of the intra-European experience to delimit warfare. Even so, Israel is reading the IHL against the grain.

The expansion of the Yishuv (the Jewish community in Mandatory Palestine) in Palestine and Israel's colonization in the OPT, however, share a characteristic: they form a *sovereignty vacuum* in which the ruling foreign power, first Great Britain and now Israel, attends to the native population's general welfare but disregards its political aspirations. Specifically, under both the Mandate and IHL, being the majority—in both cases, an Arab majority—is not a precondition for sovereignty, as it is in other nation-states: sovereignty remains suspended until the Mandate or occupation comes to an end. Starting in 1967, Israel used the occupation as the framework for the continuation of the very colonization that had established it as a country under the British Mandate. The occupation also reinforced Israel's unwillingness to set its boundaries. It is this sovereignty vacuum that has been put in the service of colonization as a strategy of state building, first by the Yishuv and now by Israel. Supported by the United States from the Cold War on and subsequently through the articulation of a "special relationship" between the two countries, Israel has been able to defy the international community's desire to bring the conflict to an end. This international context will be covered in Section IX, the concluding section of the essay.

I

In seeking to comprehend the reasons for Israel's desire to draw out its occupation of the West Bank and East Jerusalem, it is best to start with the part of the occupation that has ended. Israel conquered the Sinai Peninsula from Egypt in 1967 but agreed to restore it to Egypt as part of the March 1979 treaty between the two countries, transacting "peace for land." The agreement with Egypt has been facilitated by the fact that treaties concluded between sovereign states fit neatly into the main channel of international relations. Furthermore, there was no doubt as to the location of the international border between the two countries. The line was demarcated by Britain and the Ottomans in October 1906 and was reaffirmed in the February 1949 Egyptian-Israeli armistice agreement. By this logic, when Egypt agreed to enter into a treaty with Israel, it should have been easy to bring the conflict between two countries to a conclusion. That was not, however, the case. Israel had planned for a different future in the Sinai.

As early as 1969, Israel established the military Nachal (the military's own settlement arm) colony called Dikla in the northern Sinai just west of Gaza, as well as the town of Ofira near Sharm al-Sheikh at the tip of the Sinai Peninsula. In January 1972, General Ariel Sharon, the head of the Southern Command, evicted in short order 1,500 Bedouin families and bulldozed their houses, tents, and tin shacks. The Bedouins' orchards and fields were uprooted so that a buffer of settlements could be built in the Rafah Approach (see map 4). By severing Gaza from the Sinai, the belt of settlements was expected to end a wave of road mining, sabotage of installations, and attacks against civilians. The plan enjoyed the support of Minister of Defense Moshe Dayan and was incorporated into the Galili Document that was adopted into the Labor Party's platform in September 1973. Its promised highlight was the

Map 4. Former Israeli settlements in Gaza. Reproduced with the permission of the Foundation for Middle East Peace from "Gaza Strip—January 2002," http://fmep.org/resource/gaza-strip-jan-2002/.

construction of the city of Yamit, planned to have 200,000 residents but reaching only a population of 2,500, and of a seaport that was never built. The colonization in northern and southern Sinai was an extension of the military frontier already under way in the Jordan Valley by the same Levi Eshkol, Golda Meir, and Yitzhak Rabin Labor Party governments.

When the 1967 War yielded its first positive diplomatic Arab response, Israel was not ready to take advantage of it. In February 1971, Gunnar Jarring, the UN special envoy to implement Security Council Resolution 242, submitted his proposal for "a land for peace" accord to both Egypt and Israel. Anwar Sadat, Egypt's president of five months, declared his willingness "to enter into a peace agreement" with Israel, demanding in return Israel's full withdrawal to the pre-1967 borders. Sadat also promised "to give Israel all the guarantees she had asked for." The Jarring Plan included additional security measures as substitutes for border corrections. The Golda Meir government's reply specified that it was ready to withdraw to "secure, recognized, and agreed upon borders to be established in the peace agreement" but added that "Israel will not withdraw to the pre-June 5, 1967 line." Nor was Israel willing to accept interim plans, including one originally raised by Dayan and then taken up by Sadat, for an Israeli withdrawal from the Suez Canal in return for its opening by Egypt to international shipping. Sadat claimed that "if the United States or Israel had shown enough interest in that initiative, the October [1973] War would not have taken place."[1]

Israel's rejection of UN- and US-mediated peace plans was not based on the plans' terms. Israel's leaders might have had doubts as to whether Egypt's offer encompassed full peace or merely a lesser status of nonbelligerence in return for Israeli withdrawal. But any agreement, interim, stepwise or final, would have commenced a diplomatic process and put off or eliminated the disastrous 1973 War, the ensuing decade-long economic recession, and possibly the loss of power by the Labor Party to the Likud and the rise of Gush Emunim. Even when Israel accepted all of Egypt's territorial demands in the

March 1979 Camp David Treaty, now under Likud's prime minister Menachem Begin, it received no more than a "cold peace," very much akin to a nonbelligerence accord.

Sadat's peace feelers were refused by an Israeli government that held to its ingrained legacy of colonization. There was, however, one crucial difference between colonization in the OPT and in the Sinai. No case could be made for a "Shamgar Doctrine" in the Sinai—a claim that Israeli control there did not constitute an occupation. By colonizing parts of Egypt, Israel had, in effect, transferred its own state-building method of colonization during the Yishuv onto the territory of a foreign sovereign country. Colonizing Egyptian territory without regard to the international legal and political context was true hubris.

We need not go far to establish why colonization has such a hold on the Israeli state, society, and imaginary. Israel is unlike nation-states that were created through the unification of smaller political units, as was done in western Europe, or secession from a multinational empire, the route taken in eastern Europe. Jewish nationalism was born in the 1880s in the Pale of Settlement (the western region in Imperial Russia to which Jews were confined) in response to the checkered accomplishments of the integrationist *hasakla* (Jewish Enlightenment) in czarist Russia and a wave of pogroms directed against the most integrated communities of the southern pale. It had two major factions. The much larger faction aspired to cultural autonomy *in situ*, possibly under a liberal or socialist regime that would replace czarism. Zionism—a much smaller faction—was eager to territorialize itself and soon debated the question of just where to do so. Martin Gilbert's *Jewish History Atlas* displays a map of numerous places considered for setting up a Jewish state, from the British colony of Uganda, through Cyprus, to Gaza.[2] Palestine was the default option: it was preferred by the self-styled "Zionists of Zion," since it was the site of the Jewish kingdoms of antiquity and was the one place that would underwrite a myth of return and attract the pious eastern

Why Has the Occupation Lasted?

European Jewish masses. Immigration to Palestine for the purpose of state building required its colonization.

Zionist state building has followed from its very beginning the settler-colonial method of piecemeal colonization that also created Canada, Australia, South Africa, and the Spanish-speaking states of the New World. The history of settler colonialism has been the subject of generations of historical study; some of its best-known practitioners are D. K. Fieldhouse, George Fredrickson, Caroline Elkins, and Susan Pedersen.[3] In the past two decades, Patrick Wolfe and Lorenzo Veracini, whose perspective was shaped by their Australian experience, have rekindled interest in settler colonies. Their starting point is that settler colonialism is a distinct form of the broader genus of colonialism. While nourished by a colonial great power, settler colonists had remained autonomous of their metropole, since they were the claimants of a particularly valuable resource: their own sovereign capacity. Settlers are different from emigrants who join someone else's already existing society, since settler colonists are founders of their own society. In the cogent summary of Mahmood Mamdani, settler societies "are made by conquest, not just by immigration."[4] The primary goal of settler colonization is the acquisition of the land itself upon which settlers establish their own sovereignty. Consequently, as Wolfe makes clear, the dominant feature of their society is not the exploitation but the replacement of the native population. Replacement can take several forms: in addition to genocide and expulsion, it can come about through cultural assimilation and the political integration of a portion of the native inhabitants.

Veracini goes beyond construing the unique socioeconomic and political characteristics of settler-colonial state building by shedding light on its corresponding culture. The settler-colonial outlook is born out of the experience of being at once subordinate to the colonial metropole and superordinate over the native population. Given their "in-between status," settler colonists are notable for their ability to obscure their social formation's origins by hiding behind several facades. They sometimes present themselves as met-ropolitan colonizers—though they broke away from the metropole in order to become sovereign in their "own" land. Alternatively, they hide behind a por-trayal of settlement as a peaceful act—even when it was accompanied by considerable violence. In other cases, they shelter behind the portrayal of settler colonists as the land's future citizens—though reaching that status required the suspension of the principles of democracy along the way. Fre-quently they either characterize themselves as refugees or emphasize the pioneering labor and hardship needed to establish themselves on the land—even when pioneering was simultaneously an act of replacement.[5]

Veracini's framework allows us to address the well-known claims that Israel cannot possibly be a settler colony since it didn't have a metropole, was established by refugees or immigrants and not by settlers, and was based on socialist-inspired pioneering Jewish labor and consequently did not exploit native Palestinians. As pointed out by Veracini, all settler colo-nies had a sponsoring metropole they freed themselves from. The exploita-tion of natural resources and native labor is a central characteristic of colo-nial regimes, but, as becomes clear from observing the northern American colonies and the Yishuv in Palestine, this does not hold true for all settler colonies. Nor is socialism necessarily antinationalist.

Let me examine at some length the remaining claim, the most arresting one, that because the Jews arrived in Palestine as refugees they cannot be viewed as settler colonists. In what was the most massive wave of Jewish emigration since the expulsion from Spain, two million Jews left the Pale of Settlement and the rest of eastern Europe between 1882 and 1914. Only about 3 percent of these emigrants chose Palestine as their destination, over-whelmingly preferring other immigration options in America, in western Europe, and across the globe. Pull factors to Palestine remained weak, and immigration picked up only when other options became unavailable. Against the background of the Johnson-Lodge Act of 1923, which ended the

Why Has the Occupation Lasted?

United States' largest migration wave, and of the worldwide Great Depression, other destinations were closed off. With the spread of anti-Semitic legislation in eastern Europe and Hitler's assumption of power in Germany, Palestine remained the Jews' only refuge. On November 25, 1936, appearing before the Palestine Royal Commission (known as the Peel Commission after its head), Chaim Weizmann, the president of the World Zionist Organization (WZO) testified that in Europe there were six million Jews, "for whom the world is divided into places where they cannot live and places where they cannot enter."[6] Jewish immigrants to Palestine, consequently, had as strong a claim to being refugees as any. A massive wave of refugees reached Palestine for the first time, doubling its Jewish population in three years, which now constituted one-third of Palestine's total population. Yet the sheer size of this wave of refugees who had arrived to settle in Palestine and the corresponding rise in land purchasing alarmed the Palestinian population and led them to rise in the 1936-39 Arab Revolt. As a result of that revolt, the British issued in May 1939 a white paper that repudiated the Balfour Declaration and severely curtailed additional Jewish immigration. It was the great tragedy of European Jewry that in Palestine they were, simultaneously, refugees *and* settlers and that consequently Palestine's doors were closed to them at their hour of deepest need.

After the end of the Second World War, the world was not closer to solving the problem of Jewish refugees—the saving remnant of survivors. Though other displaced persons commonly had a homeland to return to, Jewish concentration camp survivors returning to their homes faced repeated pogroms carried out by their neighbors. In the most notorious incident, which took place a year after the end of the Holocaust, forty-two Jewish refugees were killed in Kielce, Poland, leading to the survivors' mass flight out of the country, encouraged by the Polish government, most commonly to the safety of the American Zone in Germany. At the same time, the initiative of Illinois congressman William Stratton to open the United States to four hundred thousand Jewish refugees was blocked by the State Department, and Britain fought with every available resource against the illegal immigration of survivors to Palestine. Under these circumstances the fate of the survivors and the future of Palestine were linked. Already, the Anglo-American Commission and later the UN Special Committee on Palestine (UNSCOP), both of which visited the displaced persons camps, recommended the settlement of part or all of Jewish displaced persons in Palestine. UNSCOP increased the territory allotted to the Jewish state as part of the UN partition plan so it could accommodate the refugees stranded in Europe. The Palestinian Arab High Committee was not moved by the plight of the Holocaust survivors; for its members, large numbers of Jewish refugees settling in their country signaled the loss of their sovereignty to a settler-colonial state. For Britain and the United States the Jewish question was one of settling refugees; for the Palestinians the question was one of being displaced by settlers.

Though Zionism is a settler-colonial movement that established its sovereign state through the displacement of part of the country's Palestinian inhabitants, it still matters that it consisted mostly of refugees. Without the pre- and post-Second World War refugees, Yishuv would very likely have become a failed settler colony. In fact, of all late nineteenth- to early twentieth-century colonization movements—including the French settlements in Algeria, Tunisia, and Morocco, the Portuguese settlements in Mozambique, the German settlements in Namibia, the Italian settlements in Libya, the British settlements in Kenya, the Japanese settlements in Korea and Manchukuo in Northern China (1932–45), and the Nazi settlement in Poland—the Zionist settlement alone was successful, in large part because of the haven that the British Mandate provided to Jewish refugees.[7]

The need to accommodate refugees also had a powerful impact on Zionism's territorial ambitions. In the 1920s all Zionist parties were maximalists: that is, they expected the Jewish state-to-be to include both sides of the Jordan River and to spread up to the Golan and into southern Lebanon. In the

1930s, Zionists were divided regarding their territorial aspirations. The Revisionists, the forerunners of the Likud, remained maximalists, while the Labor Settlement Movement (LSM) moderated its expectations and consented to the proposed partition of Palestine by the British Peel Commission in 1937. When the UN introduced its November 1947 territorial partition plan, the leaders of the LSM, operating under the strictest urgency, accepted the resolution (even as some of them hoped for further territorial expansion under more auspicious conditions), which would allow the establishment of a Jewish state in part of Palestine.

The partition plan, however, was unacceptable to the Palestinians in 1948. They were unwilling to cede any part of Palestinian land, since, from their perspective, the conflict was not with Jewish refugees but with Jewish settlers. These conflicting perspectives led to the two-step 1948 War: first, a civil war of neighbors between Israelis and Palestinians, then the first Arab-Israeli War between Israel and a coalition of Arab states, leading to the displacement of as many as three-quarters of the Palestinian inhabitants of what became Israel and the takeover of their towns, lands, and sometimes homes by settler-refugees. The Israeli victory in the war allowed the newly born Israel to open the country's blocked borders, leading to the entry of waves of refugees and the doubling of its population within its first three years. Israelis, as pointed out by the late Israeli sociologist Baruch Kimmerling, tend to focus on Jewish motivations for immigration to Palestine, while Palestinians are concerned with the consequences of that immigration. Only the combination of their perspectives can provide us with a complete picture. Veracini, in sum, suggests, not that settler colonists are neither refugees nor pioneers, but rather that refugees and pioneers who build new societies by colonizing land commonly do so at the expense of indigenous or native populations. Colonization of Palestine was the main strategy of Israeli state building and the core of its Zionist ethos that continued to be highly influential even after 1948.

II

Israel did not invent colonization in the wake of the 1967 War. When Defense Minister Moshe Dayan was asked in 1968 what the Labor Party should do with regard to the recently conquered occupied territories, he found it easy to answer: "The first step is the traditional one in the realm of action in the State of Israel—settlement." Yigal Allon, deputy prime minister, reiterated the purpose of Israeli colonization in the OPT in unmistakable terms:

> We accustomed ourselves and the entire world to treat [our settlement] activity as facts with particularly weighty significance. This turned into one of the weapons of our revival movement. It can be assumed, therefore, that no one will misunderstand the importance of this activity.

Israel Galili, a leader of the socialist Kibbutz Hameuchad movement and Prime Minister Golda Meir's closest confidant, reiterated in the 1971 Congress of the Labor Party that "the trust accorded the Labor Party by the public" stemmed, first and foremost, from "its settlement ethos." Thus, in Galili's words, expansion, whether to the Jordan River or to Tel Aviv, originated from the same pure source of national revival.[8]

Israeli colonization, to paraphrase William Faulkner, is not dead; it isn't even past. The tools of colonization, honed before 1948 to a sharp edge, and subsequently deployed within Israel's new boundaries, were available and ready to be pressed into service in the territories newly occupied in 1967. When the state of Israel was established in 1948, the colonizing institutions that had been instrumental in creating it—the WZO, the Jewish Agency (JA), the Jewish National Fund (JNF), et cetera—were no longer needed, certainly not in their previous forms. The WZO's settlement activities could easily have been handed over to the new state, allowing the organization to focus on its role as a bridge between Israel and supportive Jewish communities around the world. There was even less need to keep alive the JA, a coordinating body between the Yishuv and the British Mandate. The JNF, which had purchased and held the land reserves of the Jewish people in Palestine, could have vested its holdings in the state of Israel. Even the various kibbutz and *moshav* settlement movements were part of the prestate sectionalism rejected in the name of *mamlachtiyut*—the transfer of all loyalties from each sector to the new state—a principle promoted assiduously by Prime Minister David Ben-Gurion. Nevertheless, each of these colonizing institutions was held over after the establishment of the Israeli state. The WZO, the JA, and the JNF were kept because they were the tools of Jewish privilege.

Israel preserved its state-building settler-colonial institutions precisely because they were not branches of the new state and, consequently, did not have to provide services to Israel's Palestinian citizens (in the way that a state operating on the basis of the equal treatment of all its citizens would have been obliged to). In the years following the 1948 War, Israel expropriated the land of about 70 percent of Palestinian localities, and an even larger share of the land previously belonging to the Bedouin of the Negev. It then employed such nonstate institutions as the WZO, the JA, and the JNF to colonize this land. The post-1948 settlement was carried out under the innocuous slogan of "population dispersal," though in fact the Israeli government sought the wider dispersal of the Jewish population and the simultaneous concentration of the remaining Palestinian population within smaller areas. Between March 1950 and December 1966, while Israel was settling hundreds of thousands of new Jewish immigrants along its newly acquired borders, it was placing its Palestinian citizens under military government, which served as one of the tools enabling the continued territorial dispossession of privately owned Palestinian land. In the wake of the 1967 War, the self-same institutions were pressed into the service of colonization in the OPT, this time jointly with Israeli ministries and under the auspices of the Israeli government.

A clear illustration of the continuity of settler colonialism across the divide of the 1967 War is found in the adjudication of the 1972 Rafah Approach appeal. This was one of the first High Court of Justice (HCJ) cases to examine the reasoning behind an order of the military government in the newly occupied land. It became a precedent-setting ruling. Following the eviction of 1,500 Bedouin families (see Section I), Israel established in that newly abandoned territory a Nachal military settlement to serve as a security buffer. In 1972, Bedouin sheiks, assisted by nearby socialist kibbutzim, sued the military for having founded this settlement for political rather than security reasons. Justice Witkon accepted the deposition signed by General Israel Tal and ruled that "settlement of Jews . . . in itself, in this case, is a security measure."[9] In the subsequent Beth El ruling from 1979, the same security reasoning was accepted, though the settlements of Beth El and Beka'ot (which were built on expropriated private Palestinian land) were civilian from the start. Of course, viewing settlements as performing a military task potentially renders them legitimate targets of attacks. But more importantly, by accepting that civilian settlements were part of the military's regional defense plan, the HCJ incorporated into its interpretation of IHL the Israeli state-building method of colonization. IHL allows for the protection of the occupying forces' security, but by treating civilians as soldiers and settlements as military camps, the HCJ molded IHL to fit Israeli history and not only stretched it beyond recognition but annulled its prohibition on colonization.

General Tal later conceded that he had only supplied the signature on the document placed before him. His confession raises the question, Just how important is colonization in the OPT for Israeli security? According to a telling 2012 report from the Council for Peace and Security, a body composed of retired Israeli military and security experts, "The settlement project not only does not contribute to the overall security of the State of Israel, but it incurs significant security, political, economic, and social prices and risks."[10] The report goes on to suggest that it is the presence of military forces, rather than settlements, that increases security, contradicting General Tal's affidavit and the court's approval of his approach. It is, of course, not surprising that colonization inevitably leads to conflict with those it displaces. But the willingness to undertake colonization in spite of the risks it incurs indicates that—instead of enhancing Israeli security—colonization merely marks the boundaries of land Israel wishes to eventually annex.

The Rafah Approach settlements were part and parcel of the same "military frontier" colonization that Israel had already commenced in the OPT. The 1973 War and the rapid evacuation of settlements on the Golan in the face of the advancing Syrian military raised even more serious questions as to the ability of military colonization to achieve its declared aim of achieving security. Even so, after a short lull the tail end of Labor Party's rule witnessed the expansion of settlements in all parts of the OPT more rapidly than at any other time since 1967. If additional proof was needed, the March 1979 Camp David peace treaty with Egypt demonstrated most clearly that Israeli security could be attained without the construction of settlements altogether. Detaching the goal of security from the means of military frontier settlements left continued colonization as an end in itself without justification. But already other interests and groups were waiting in the wings to justify settlement in new terms so as to continue and expand the venture that had begun in the Labor Party era. New patterns of colonization required a new and more radical legitimation, which was provided by a refocused and reinterpreted Judaism.

There is another, related, urgently important difference between colonization by the LSM during the Yishuv (up until 1977) and by Likud-led Israeli governments after 1977. Similarity, even continuity of the two practices does not imply their identity. *Si duo faciunt idem, non est idem.*

The vineyards and orchards planted by the earliest wave of Jewish settlers who arrived between 1882 and 1903—the First Aliya—thrived on the employment of low-paid Palestinian workers. Second Aliya members, who reached Palestine from 1903 to 1914, sought to persuade First Aliya farmers to hire them instead, in solidarity with other Jews, instead of Palestinian laborers.

But Jewish agricultural workers were unable to subsist on the low wages paid to Palestinian workers and wanted European wages. By 1908, their futile struggle for "Hebrew labor"—through the "conquest of labor" from the lower-paid Palestinian workers—was supplemented by a more promising tactic, the "conquest of land." This transformation took place through an alliance of the LSM with the WZO and the linkage of their respective institutions the JNF (the WZO's land-purchasing arm) and the Histadrut (the LSM's trade union). The colonization led by the LSM was separatist in intent: instead of employing Palestinian laborers it resorted to forming its own distinct—and exclusively Jewish—cooperative economy, starting in the Ottoman period. The respective aims of the JNF and the Histadrut were to close Palestine's land and labor markets to Palestinians and to make these "closed shops" available to Jews only. These institutions were the mainstays of the Israeli-state-to-be and the LSM leadership. This separatism, however, was the result, not the cause, of the Jewish-Palestinian conflict.[11]

What was the significance of the LSM's separatist method of state formation for the Jewish-Palestinian conflict? In the astute observation of the historian Anita Shapira,

> The ideology of Hebrew Labor . . . brought about the reduction of the settlement area in Eretz Israel. In the long run, the establishment of separate Jewish areas of settlement entailed the relinquishment of those areas that did not possess a Jewish majority. This decision was the first step on the way toward Eretz Israel's partition.[12]

It was from the LSM's mainstream that the majority of the supporters of the various partition plans emerged, the plans being the 1937 Peel Commission's Plan and the 1947 UN plan. If by the mid-1930s partition was already grounded in Palestinian reality, this was in large measure due to the LSM's strategy of state formation. Having supported economic bifurcation and consequently being less dependent on Palestinian labor than any other Jewish group, the LSM was best equipped to support de jure partition. In this

Why Has the Occupation Lasted?

they radically differed from the white South African mining economy or the southern plantation economy of the United States. Being militant in its demand for *exclusive* Jewish employment, the LSM had become more *modest* in its demands for territorial expansion. To increase the ratio of population to land, the LSM agreed to have the latter diminished so that the density of the former would grow. Prioritizing demographic strength over territory was in the natural interest of the LSM, which, on the basis of its formative experience in the labor market, grasped the demographic limits of Zionism. The LSM recognized that an effective demographic presence was necessary to secure the Jewish population's permanence and safety in Palestine. This recognition predisposed the LSM to entertain territorial compromise in order to enable the entry of Jewish refugees both before and after the Second World War. The aim of the LSM became the realization of a homogeneous (i.e., Jewish) settlement society *within* Palestine.[13] Such homogeneity in the conditions of a small country like Palestine would always be partial: even within the boundaries of Jewish state set by the 1948 UN Partition Resolution, the Arab population was to make up 45 percent, though the arrival of Jewish refugees from DP camps in Europe was expected to change the ratio rapidly.

The Allon Plan, as we observed in the first essay, supported colonization mostly in the less densely populated part of the West Bank in the Jordan Valley, though Allon soon gave in to new temptations and incorporated into his map the Gush Etzion and Hebron settlements—even though Prime Minister Rabin had ejected Gush Emunim's unauthorized Elon Moreh settlement nucleus eight times from the densely populated mountain range of the northern West Bank (Samaria).[14] The post-1977 colonization of the West Bank overthrew this demographic calculus and prioritized territory over demography.

Ironically, the Likud had not engaged in settlement or had settlement institutions or potential settlers. Consequently, the Likud turned to Gush Emunim to be its foot soldiers. Through Gush Emunim, colonization took a big leap from its demographic to its territorial version. The day after the May 1977 election that made the Likud the largest party for the time in Israel's history, Begin visited the settlement of Ellon Moreh and declared, "We stand on the land of liberated Israel. There will be many Ellon Morehs." Without Gush Emunim's religious commitment, most post-1967 colonization would have taken place in the less densely populated parts of the OPT—in the Jordan Valley and along the Green Line—rather than in the heart of the densely inhabited West Bank. By 1981, the Likud would offer its own plan for intensive colonization, the Drobles Plan, which opened up the whole of the OPT to settlement. It combined demographic and territorial colonization in one package. The Drobles Plan and the Likud's colonization efforts differ in one additional way from earlier colonization under the Allon Plan. New waves of Jewish immigrants, such as those from the USSR, could have been accommodated within the state of Israel, but the Likud government sought to direct them (and the even larger flow from the USSR's successor states) to the new colonies, though most of these immigrants would have preferred to live in Israel's urban centers within the Green Line.

Begin's colonization and the settlements of Gush Emunim members in the densely populated parts of Palestine were intended to make territorial partition impossible and colonization irreversible. The new radical geography-centered approach to colonization replaced the demography-centered approach of the LSM, intensifying the Israeli-Palestinian conflict. It also led to the first large-scale, coordinated Palestinian resistance movement to Israel's military rule in the West Bank, which lasted through the late 1970s and early 1980s.

III

A particularly effective way of examining the (dis)continuity of the colonization project in Israel is to trace it through the generations. Since generations overlap and rarely possess beginning and concluding dates, they are a notoriously amorphous social phenomenon. But occasionally, as suggested by Karl Manheim, the biological and historical cycles interlock. At such times, under the influence of a singular historical event, a cohort is politicized and converted into a self-conscious generation. In Israel, the 1967 War played such a formative role.

The founding fathers and mothers of Israel—David Ben Gurion, Itzhak Ben-Zvi, Golda Meir and others, who arrived in the Second (1904–14) and Third Aliyas (1918–24) waves of immigration—were followed by the first native-born generation of Israel, which overlapped with the second generation of the LSM. Led by Moshe Dayan, Yigal Allon, Israel Galili, and Yitzhak Rabin, this *sabra* generation devised the "Stockade and Watchtower" form of military settlement during the years before the Arab Revolt of 1936–39. This first native Israeli generation not only militarized colonization but later commanded the military units that fought in the 1948 War. They were groomed to take over leadership from the state's founders, but according to Yonathan Shapiro they remained dwarfed by the founding fathers' generation, never developing an independent worldview of their own. Consequently, this first native generation merely reproduced the outlook of the previous generation and adopted and expanded its goals. In doing so after 1967, they legitimized the colonization project and found justification for their own life project.[15] Though there was much talk of expanding the colonization of the OPT, the Labor Party government only halfheartedly implemented the settlement planks of the Allon Plan. The LSM could no longer summon its erstwhile commitment to its own Zionist pioneering ethos. All in all, at the end of the Labor era in 1977, there were fifteen settlements in the Jordan Rift, one or two established per year, still directed by a demographic framework for colonization. The area—once planned for a population of 20,000—was inhabited in 1986 by only a few thousand settlers.[16] Having reopened the door of settlement, however, the Labor Party could no longer close it.

The driving force behind Israel's second era of colonization belongs elsewhere. The decisive victory of the 1967 War—which achieved the conquest of the biblical land of Jewish antiquity (the West Bank or Samaria and Judea) was a generation-forming experience for the religious Zionist community. This generational cohort interpreted the victory as an advanced stage in the course of messianic redemption and proclaimed its convictions in the context of its own intergenerational experience. In contrast to the Labor Party, with its formidable foreign-born leaders who were the state's founders, religious Zionism (organized in the National Religious or Mizrachi Party, today the Jewish Home Party) remained a junior partner in the performance of national pioneering tasks rather than a leader. Religious Zionism served at most as an interest group or a religious lobby representing sectoral interests with leaders fearful of losing the group's youth to assimilation in secular Israeli society. The first generation of religious Zionist leaders signed up for Zionism to "solve" the practical concerns of diaspora Jews but not of Judaism. Having rejected the anti-Zionist ultra-Orthodoxy of Agudat Yisrael (which left redemption in the hands of providence), but becoming only a pale imitation of the LSM, they were ultimately criticized and humiliated by both camps.

Taking on the mission of frontier expansion allowed the second generation of religious Zionists to place itself on a new footing. From its ranks emerged the Gush Emunim (Bloc of Faithful) settlement movement, which also served as a powerful lever in the intraparty generational conflict. As pointed out by Shmuel Sandler,

> By turning the issue [of settling the West Bank] into both a national and a religious cause the Mizrachi camp emerged as a leading force in both areas, for in taking the lead on settlement in the territories, it could demonstrate its loyalty to the sacred ideals of settling the land and security, while at the same time criticizing Agudat Yisrael for their disloyalty to the Land of Israel.[17]

Gush Emunim arose from the well-integrated network of Israel's religious Zionist educational institutions. These schools—which have autonomy in determining their curricula, even though they are funded by the state Ministry of Education—transition religious Zionist youth from kindergartens, elementary schools, and the Bnei Akiva youth movement into the *yeshiva tichonit* high school network (where high-level traditional religious studies are coupled with secular education) or into the military *yeshivat hesder* and all the way to the national religious university, Bar Ilan. Religious Zionist, as well as *haredi*, education has flourished under this arrangement, which allows a measure of separation between religious and secular Jews. It has been an anomaly in Israel, given that under the Labor government of Prime Minister Ben Gurion, nonreligious independent schools were unified under state authority and paramilitary forces were folded into the IDF.

From within the second generation of religious Zionists, a particular subset received their graduate education at the Merkaz Harav yeshiva. This group was best equipped to claim the mantle of leadership. Unlike the Mizrachi, which joined the LSM mostly for pragmatic reasons, the yeshiva's spiritual leaders—Rabbi Abraham Isaac Kook and his son Rabbi Zvi Yehuda Kook—took a more sympathetic view of the LSM and Zionism in general. For the rabbis Kook, Israel has not only practical but divine significance. Secular Zionists, in the Kooks' view, were the unwitting tools of a messianic design whose beginnings were slow but whose forward direction was certain.[18] Zionist immigration was the first step in the providential fulfillment of the process of redemption (*atchalta degeula*). It is therefore no surprise that the occupation of the Old City of Jerusalem and the other holy sites of the West Bank was seen by students and graduates of Merkaz Harav as the vindication of their faith and as a decisive step toward complete redemption.

As heirs to the settler-colonial project, Gush Emunim succeeded in mobilizing support not only from within the national religious camp but from nonreligious groups and individuals as well. Several political bodies in which secular activists joined with religious settlers played a crucial role in transferring the mission of pioneering from the LSM to Gush Emunim. The new movement replaced the old and, in the process, synthesized Rabbi Kook's faith with the aspirations of the Second Aliya. LSM veterans supported Gush Emunim precisely because it followed the traditional course of settlement, which had an aura of legitimacy in a society where pioneering had been a core element of nationalism and a major source of prestige and influence. Even Prime Minister Rabin, who fought hard against early Gush Emunim settlements, found it useful to express his admiration for their "pioneering zeal." [19] Individual LSM leaders, among them Allon, Rabin, and Peres, acted as mentors and facilitators for the settlements of Qiryat Arba, Ofra, and Kadum, which would not have been established without their help.

Though Gush Emunim claimed the mantle of the LSM, its colonization project was a "revolution within a revolution," both different and more radical in three important respects. First, the kibbutz and the *moshav* (a cooperative community of individual farms)—the agrarian settlement colonies of the LSM—were replaced by the semiurban, nonagricultural middle-class *yishuv kehilati*. After an initial period of resistance, in 1977 the WZO's Settlement Department recognized the *yishuv kehilati* as a "pioneering settlement," making it eligible for financial support from the Zionist movement.

Second, though Gush Emunim took great pride in presenting itself as what Rabbi Moshe Levinger, a settlement leader from the Qiryat Arba settlement near Hebron, called "the direct and legitimate offspring of the pioneers of Zionism," Hanan Porat, the other prominent Gush Emunim leader from Kfar Etzion, rudely told LSM opponents, "You finished your role, just don't interfere with our attempt to continue it." In short, to gain national legitimation, Gush Emunim made the great legacy of colonization its own even as it reinterpreted it through a religious lens. After a conversation with Gush Emunim representatives in July 1974, Shimon Peres concluded: "We are living in two separate countries. You live in a country that needs to be set-tled, while I live in a country that needs to be defended." Porat rejected the assertion that the role of Zionism was to constitute a safe haven for Jews so they could hold their own in the world. Gush Emunim viewed Zionism dif-ferently, as "the process of redemption in its concrete sense—the redemption of the people, and the redemption of the land—and in its divine sense—the redemption of the godhead, the redemption of the world." Just how far Gush Emunim had distanced itself from the idea of maintaining a "military fron-tier" may be seen from its rejection not only of the principle of security but also of the goal of peace. "A secular peace," said another founder of Gush Emunim, "is not our goal." [20] Its starting point with regard to peace was reli-gious and messianic, so it saw peace as attainable only in the end of days.

Third, Gush Emunim colonization rejected demographic criteria for choosing the location of Jewish colonies. The odd "N"-shaped pattern of col-onization during the Yishuv—running from Upper Galilee down to the Bet Shean Valley and then diagonally across the Jezreel Valley (Marj Ibn-Amer) up to Haifa and Nahariya, and down again to Gedera—followed the layout of the valleys and coastal areas, less secure during Ottoman times and conse-quently less densely inhabited by Palestinians. Gush Emunim colonization, in contrast, was aimed at the mountainous regions where the vast majority of Palestinians resided (see map 2). As Gush Emunim saw it, Jewish settle-ments up to the 1948 War had spread out over the "wrong" part of the Pales-tine, the coastal region that in antiquity was inhabited not by the Jews but by the Philistines. Gush Emunim wanted not only to correct this pattern and restore history by moving Jews into the lands they had held in biblical times but to join the ancient homeland to Israel within the Green Line. In the process, Gush Emunim tossed overboard the LSM's goal of creating an eth-nically homogeneous colony. It advocated pushing settlement into the loca-tions of ancient Jewish towns and villages that had a dense Palestinian pop-ulation in order to undermine the possibility of territorial partition. It also raised the Israeli-Palestinian conflict's stakes by leaving little contiguous territory for a potential Palestinian state, increasing friction, and producing higher levels of violence in which the settlers themselves played the role of both vigilantes and soldiers drafted into regional military units that protected their settlements.

These transformations—and the corresponding religious radicalization among Palestinians—have been lengthy, yet they remain incomplete—not a "religious turn" but maybe half a turn. Religious vanguards have mobilized a large enough portion of their respective populations to form an alternative system of institutions and even penetrate the ruling echelons but not to effect a revolutionary takeover of the central political and military institutions or to impose an exclusive religious law, either *halacha* or *shari'a*. These religious turns are incomplete in another way: within both Gush Emunim and Hamas, religious, nationalist, and socioeconomic aspirations and interests compete with each other. Far from being strictly or exclusively theocratic turns, they offer more radical interpretations to erstwhile nationalist aspirations and mobilize on their behalf quietist, or politically marginalized, social strata. Gush Emunim bundles a culturally based interpretation of Judaism with aspirations to social mobility. Meanwhile, Hamas joins an Islamic lifestyle with the satisfaction of the dire need for social services among both its followers and larger cross sections of the Palestinian population. Hamas's religious sway has been further moderated through its continued engagement in pragmatic coalition building with competitors. Though the import of each religious half turn is far-reaching, neither religious Zionism nor Hamas has achieved hegemonic status. In fact, both movements encounter considerable hostility within their respective societies. These half turns account for the turmoil of Israeli and Palestinian politics and for deep internal conflicts among both Israelis and Palestinians. This internal polarization finds its expression in corresponding territorial divides: the division between Hamas's control over Gaza and Fatah's and the PNA's sway over

Areas A and B in the West Bank, as well as the division between what is colloquially termed the settlers' "State of Judea" in the West Bank and the liberal and secular-minded "State of Tel Aviv." At this historical juncture, the Zionist Camp Party (the old Labor Party), Yesh Atid, and in particular Meretz—Israel's center-left and center nationalist parties and its human rights and civic NGOs—offer a bulwark against the comprehensive realization of religious Zionists' and Likud's aspirations but are unable to supplant them.

I V

Gush Emunim itself was not made of one cloth. A sharp disagreement divided the nascent movement: Should it undertake whatever actions were deemed necessary to maintain the momentum of the redemptive process, even at the expense of isolating itself from the rest of Israeli society? Or, should the movement seek "to settle in people's hearts"—that is, to engage in the painstaking process of preparing the majority of Israelis, educationally and politically, for the new reality the movement sought to create? Those who embraced the first option were ready to break with the system of Israeli democracy by engaging in violence, while the consensus builders sought to remain within the framework of *mamlachtiyut,* namely unity even at the price of slower progress toward the redemption of the Land of Israel.[21]

The "by all means necessary" faction was formed early on with the Gush Emunim's proclamation of a messianic frontier and the consequent radicalization of Israeli colonization. With the ascent of the first non-LSM government in Israel's history under Menachem Begin in June 1977, Rabin's policy of resisting Gush Emunim's settlement attempts was overturned. The religious Zionist settlers received massive assistance, mostly in the form of subsidized housing and employment and tax benefits, and the second Begin government adopted the Drobles Plan for opening up the whole of the West Bank to colonization. As Palestinian resistance grew, the Begin government suppressed the elected Palestinian municipal leadership, an underground was formed by prominent members of Gush Emunim's vanguardist wing in 1979. Its main leader was the chairman of the Municipal Council of the settlement of Qiryat Arba. Its assaults were motivated not only by revenge but also by the aim of causing Arab flight. The Jewish Underground, as it was eventually called, attempted to assassinate and successfully maimed Palestinian mayors, they sprayed gunfire into a crowd of students at Hebron's Islamic College, and in 1984, one of their cells was caught in the nick of time while placing bombs in five Arab buses in East Jerusalem. During their interrogation, members of the Underground divulged that their ultimate goal was to blow up the Dome of the Rock (either by using explosives stolen from the Israeli military or by crashing an explosives-packed plane into it), an act of messianic awakening viewed as preparation for the construction of a Third Temple.[22] Had this terror plot been successful, it would very likely have led to a confrontation between settlers and Palestinians in the OPT and, more broadly, between Israel and the Muslim world.

The members of the Underground were sentenced to short prison terms. The ringleaders had their sentences commuted and were released by 1990. By then, however, Gush Emunim's moderate wing, led by Rabbi Joel Ben-Nun and others, that espoused the option of "settling in people's hearts," had seized the initiative. Ben-Nun denounced settlers' "violent, strong-armed, materialistic, indeed savage" approach to fulfilling Gush Emunim's messianic aims and their hostility toward Israelis who were left of center politically.[23] If the Israeli public opposes the settlement project, he explained, it will not matter how many settlements there are. Instead of appearing to be a narrow-minded interest group, the settlers had to "close the gap with their brother-enemies, to soften their opposition, to convince them"—in other words, to lead them in a new direction. The violence of the vanguardists has not disappeared altogether today; it finds its repeated expressions in vigilante attacks on Palestinian property and villagers, most recently through self-designated "Price Tag" operations against those who dare to resist the expansion of religious Zionist settlements.

Since the mid-1980s and for the better part of a generation, religious Zionists have left an indelible impression on secular Israeli society by their energetic, creative, and monomaniacal pursuit of the goal of colonizing and gaining possession of the Land of Israel. Some of their impact—for example, the partial "reenchantment" of Israeli secular culture through a deepening of Jewish consciousness—would have taken place under most circumstances, since similar religious turns were occurring elsewhere in the 1970s and 1980s. But in the case of Israel, the growing impact of the second and third generations of religious Zionists was also helped by their social mobility, which took them into prominent social positions. As observed by Nissim Leon, religious Zionist youth were driven by both religious zeal and individual ambition. Their professional aspirations were based on the high quality of the education in secular subjects offered in their yeshiva high schools—unlike *haredi* schools, where secular topics were underemphasized if not altogether ignored—as well as by their attraction to opportunities in Israel's growing market economy and their increasing access to middle-class status.

The contrasting socioeconomic profiles of the first three religious Zionist generations are telling. The founding generation is generally viewed as belonging to an older, staid, petty bourgeoisie of shopkeepers, merchants, and teachers. The Gush Emunim generation that followed it put educational preparation to good use and took advantage of the robust economic growth Israel enjoyed following the 1967 War and the end of its first recession (*mitun*). The third, contemporary generation has taken a further turn away from the cooperative LSM-dominated economy and toward a privatized, knowledge-intensive economy that is well integrated with the global economy and that has opened up many more channels of social mobility.[24] In many respects, Israel's religious Zionists today resemble the modern Orthodox in the United States.

The social mobility of the religious Zionists was not based solely on their educational achievements and individual ambitions; it was considerably enhanced by their commitment to the settlement project and their ability to turn it to their advantage. As summed up by the director of the Adva Center for Research on Equality and Social Justice in Israel, Shlomo Swirsky, championing colonization empowered the religious Zionist group and "established it in the ranks of the upper middle class." [25] Israeli governments pour probably as much as 2 percent of the annual GDP into the colonization of the West Bank—in addition to ongoing infrastructure, construction, and security expenses—by way of inexpensive mortgages and innumerable grants designed to attract settlers into the new colonies. The higher quality of life in settlements—which featured houses with a backyard in comparison with high-rise apartments in crowded cities—had its own appeal. With the decline of the Israeli welfare state and growing inequality within Israeli society (making it the most unequal of Organisation for Economic Co-operation and Development countries after Mexico), the OPT remained a last vestige of the Israeli welfare state without, of course, appearing to be so. Championing the settler-colonial state-building strategy afforded Gush Emunim and the settlement movement considerable social mobility. Upward mobility and colonization reinforced each other.

There are three social spheres in which the growing influence of religious Zionists is manifest and well documented and is directly connected with their role as champions of colonization: in military service, media, and national politics. In Israel no sphere of life is more "sacred" and more closely tied with colonization than military service. During the Yishuv, settler and soldier roles were closely associated and were vested with privileged citizenship for their commitment to the common good. Service in elite units functioned as the proving ground of the LSM's up-and-coming political leaders. Just one year after the 1967 War, a special arrangement was established to draw religious Zionist youth closer to the military: the *yeshivat hesder,* a new military-religious institution in which students alternated three years of religious study with thirteen months of military service (usually in their own separate units)—a period much shorter than the three years that were mandatory for male citizens in general. Yeshiva students were authorized by their rabbis to take part if they wished but were not required to do so.

Yeshivas and the military became even more closely associated two decades later. Notable secular members of the Israeli military—later to occupy prominent positions in the Labor Party—invited religious Zionists to take on a greater military role. In the wake of the public demoralization that resulted from Israel's poor showing in the 1973 War, Lieutenant General Motta Gur, the Israeli military's chief of staff, hailed the dedication of religious Zionist soldiers and urged them to serve in all military units. Major General Amram Mitzna, the head of Central Command during the First Intifada and between 2002 and 2003 the leader of the Labor Party, was even more explicit. Against the background of the harsh internal debate that had erupted in response to the massive wave of Palestinian resistance, he demanded that religious Zionists assume greater responsibility for Israel's future by becoming professional soldiers army after their mandatory service. "The military," he stated, "needs you and the values you bring, especially today, when cracks open up in both the values of Israeli society and the motivation to serve the military. Now we need you more than ever." [26]

In 1988, Rabbi Yigal Levinstein and Rabbi Eli Sadan, a graduate of Rabbi Kook Merkaz Harav Yeshiva, took up Mitzna's call. They established Bnei-David, the first premilitary preparatory yeshiva, in the Eli settlement, with the aim of strengthening the faith of religious teenagers in a "gap year" between the end of high school and the beginning of military service to better fortify them to encounter the secularism of the military. Bnei-David has cohorts of five hundred students and, by now, several thousand graduates, the vast majority of whom have served in combat and even elite units. Out of the currently existing forty-four preparatory schools in Israel, eighteen are religious; of these, eight are in the West Bank and another two on the Golan Heights. Though most of these are smaller and have cohorts of about fifty students, the share and influence of religious Zionist soldiers in the military has changed considerably. While in 1990 only 2.5 percent of infantry officers were religious Zionists, by 2007 their number had jumped to 31.4 percent, three times greater than their representation in the national population. The rapid rise in the percentage of religious officers, combined with a declining share of secular combat soldiers and officers who hail from kibbutzim, has altered the character of the IDF.

In 1988, the same year in which the first premilitary preparatory yeshiva was set up in a West Bank settlement, the prominent religious Zionist journalist Uri Orbach published a call in *Nekuda*, the settlers' weekly. Speaking for *Nekuda*'s journalists, he bemoaned the chasm between the settlers and the world of the media. To close the rift, he advised high school graduates to break into the field by seeking to become reporters for Galei Tzahal, the military radio station, and place equal importance upon service in the media and service in an elite military unit. Orbach self-consciously conceived of gaining a religious foothold in the media as a military operation. This goal was evident throughout the operation's recruitment efforts: from Orbach's slogan "The best to the media" (a variation on the Israeli Air Force's popular call "The best to the pilot academy") to his identification of a goal "to penetrate the media," or, in the words one of Orbach's colleagues, to achieve "the conquest of the media." [27] By 1998, religious Zionism was heavily invested in this domain. Its high schools offered as many as thirty media, movie, and TV courses, and several elementary schools were designated as "media schools." Additionally, a school for movie and TV opened, and the pirate radio Channel 7 was established, later to become an Internet-based radio and TV channel. This expansion benefitted from the explosive growth of private Israeli media in the 1980s and 1990s. Today, religious Zionist broadcasters, correspondents, and journalists are no longer confined to religious publications (in fact, *Nekuda* was discontinued); they now operate in the heart of Israeli media, advancing their prosettlement agenda.[28] Religious Zionist broadcasters frequently invite settlers or their political representatives to talk shows without seeking to balance them with opponents of the colonization movement.

Finally, religious Zionists occupy important posts in the public sector. The importance of the religious Zionist party, the Jewish Home in its current designation, precedes the 1967 War. It has commonly been able to tip power within the Knesset to either left- or right-wing coalition governments. Until 1977, it always allied itself with the LSM, but since then its second-generation leaders have moved the party decisively to the right while propping up Likud governments. In the few instances in which Labor returned to run the country, the religious Zionist party acted to restrain it while negotiations were under way with the Palestinian National Authority (PNA). In 2012, the Jewish Home party, led by Naftali Bennett, undertook a strategic opening toward secular Israelis, calling them "brothers" in public pronouncements. Bennett placed on the party's list of candidates a secular woman, Ayelet Shaked, and, after the 2015 elections he secured her a position as the minister of justice. In 2016, the heads of the Mossad and the police, and the government's legal adviser—all appointed governmental positions and gatekeepers to the judicial system—are religious Zionists. This presents a consolidation of power that is highly telling of religious Zionists' political sway in Israeli social and political life.

Under the influence of its third generation religious Zionists are no longer merely an interest group in search of public funding for their schools, synagogues, *mikvot* (ritual baths), and other institutions. They are also not satisfied with being the state of Israel's "kashruth supervisors." Instead, they have become a broad-based ideological movement striving to change Israel's character and direction. Gush Emunim itself has been replaced with two formal organizations: Amana, a settlement arm, and the Yesha Council, which represents settlers and is commonly dominated by its religious Zionist wing. The role played by Judaism within the IDF illustrates this change. According to Yagil Levy, the Israeli military is undergoing a process of theocratization, in which military rabbis are not limited to supervising the accommodations made for religious soldiers but instead exert growing influence on all soldiers and on military commanders. Both formally and informally, commanders consult with the religious rabbinate corps as well as with the rabbis of religious military preparatory schools. The topics of consultation include troop deployments in the OPT, the regulation of Sabbath practices, and the integration of women into combat and field units. Rabbis are asked to rule in cases of conflict between military commands and religious commandments, in effect creating a dual source of authority deviating from the norm of civilian control over the military in democratic societies. The rabbinate corps has also seized a prominent role in enhancing soldiers' "Jewish consciousness." The IDF entered this process through an understanding that the preparatory schools and yeshivas would supply the military with the manpower needed to carry out its tasks. Consequently, the IDF has become more willing to accommodate, and sometimes even to encourage, religious motivations for carrying out its tasks.[29]

The culmination of the tendency toward growing theocratization in the IDF was a communiqué issued by Colonel Ofer Winter, the commander of the Givati Brigade, to his battalion and company commanders on the eve of the third Gaza war, Operation Protective Edge, in July 2014. Colonel Ofer Winter called for divine aid in fighting a foe that "abuses, blasphemes, and curses the God of Israel's [defense] forces."[30] This call intermixed military duties with religious faith and sought to transform the war into a religious conflict.

Such theocratization is a significant development with far-reaching implications not only for the future of Israeli colonization and the occupation in general but for the state of Israel as well. However, it is far from becoming a completed or an unchecked process. It is equally important to recognize the powerful tendencies that seek to limit the growing sway of the military rabbinate and religious military preparatory schools and their rabbis. In fact, Rabbi Yigal Levinstein, the cofounder of the religious military preparatory school in the settlement of Eli, sees the IDF's educational corps as a formidable rival. In July 2016 he savagely attacked the IDF for educating officers and soldiers on human rights and pluralism and thus, he alleged, weakening their resolve.[31] Since the appointment of the new chief of the IDF's general staff, Lieutenant General Gadi Eizenkot, in February 2015, the tide has been turning against the military rabbinate and its attempts to spread its influence among the soldiers. Eizenkot returned the rabbinate corps to its original role of providing religious services and transferred its education role to the education corps. According to Levy, there is still a long way to go before the IDF would become a theocratic military, and the existing theocratic trends have not made headway outside the army, which has a higher percentage of religious soldiers than the other military branches.

The religious Zionist community has grown in influence, but in addition to receiving external pushback it is being weakened by internal divisions. The most important dividing line recreates the debate within the early Gush Emunim between in its own internal vanguardists and the consensus builders. Today the former, the followers of Rabbi Avraham Shapira, place commitment to religious law above state law and democratic decision making. In case of a governmental decision to remove settlers from the West Bank, they would call on soldiers to disobey the evacuation order. The latter, followers of Rabbi Tzvi Tau, are more numerous than the former and are organized in the so-called *yeshivot hakav*, or the "yeshivas that follow the line," (*yeshivot hakav*), meaning the principled line of *mamlachtiyut*, to which they give a uniquely religious twist by holding that one must not defy the democratic will of the people and must instead remain loyal to the state of Israel because it has sacred value. The religious settlers within Israel who live closest to the Green Line, in particular in the Gush Etzion settlement bloc (see map 5), are pro-*mamlachtiyut* and worry that attacks by settlers from the pirate outposts against their Palestinian neighbors reflect on them badly. Finally, a significant portion of the religious Zionist community has become more Orthodox over the years, earning the nickname *hardalim* (short for *haredi leumi*, nationalist *haredi*). Their political and religious loyalties cut across the pro- and anti-*mamlachtiyut* division. Though the influence of the religious Zionist community, which incubated the Gush Emunim settler movement, has spread through the institutions of Israeli society, its size and reach are limited and it continues to rely and remain dependent on its secular Likud allies.

Settling in the midst of the densely inhabited heartland of Palestine required Israeli governmental authorization (or at least tacit support, as was the case for the squatter settlers of the outposts), but it was also an individual choice that benefited both individual settlers and their families materially, as well as the religious Zionist community politically by giving them a seat at the national political table. At the same time, aside from the soldiers posted to guard them, the religious Zionist settlers suffered the brunt of the casualties of the overall settler population, since they encroached most directly on, and lived in closest proximity to, the Palestinian population. Indeed, secular Israelis observe with consternation the willingness of religious Zionist settlers to expose their families and children to potential attacks in their settlements and on the roads leading to them. Most commonly, their response to loss of life among their fellow settlers is a combined emphasis on their mental strength and commitment, steadfastness, and demand for additional Jewish homes or the establishment of yet another squatter outpost to buttress the colonization project.

A social network posting of Eliraz Eitam, a young woman from the Otniel settlement, provided an exceptional glimpse into the privately admitted

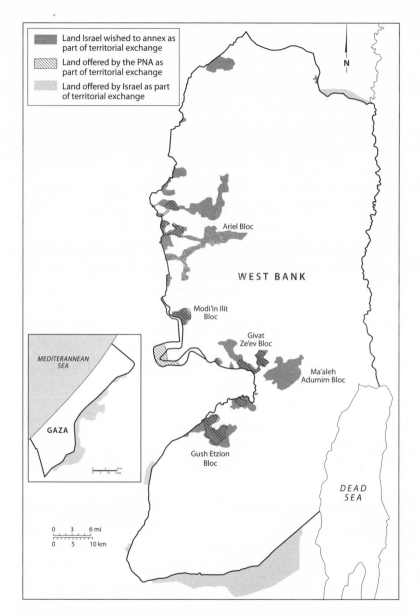

Map 5. Settlement blocs and proposed territorial exchange in Annapolis talks, 2008.
Used by permission of Shaul Arieli. Based on "Annapolis Process (2008): Palestinian
Proposal (approximation)," www.shaularieli.com/image/users/77951/ftp/my_files
/maps/pal_pro_anapolis08.jpg?id=7718585, and "Annapolis Process (2008) Israeli
Proposal (approximation)," http://etsuv.com/image/users/77951/ftp/my_files/maps
/israel_pro_anapolis08.jpg?id=7718576.

impact of attacks. In July 2016, following the killing of a neighbor driving a car, Eitam wrote of her own and her fellow settlers' reaction, "We won't show you what great heroes we are, because we are not. We will not get up to go to work, we will stop going shopping, since our lives have come to a halt." [32] After a short public upheaval, the customary claim that losses strengthen rather than weaken the settlements was reasserted. The public face the settlers show the world is illustrated by the appeal of Amana, the organization that took over the settlement function of Gush Emunim, to potential settlers: "Become part of a communal puzzle and live in complete harmony." [33] Equally arresting is a guidebook titled *Yesha Is Fun: The Good Life Guide to Judea and Samaria*. Its authors still use the acronym Yesha, which stands for Judea, Samaria, and Gaza, though Israel withdrew from the latter in August 2005.[34] Neither the Amana recruitment materials nor the guidebook as much as mentions the word *Palestinian*, despite their massive presence. The propinquity of Palestinians—those whom the settlers help dispossess and whose enmity the settlers incur—suggests these settlements cannot always be "fun," let alone "harmonious." Such denialism on a grand scale is very likely a means for settlers to reassure themselves about their communities' future prospects, but those communities are riven by an unacknowledged and unspoken fragility.

V

It is time to turn to one of the most formative events of the Israeli-Palestinian conflict: the attempt to resolve the conflict through the diplomacy of the Oslo Accords, or "Oslo," as the process is often called in shorthand. Oslo offers an opportunity for examining the relative weight of both Gush Emunim and Hamas, the influential Israeli and the Palestinian religious movements, in the breakdown of the peace process and the continuation of the occupation. In this section, I will focus on the way the conflict over Oslo played out within Israeli society, particularly between the supporters of the process and the religious Zionist community and its Gush Emunim settlers, who opposed it vehemently and sometimes even violently. It is just as important to examine a parallel process—the role played by Hamas in catalyzing the opposition in Palestinian society, which enabled Hamas to differentiate itself from Fatah and its conciliatory approach expressed through the Oslo Accords, and I shall do in the next section. The roles played by Gush Emunim and Hamas are vastly different: the former set up the major roadblock to peacemaking through its colonization project, while the latter reacted to the Israeli refusal to remove Gush Emunim's colonies. Even so, the dissension between the two leading Palestinian bodies made peacemaking even more difficult, weakening international pressure on Israel and contributing indirectly to the perpetuation of the occupation.

The Oslo Declaration of Principles (DOP), as explained by Ron Pundak, one of its negotiators, is not a peace accord but a framework for one—a declaration of intentions and a road map. The accompanying letters, in which the two sides accepted each other's legitimacy—the Palestinian Liberation Organization (PLO) recognized Israel and the latter recognized the PLO as the representative of the Palestinian people—were the key to the Oslo negotiations' breakthrough. This mutual recognition remains in effect. The greatest shortcoming of the DOP was its failure to state the political end its signatories sought to achieve. Israel's unwillingness to do so—its denial of the right of self-determination to the Palestinian Arab people already recognized in UN General Assembly Resolution 181 to partition Palestine to two states—was the Achilles' heel of the Oslo process. The Israeli signatories of the DOP floated alternative ideas, running the gamut from an autonomy plan, to a federation between Jordan and the West Bank, to an Israeli-Palestinian-Jordanian condominium in the West Bank, before considering the establishment of a Palestinian state in the OPT. In the absence of a clear political aim and a willingness to speak of a territorial partition leading to the coexistence of two nation-states side by side, the core issues of the conflict were open to negotiation and thus were turned into hostages for both sides' extremists.[35]

Two of the most common explanations for the breakdown of the Oslo process are that Israel's goal was not to terminate the occupation but to place it on more sustainable grounds. An alternative view holds that Rabin's assassination on November 4, 1995, by a sympathizer of the religious settlement movement cut the process short, stopping it from its likely evolution toward territorial partition. Each of these interpretations presents us with a different Rabin, and indeed Rabin expressed contradictory positions. Rabin was sharply critical of the religious settlers and projected to the Israeli public a willingness to compromise. He clarified that there was a price to be paid for peace and recognized the PLO as the legitimate representative of the Palestinian people. He thus acknowledged collective Palestinian demands, including the withdrawal of Israeli forces, at first from Gaza and Jericho. Rabin was murdered after signing Oslo II, the most-far-reaching agreement for Israeli withdrawal from the West Bank. At the same time, he never crystallized a clear position on whether he would support the formation of a state of Palestine, and even his successor Shimon Peres accepted this idea only years after Rabin's assassination.[36]

Instead of adopting one or the other of these interpretations, I wish to emphasize the danger of reading history backwards and giving inordinate importance to personality and intention at the expense of the complex dynamics of competing social forces. The peace process—to borrow the criticism of the late George Fredrickson, who wrote on the different but related topic of white supremacy in South Africa and the United States—is, "from a historian's perspective, a complex and uneven one that cannot be fully appreciated in teleological terms, or merely looking at the final outcome as a predetermined result of . . . attitudes, motivations, and advantages." [37] I also find little value in guessing at, or attributing so much explanatory power to, the intentions of the Israeli architects of the Oslo process, in particular of Rabin. We should pay as much, if not more, attention to Oslo's opponents.

The first signs of the downward spiral of the peace process became visible as soon as the implementation of the Oslo DOP collided with prior Israeli colonization. Under Rabin, colonization in the West Bank continued apace during the Oslo process. But it is worth recalling that Rabin froze the building of further colonies and that the vast majority of the settlers who relocated to the West Bank were *haredim* who settled in two large towns adjacent to the Green Line rather than in its heartland, as Gush Emunim did. Rather than Rabin, what stood most clearly in the way of the promised Israeli withdrawals was the pervasive influence of the Yesha Council—the organization of the existing settlements, the major interest group committed to continuing, unbridled colonization. Settler representatives as well as the Israeli military establishment played an inordinate role in negotiating the extent and layout of the phased Israeli withdrawals. The negotiations were led by the Israeli military, especially the Central Command in charge of the West Bank, which were expected to cater to the settlers' needs. Central Command sought to retain control over vital roads and demanded the construction of "bypass roads" to ensure the settlers' safety. Before the Second Oslo Accord was approved, the secretary general of Gush Emunim's settlement arm was allowed to recommend changes to the agreement. When it was discovered that the provisions of a map already approved by the Knesset hurt settlers' interests, the map was surreptitiously changed to ensure that the settlers' communities would not be subject to the Oslo provisions. Not surprisingly, the settlers took the credit for the changes. In one article with the telling title "The Maps of the Oslo Accord Are the Maps of Jewish Settlement," a settler leader triumphantly concluded that "the Oslo process is the best example . . . of the influence of Jewish settlement on the political process." All these examples demonstrate that the very settlers who were an obstacle to territorial withdrawal had considerable influence over the negotiations that were to finalize the withdrawal's details.[38]

There was a historical opportunity to curtail the continued influence of Gush Emunim, but Rabin chose not to take it. Both Hamas and the Israeli Right vocally opposed the Oslo Accords and sought to wreck their implementation. The First Intifada did not die down with the Oslo DOP. Between the signing of Oslo I (on September 13, 1993) and February 24, 1994, ten Israelis (mostly soldiers, and half of them in Gaza) were killed in stabbing or shooting incidents. On that day Baruch Goldstein, a settler in Qiryat Arba on the outskirts of Hebron, donned his military uniform and opened fire on the Arab worshippers in Hebron's Mosque of Abraham (Me'arat Hamachpela, or "the Cave of Patriarchs" for Jews), who prayed there. Goldstein killed twenty-nine Muslim worshippers before being bludgeoned to death by the survivors. This assault, so clearly aimed at derailing Oslo and inciting hatred and retribution, was carried out by a physician and disciple of Rabbi Meir Kahana (whose party was banned by the Knesset because of its racism). An attack of this magnitude carried out by a member of the right wing of the settlement movement would have been a golden opportunity for Rabin to remove the approximately four hundred Jewish settlers from the old Jewish quarter of Hebron. Given that Israel was soon to start negotiating with the yet-to-be-formed PNA over withdrawal from all West Bank cities, the removal of the settlers from Hebron, the West Bank's only mixed and most contentious city, would have solved one of the thorniest issues of Oslo. Israeli public opinion was behind Rabin, and even his opponents had been unnerved and silenced by the sheer brutality of Goldstein's assault. The removal of this group of settlers would have created a precedent to be followed elsewhere. Rabin let this opportunity pass.

As we know, Rabin's hesitation did not save the Oslo process or himself. He was murdered one week after signing the second, and most substantial, Oslo accord (also known as the Taba Accord), which created the self-governing PNA, delineated Areas A, B, and C, and committed to Israeli withdrawal from the Palestinian cities of the West Bank, except for Hebron (see map 1).

A special and uniquely unsatisfactory withdrawal agreement was worked out for Hebron in January 1997 by Prime Minister Netanyahu. At Netanyahu's insistence, in order to retain the settlement of 450 Jews amid some 20,000 Palestinian residents in Hebron's Old City, the accord agreed to keep Hebron a mixed city. The largest part of Hebron became Area H1, which was turned over to the PNA and treated as part of Area A, while Israeli troops remained in H2, an Area C enclave. This arrangement choked the life out of Hebron's Old City.[39] The influence of the Yesha Council and the settlers expanded further under Netanyahu. The committee charged with preparing the map for the three withdrawals agreed to at the Wye Plantation Accord of October 1998 was composed entirely of settlers, representing the various Israeli ministries and even the military itself, instead of the civilian authorities that had negotiated the original Oslo DOP.[40]

The role played by settlers in the withdrawal process and the continued support they enjoy in Israeli society demonstrate the depth and reach of Israeli religious Zionists, even in the face of serious opposition. Two unprecedented acts of violence—the massacre carried out by an individual settler in a place of worship in Hebron and the assassination of Israel's prime minister during a peace rally in Tel Aviv by a sympathizer of the settler movement—each at a crucial stage of the post-Oslo talks, demonstrate the length to which Oslo's opponents were willing to go to stop peacemaking and the attendant settler withdrawals. But the influence exerted by the settler movement on the implementation of the Oslo Accords was equally important. The transfer of growing responsibility over the negotiations from the political echelon to the military, the police, the Shin Bet, and the Civilian Administration, which were in charge of ensuring the security of Israeli settlers and settlements, and in June 1996 from the Labor-led government, which possessed the "Oslo spirit," to Netanyahu's Likud government, which opposed Oslo in principle, favored Israeli and particularly settler interests at every point. The settlers' efforts in the ensuing rounds of negotiations—as much as the original, ambiguous intentions of the Israeli signatories of Oslo—maintained the balance of power in favor of the colonial power over its subjects.

One of the most astute analyses of the causes behind the collapse of the Oslo process has been offered by political scientist Ian Lustick. Lustick draws on the "Iron Wall" political strategy of building a Jewish state in the face of Arab opposition, offered by Ze'ev Jabotinsky, the leader of the Revisionist Party (from which the Likud emerged), and transforms it into a tool of political analysis. Concluding that indigenous Palestinians, like other indigenous peoples, "will resist their colonizers as long as they see any hope of ridding themselves of the danger of colonization," Jabotinsky asked how Zionism could overcome that opposition. Lustick lays out Jabotinsky's five-stage approach: (1) constructing an "Iron Wall" (combined Jewish militia and British Mandatory military power to suppress resistance); (2) continuing to defend the Iron Wall in the face of Palestinian hostility; (3) repelling Palestinian attackers and imposing costly defeats on them that strengthen moderate Palestinians; (4) on perceiving a willingness for moderation among the Palestinian antagonists choosing to compromise; and (5) reaching a settlement with the other side that is based on mutual recognition.[41]

Lustick then maps the actual phases of the Israeli-Palestinian conflict on Jabotinsky's five stages and argues that in the 1967 War Israel indeed imposed a costly defeat on its Palestinian attackers and their allies, thereby strengthening moderate Palestinians (stage 3), but that it did not continue pursuing the Iron Wall strategy to stage 4. In Oslo, Israel made only a halfhearted attempt to reach the kind of compromise that Jabotinsky's stage 5 anticipates. Lustick equivocates as to the reasons for Israel's unwillingness to accept that it had finally achieved what it wanted: recognition of its legitimate existence on the part of the PLO. At times Lustick suggests that the siege mentality Israelis had developed during the earlier stages of the conflict made it impossible for them to trust Palestinians, and at other times that the sweet result of military victory led Israel to escalate its demands, making a territorial compromise impossible.[42] I would suggest that it is just as likely, as we have seen throughout this essay, that Israel has changed since Jabotinsky's time in another way. As much as psychological impediments or military conquests matter, what radicalized Israeli strategy was the rise of the religious Zionists, who helped chart an alternative course. Religious Zionists continued the colonization process even in the face of Palestinian moderation.

V I

"Oslo" supplies an equally important opportunity to examine the spread of religious opposition among Palestinians under occupation. Just as the settler movement could not fully stop the peace process but could constrain and thwart it, the same was true for Hamas. The dynamic in the two cases, however, was different. Hamas's influence on Palestinian decision making was already manifest before Oslo. Support for Hamas was due to that organization's involvement in the provision of social services and its continued willingness to resort to gruesome violence against Israeli targets. To assess Hamas's influence, I will start with the question: Why did Yasser Arafat, his Fatah, and the PLO sign an agreement to end close to thirty years of violent struggle in return for Israel's recognition of the PLO as the legitimate representative of the Palestinian people, but without getting Israel to offer a Palestinian state in the OPT? Why did Yasser Arafat sign such an unfavorable, even flawed, agreement?

By 1987, the PLO, which had taken over the leadership of the Palestinian national movement in the wake of the 1967 War and had amassed international recognition in the 1970s, was a shell of its former self. A first step in the loss of the PLO's dominant status was its eviction from Beirut as a result of Israel's first Lebanon war in 1982. Being headquartered in Tunis deprived the

PLO of military options. Simultaneously, its Tunisian "exile" detached the PLO from the population of the OPT—which developed its own leadership during the First Intifada—and left a political vacuum that began to be filled in by Hamas. To make up for these vulnerabilities, Arafat cozied up to Saddam Hussein and in 1990 supported his invasion of Kuwait. This pattern of behavior mirrored similar cases of intervention by Palestinians in intra-Arab affairs that were intended to strengthen Palestine's position or find a champion for the Palestinian cause or both: for example, attempts to topple King Hussein of Jordan in September 1970 and intervention in Lebanon's civil war from 1975 on. These collaborations led to disastrous consequences for the Palestinians—the expulsion of Palestinian leaders and militants, and even, in some cases, most of the community from their host societies. Arafat's support for Iraq proved equally disastrous. Though the PLO managed to assert a measure of authority over the First Intifada, a local, and potentially competing, authority emerged from among its leaders. In addition, Hamas's dedication and zeal gained it growing respect among the occupied Palestinians. To reassert its authority, Fatah needed a new approach.

A great deal can be learned about intra-Palestinian politics and subsequent problems that beset the Israeli-Palestinian peace process from the simultaneous existence of two negotiating channels. Early 1990s' diplomacy was a tale of two cities—Madrid and Oslo—offering a tangled skein with two plots and several subplots, which pitted a bruised Israel against a defensive PLO. The 1991 Madrid talks were unprecedented. In the wake of the First Gulf War, the United States was able to put together a face-to-face conference between Israel and all Arab states, including Syria, as well as several international sponsors. Though the PLO was rejected by Israel as a participant, Palestinian representatives were part of the Jordanian delegation. The talks started in October 1991 and lasted for about two years but, besides breaking the ice, remained fruitless. Only after the Likud prime minister Yitzhak Shamir was defeated by Yitzhak Rabin in 1992 was progress recorded, but not in the Madrid talks. Thereafter, an equally groundbreaking set of secret and semiofficial talks between a pair of Israeli academics and representatives of the PLO commenced in Oslo and concluded in the now equally famous and infamous Oslo DOP, signed on September 13, 1993. Though Haider Abdel-Shafi and Hanan Ashrawi, the Palestinian delegates to the Madrid talks, demanded that at the end of an interim process Israel accept the establishment of a Palestinian state, the Oslo DOP did not clarify the end result of the peace process.

Following the elections mandated by the first Oslo Accord, a Palestinian Legislative Council and the Palestinian Authority, later called the Palestinian National Authority (PNA), were constituted and assumed power in parts of the OPT. Once the council began operating, Arafat's supremacy was assured. By bypassing the Madrid talks, the external (i.e., Tunis-based) leadership of the secular Fatah resistance sidelined both the local leaders and Hamas.[43] Arafat's primary goal in signing on to the Oslo DOP appears to have been survival. The imbalance of the Oslo Accord's concessions led to the formation of a "survivalist" PNA that had sunk all its capital in the peace process and could not abandon the agreement. Admittedly, Arafat was far from being fully committed to the Oslo processes and contradicted himself throughout the negotiations. But the unsatisfying compromise of Oslo contributed to Fatah's weakness vis-à-vis Hamas as time went by. Over time, Fatah's survivalist approach left the door open to ever more embarrassing policies: it continued cooperating with Israel in the peace process even after Israel stopped offering to withdraw from additional areas in the West Bank. Collaboration without real signs of movement toward a Palestinian state shredded the PNA's legitimacy.

Hamas's challenge to Arafat's leadership ability was already evident at the early stages of the Oslo process. At the most auspicious moment of peacemaking between Israel and the PLO, Hamas played the same destructive a role for Arafat that Gush Emunim and Rabbi Kahane's followers did for

Rabin. Terror attacks against civilians opened a Pandora's box of fear and retaliation. The destructive impact of terror attacks is particularly potent when the terrorized population holds responsible not the extremists of the other side but all Arabs or Jews. It was convenient for Hamas to view the perpetrator of the Hebron massacre as standing in for all Jews and to carry out a series of suicide bombings within Israel towns, just as it was convenient for the religious Zionist setters to characterize these attacks not as "Hamas terror" but as "Arab terror."

The subject of terror opens up a dark passageway into an examination of the strategy of resistance, the choice of the victims and the timing of attacks. Terror had been a tool of propaganda and recruitment as far back as the Russian nihilists and European anarchists. Such groups targeted innocent noncombatants with the express purpose of provoking a disproportionate and panicked governmental response that would increase solidarity for terrorists' causes. "The victim's innocence," as Michael Gross points out, "is a necessary condition for terror, without which its perpetrators fail to provoke moral outrage of sufficient intensity to elicit the response they desire."[44] Israel's definition of terrorism has always been broad, resembling that of authoritarian regimes rather than the definitions of other democracies. Before the Oslo DOP, it encompassed not only the politically inspired infliction of pain and death indiscriminately on civilians, as the term is most commonly defined, but also all manifestations of Palestinian nationalism. Today, attacks carried out against both Israeli armed forces—soldiers, police, border patrol, and private security guards—and civilians are classified as terrorism. Such an approach leaves no room for legitimate military resistance and for viewing captured attackers as POWs. At the same time, Hamas has not tried to restrict its attacks to military targets or members of the uniformed armed forces.

A particularly significant aspect of terror attacks is their timing. Terror has often been unleashed when other, less violent options of reform and change became available. As Andrew Kydd and Barbara Walter explain, "Extremist violence plays on the uncertainty that exists between moderate groups and can lead them to reject a peace settlement even if the majorities on both sides initially favored the deal." [45] Moderates around the world have been murdered for their contributions to peace making: Alexander II in Russia; Walther Rathenau in Weimar Germany; Neelan Tiruchelvam in Sri Lanka. The worst terrorism by the Basque separatist group Euskadi Ta Askatasuna was directed not against Franco's regime but against the newly emergent Spanish democracy. The peak of the Irish Republican Army attacks dates not to the Protestant Ascendancy but to the 1970s, when the British government sought to improve Catholic citizenship rights. Similarly, organizations at odds with the mainstream Fatah, whether from left or right, sought to subvert peacemaking efforts. When Margaret Thatcher, in sharp departure from US policy under President Reagan, invited two Fatah members of the Palestinian National Council for a meeting in October 1985, members of a radical organization within the PLO hijacked the *Achille Lauro* cruise ship in the Mediterranean and murdered a disabled American Jewish passenger, leading to the cancellation of the meeting.[46] The Second Intifada broke out not under Netanyahu but under Barak in 2000. The deadliest suicide attack was carried out by Hamas on March 27, 2002, during a Passover seder in Netanya the evening before Prince Abdullah's Arab Peace Initiative (API), endorsed by Arafat, was adopted by the Arab League in Beirut. And, of course, a Jewish terrorist murdered Yitzhak Rabin, the signer of the Oslo DOP. Kydd and Walter's study of Hamas terror attacks between 1993 and 2001 leads them to conclude that "terrorist attacks . . . show a clear and recurrent pattern: violence is timed to coincide with major events in a peace process." [47]

Hamas was not alone in timing its attacks to thwart the peace process. Israeli governments also authorized assaults during lulls in the violence, usually in the form of targeted assassinations, not only to assuage domestic

fears but also to rouse higher levels of violence by Palestinians and thus sty-
mie negotiations. Between August 1995 and February 1996, following the
implementation of the Second Oslo Accord, a truce prevailed between
Hamas and Israel, and representatives of Hamas joined Israeli-Palestinian
talks in December 1995.[48] But when given the opportunity to assassinate
Hamas's much hated bomb maker Yahya Ayash, Prime Minister Peres concluded that he could not let the opportunity pass. The assassination led to
the worse spate of revenge suicide bombings by Hamas in Jerusalem and Tel
Aviv and undoubtedly played a major role in Peres's defeat in the subsequent
elections. During the Second Intifada itself, Israel undertook such assassinations in what the historian Charles Smith has called "strategic intervals." In
November 2000, during a meeting between Arafat and President Clinton,
the target was Thabet Thabet, a member of the Palestinian peace camp with
strong ties to Israel's Peace Now movement. A year later, in December 2001,
during a visit by President Bush's envoy General Anthony Zinni, who wished
to parlay a period of calm into renewed peace negotiations, Prime Minister
Sharon ordered the assassination of Raed Karmi, a leader of Fatah's al-Aqsa
Brigade who was responsible for multiple attacks against Israeli soldiers and
civilians, thereby undermining Zinni's mission.[49] It is quite likely that the
timetable of these assassinations was subject to multiple and conflicting
considerations. By the time the intelligence that would ensure an effective
targeted assassination had been gathered, the uptick of violence had calmed
down, but the operations were not called off.

Though the two sides sought to continue the negotiations in spite of the
mounting violence, the Oslo process was stalled. The last attempt to unstick
it took place during face-to-face negotiations between Arafat and Israel's
new Labor Party prime minister, Ehud Barak, with the active participation
of President Bill Clinton, in July 2000. They resulted in no meeting of minds
and ended on a deep note of disappointment. By September 2000, when the
Second Intifada broke out, it was no longer possible to generate a nonviolent,

community-driven uprising akin to the First Intifada. The creation of Areas A, B, and C had subdivided the West Bank into small enclaves (see map 1), and Palestinian civil society activists could no longer mobilize large groups across the OPT. In addition, firearms were available to the PNA's security forces on a large scale. Under these conditions, Palestinians' resort to violence was unsurprising.

The goal of the Second Intifada, according to Nada Matta and René Rojas, was to rebalance asymmetrical Israeli-Palestinian power relations by "out-suffering" the adversary. But in analyzing Hamas's strategy during the Second Intifada, Matta and Rojas conclude that it was a dual-arena strategy, aiming both to raise Israeli fatalities and casualties to unbearable levels and to marginalize Fatah, its main domestic rival, thereby undermining its conciliatory approach toward Israel. Hamas, in fact, was successful in crippling the security cooperation between the PNA and Israel during the Second Intifada and replacing it with coordination between Islamic and national resistance forces. By 2002, all rival Palestinian factions, including Fatah's Al-Aqsa Brigades, Islamic Jihad, and the Popular Front for the Liberation of Palestine, had carried out suicide bombings inside the Green Line. Israel's harsh retaliation—in particular, its targeted assassination of Hamas operatives and leaders—demonstrated the limits to an out-suffering policy. Even so, as Matta and Rojas explain, "Once the failure of terror in the external arena became indisputable, an inward-oriented approach assumed strategic primacy," and Hamas continued suicide bombings during 2003 and 2004, though at a reduced rate, in order to maintain its pressure on Fatah.[50] As Mia Bloom has explained, terror is "a policy to outbid rivals for political market share."[51]

Arafat had vacillated between peacemaking and supporting the Second Intifada, and his death in November 2004 delivered the PNA to his second-in-command Mahmoud Abbas, who, unlike his predecessor, was committed to conciliation with Israel. Abbas proceeded to suppress Fatah's own

Al-Aqsa Brigade's terrorist attacks. Given Israel's continuing repression, and the United States' promotion of democracy in the Middle East that accompanied its entry into the Second Iraq War, Hamas ended suicide bombings and turned to elections as an alternative resistance tactic. In the 2006 elections, it won seventy-four seats to Fatah's forty-five in the Palestinian Legislative Council. But it continued firing missiles from Gaza into Israel. Such attacks—between 2001 and 2008, amounting to some 11,485 rockets and mortars—were inspired by Hamas's opposition to the Oslo process, by the construction of a Separation Wall around Gaza, and by Israel's continued control of Gaza from outside the wall. As many as half of the rockets and mortars were fired after the 2007 coup that made Hamas Gaza's sole ruler. Since their imprecision resulted in 674 missiles per one Israeli fatality, their firing was no longer part of the "out-suffering" strategy to maximize Israeli civilian fatalities. According to Matta and Rojas, it was done to satisfy "the internal need to promote the resistance bloc by differentiating Hamas from its new electoral rivals, preventing militant defections, and mobilizing popular support." [52] Hamas played its role in undermining Oslo and, in the process, weakening Fatah as well.

Adopting the weapon of suicide bombings and, in particular, aiming it against all Israeli civilians was the most grievous error of the Palestinian resistance movement. According to the historian Rashid Khalidi, such attacks showed an "inability . . . to understand the limits of violence" and proved "disastrously counterproductive." [53] Suicide bombing, a tactic introduced to the Middle East by Hezbollah in Lebanon in 1982, was at odds with Islamic traditions and tenets of warfare, martyrdom, and suicide and required Hamas, Islamic Jihad, and, later, Fatah's al-Aqsa Martyrs Brigade to reinterpret or radicalize those traditions. Further, international human rights organizations deplored suicide bombings as an illegal form of resistance: for example, Human Rights Watch designated them—even when perpetrated on settlers—as a war crime and a crime against humanity. [54]

Attacks not only against settlers in the OPT but against residents within Israel erased the Green Line and deemed Israel itself as occupied territory. Consequently, these attacks undermined support for withdrawal from the OPT and for the peace process among Israeli moderates and saw the election of Sharon as Israel's prime minister, the reoccupation of Palestinian towns for two months, raids, targeted assassinations, closures, and the construction of the Separation Wall. With these Israeli responses, the peace process had effectively come to a screeching halt. When the Oslo Accords were supplemented by President Bush's Road Map in April 2003, the peace process became "performance based": that is, it stipulated that no additional Israeli withdrawals would take place as long as terror attacks persisted. But the two sides were already deadlocked in its first stage and the Road Map was never implemented.

It would be, however, a mistake to describe Hamas as committed exclusively to a violent strategy of resistance. Hamas has neither accepted nor fully rejected the Oslo process; after all, in January 2006 it participated in the elections to the second Palestinian Legislative Council that was constituted as part of the Oslo process. Its opposition to Oslo was justified by religious commitments, and they clearly serve as a bulwark to prevent Hamas from losing its legitimacy as Abbas did through continued cooperation with Israel. Hamas, however, also shows periodic signs of keeping the door open to more pragmatic considerations.

Shaul Mishal and Avraham Sela observed in 2000 that Hamas's decision making was best viewed as balancing its dogmatic ideology with a pragmatic approach to political and institutional survival. They categorized the resulting adjustments as "controlled violence" vis-à-vis Israel and calculated conflict and coexistence with the PNA. They concluded,

> Although it is doubtful that Hamas will revise its ultimate goal against and its public attitude toward Israel, it may find that it can accept a workable formula of coexistence with Israel in place of armed struggle. After all, it is

not unknown for individuals, political groups, and social movements to pro-
fess publicly a determination to fight the existing order while at the same
time not excluding the possibility of becoming part of it.[55]

More recently Sara Roy reiterated the same view. "Hamas," she wrote, "not
only remains open to power sharing, but also has a history of nonviolent
accommodation and political adaptation, ideological reflexivity and transformation, and political pragmatism that the West should welcome." [56]

Israel's blockade of Gaza, which started after Hamas successfully carried
out a coup, most likely in advance of a Fatah coup, has failed to dislodge
Hamas. In fact, Hamas maintains a firm hold over Gaza in spite of the deprivation, unemployment, and sense of claustrophobia—some observers call
Gaza the world's largest prison—imposed on its population. Even the devas-
tation and massive loss of life inflicted by Israel in the three Gaza wars
(2008-9, 2012, and 2014) and the unpopularity of Hamas's restrictive religious actions and repression of political opposition do not seem to have seriously weakened its standing. Not only are many components of the blockade
counterproductive, but it is clearly no longer possible to engage in a political
process solely with the PNA, excluding the party to which Palestinians gave
the majority in the 2006 elections. The construction of a port in Gaza, long
ago agreed to by Israel but never implemented, would be a step toward a
relationship based on mutual interests and could eventually facilitate other
forms of cooperation.

Observers can easily point to many statements by Hamas—such as one in
a July 2006 interview of its leader, Khaled Mashaal, that Hamas would
accept a Palestinian state along the Green Line, with East Jerusalem as its
capital, and a guarantee of the Palestinian refugees' right of return—as evidence of its potential moderation.[57] Sometimes members of the organization
have described such an agreement as the gateway to a *hudna*, a traditional,
decade-long Islamic truce, with Israel. But while Mashaal and other Hamas
leaders have floated such feelers, Hamas, as an organization, has never for-

mally made a peace offer. Nor is it clear why Israel would agree to a ten-year truce with Hamas in return for conditions that would lead to a peace accord with the PNA. Furthermore, the *hudna* is an Islamic juridical concept and as such cannot be adjudicated through international law or by the bodies of the UN but only by Islamic religious authorities, putting Israel at an unacceptable disadvantage. In general, Hamas has kept at arm's length all formal human rights and even IHL. For example, it never allowed the International Commission of the Red Cross to visit Israeli captives it held in the past, a practice that continues in 2016. Hamas has also dismissed UN reports documenting war crimes Hamas has committed against Israel in the three Gaza wars. Signing up for international human rights and IHL would signal a turn by Hamas that could be rewarded with the opening of a new diplomatic process. After all, until September 1993, Israel also held Fatah and the PLO to be terrorist organizations, only to accept them as diplomatic partners in the Oslo DOP.

VII

Hamas is most frequently examined from the perspective of counterterrorism experts as a species of contemporary terrorist organization. In contrast, Glenn Robinson from the Naval Postgraduate School in Monterey holds that to understand Hamas we should study it as a social movement that has broad goals and is subject to widely recognized social dynamics.[58] I will expand on Robinson's suggestion by studying Hamas comparatively. Hamas, as a second-generation religious nationalist movement, I will argue, bears intriguing and unexplored parallels with Gush Emunim.

Hamas was founded in 1987 as an offshoot of the Muslim Brotherhood of Palestine. The first generation of the Brotherhood had been led in the 1940s by an urban upper class of merchants who benefited from strong financial ties with the Gulf States and Jordan. They were allied with other non-Islamic but wealthy Palestinian elites and were correspondingly cautious. The defeat of the Palestinians and Arab states in 1948, in their view, resulted from insufficient religious devotion, and the movement's goal was to rekindle religious fervor through education and personal role modeling. The Muslim Brotherhood was caught in between the traditional ulema (law doctors), for whom the Brotherhood remained a lay Islamic movement that lacked the authority to make religious rulings, and other Palestinian nationalists, who criticized its emphasis on greater personal piety for leading to passivity in the face of the occupation.

The younger generation of the Brotherhood were more likely than the founders to have risen out of the lower class, to reside in refugee camps, and to be university educated. Islamic Jihad proved to be the model for what the Palestinian Muslim Brotherhood became later, using the prestige of striking against Israeli targets to advocate for deeper personal piety. The outbreak of the First Intifada in 1987 led the younger-generation leaders to carry out an "internal coup" and to form Hamas as the Brotherhood's new face.[59] By participating in the intifada, the younger religious generation was able to push aside the older generation that was compromised by its cautiousness. In rising to power, the second-generation Brotherhood leaders resembled the second Israeli religious nationalist generation, the youth of the National Religious Party who ended up founding Gush Emunim. The rapid succession of violent events punctuating Palestinian history has accelerated general change: Hamas's quick rise at the outbreak of the First Intifada resembles Arafat's quick replacement of the PLO leadership in the wake of the 1967 War.

Gush Emunim was born out of the religious Zionist National Religious Party as the second generation's opposition to Israeli withdrawal from the Sinai and its advocacy of unbridled colonization. Hamas was born out of the Muslim Brotherhood in the crucible of the 1987 Intifada. In both, second-generation participants pushed against weak elders with negligible influence. Seeking out the role of a vanguard, the second generation of combatants gave a clear boost to the religious definition of the conflict and legitimated sweeping goals. In both societies, these religious movements contrasted with their secular nationalist counterparts, co-opting some and overshadowing the rest. Their growing prominence signaled deep opposition to territorial compromise on both sides. Refusing to part with land promised to the seed of Israel met its counterpart in the view of the whole of Palestine as a waqf, a religious endowment to Muslims for all generations. The messianic legacy of the settlers catalyzed the emergence of Islamic opponents of colonization.

At this point an important gap opens up between the two movements. While both have found their source of energy and motivation in identifying a solution to their elders' quandary, Gush Emunim was swept along a path of upward social mobility into the middle class of a rapidly modernizing society, while Hamas was a purveyor of social welfare to low-income strata of Palestinian society. The religious Zionist cohort of Gush Emunim was able to greatly enhance its social mobility by tying itself to the state-financed and subsidized colonization project, while Hamas was able to expand the range of its charity institutions as its involvement in the nationalist struggle reinforced its prestige, particularly during the years of the Oslo process. Gush Emunim's and Hamas's different social constituencies and their different relation to their state—close for Gush Emunim in Israel and, until 2006, nonexistent for Hamas in Palestine—propelled them toward different socioeconomic goals. Both movements, however, are as much social as political and religious, and their success has been dependent on that very combination. Socioeconomic progress and rising standards of living have reduced the influence of Hamas in Palestinian society, while similar changes have had much less influence on the role played by religious Zionists in Israeli society.

Hamas's *da'wa* (proselytizing for Islam) rests not only on moral education and the propagation of the faith but also on a wide array of social service and welfare institutions. The coexistence of religion and social support in the mosque—which serves as both place of worship and provider of social services—begets loyalty with benefits. Like other branches of the Muslim Brotherhood, Hamas fills the demands for medical, educational, and social services that are unmet by states and, in the Palestinian case, fills them in the absence of a state. The Israeli Civil Administration permitted both extensive mosque building and *da'wa* institutions in Gaza and the West Bank before the First Intifada. One example is the al-Mujamma al-Islamiya (the Islamic Center), which by 1987 incorporated about half of the mosques in Gaza and would become Hamas's major social welfare institution and a counterweight to the PLO's activist nationalism. The range of charitable or welfare institutions that buttress Hamas and that the organization is able to finance and operate includes educational institutions; nursing schools; refugee, orphan, and poor relief bodies; women's associations; organizations supporting the elderly; radio and TV stations; sports clubs; and so on. Hamas's Scientific Medical Association, established in 1997, runs dental clinics, medical centers, and a blood bank. The Hamas-sponsored Association for Science and Culture offers education from kindergarten through eighth grade, and the al-Mujamma runs the prestigious Islamic University in Gaza. Given their extensive reach and breadth, these Hamas-run institutions cannot be replaced by the PNA. When some of these service providers were closed down at the beginning of the Second Intifada, they were usually allowed to reopen under a different name.[60]

The balance between social services and violence, including against civilians, is a key to the religious half turn in Palestinian society and consequently requires close examination. Western counterterrorism analysts focus almost exclusively on the role of these social service institutions—Hamas's welfare network—as recruiters, supporters, and legitimizers of its terror activities.[61] But the economist Eli Berman suggests in his book *Radical, Religious and Violent* that Hamas shares important characteristics with other tightly knit "clubs" that engage in collective activities, provide social welfare, and require devotion. When they turn to violence, these religious "clubs" have a significant advantage over other militant groups, since they have fewer free riders, cheaters, and shirkers.[62] In contrast to Islamic Jihad, which does not have a network of social services and thus enjoys limited social support and sits out elections to the PNA, Hamas used its *da'wa* network of services to translate its social roots into political power in the January 2006 elections to the Palestinian Legislative Council. Hamas has also enjoyed support among secular Palestinians who believe that the organization's promise of honest and effective government is an extension of the provision of such services. In other words, Hamas's social service network allows it to become not just a terrorist organization but a political party, which can potentially negotiate agreements with Israel.

Lori Allen provides another comparison: attitude toward human rights. As a result of the Oslo process, the PNA and Palestinian civil society have become deeply dependent on funding offered by international NGOs, the World Bank, and foreign state agencies, all of which require the adoption of a professionalized human rights approach. The claims and practices of such an approach, including the human rights training of security forces, have produced, in Allen's estimation, only "performances" of human rights. The PNA goes through the motions while simultaneously violating human rights in practice, even to the extent of torturing Palestinian detainees in Palestinian jails. Allen draws a sharp distinction between human rights as such and the "human rights industry" of the PNA, which she sharply criticizes. The alleged professionalization through human rights education moderates and depoliticizes Palestinian resistance and indirectly legitimates the corruption endemic to the PNA's ministries, functionaries, and security apparatuses. In contrast, the absence of a human rights industry associated with and supportive of Hamas allows the organization to present itself as standing for sincerity and honesty while serving the Palestinian people, even if its human rights record is abysmal.[63]

The current falling out between the PNA and Hamas was the culmination of the opposing approaches taken by the two organizations and is a serious obstacle to a successful peace process. The surprising victory of Hamas in the January 2006 elections, due to popular trust in Hamas's religious commitment to stay honest and to reject the PNA's corrupt ways, deepened the division between the two. When Hamas rejected the demands of the Quartet (the United Nations, the United States, Russia, and the European Union) to commit to abstaining from violence and to recognize Israel as well as the previous agreements signed with it, foreign assistance was withheld, and Israel imposed crippling economic sanctions. The political division serves as a major excuse for Israel's refusal—supported by most of the international community—to negotiate with Hamas and to proceed with effective negotiations.

VIII

The religious vanguards in Israeli and Palestinian societies have appeared against the background of, and filled in the gap left by, the ineffectiveness of the international community and IHL to push Israel forcefully for a concluding agreement along two-state parameters. Indeed, the last two forces that have prolonged the occupation are the direct enabling role played by US foreign policy and the indirect enabling leverage provided by IHL. Growing Israeli intransigence, indeed hubris, rides on the increasingly pro-Israeli US foreign policy under successive administrations since 1967. The United States transitioned from a position of relative neutrality—to the point of forcing Israel to withdraw from the Sinai in 1957, and remaining ambiguous with regard to the Israeli decision to launch the 1967 War—to one of unbending support since the early 1970s.

The growth and acceleration of the pro-Israeli stance in American foreign policy have two main sources—international and domestic—and the nature of US-Israeli relations at any given time is determined by their balance. The former is an expression of national security considerations, while the latter is articulated in the form of a "special relationship." So-called special relationships are a goody bag commonly filled with ill-defined and amorphous benefits that have been repeatedly added and subtracted over time. Though by their very definition special relationships should remain immune to the vagaries of crass interests, the record suggests that the specialness of the US-Israeli relations has been contingent on the salience and interpretation of US national security interests. In this section, I will survey the history of political and military ties between the two countries and will then turn to the evolution of their symbolic dimension in order to assess the role played by the United States in prolonging the Israeli occupation.

Though under President Truman the United States was the first country to recognize the newly declared state of Israel in May 1948, it trailed the USSR in recognizing Israel *de jure*. For most of Truman's and Eisenhower's administrations, Israel was viewed as "a major political and security liability," to borrow the words of the political scientist Robert O. Freedman.[64] Israeli-US relations thus began at a low point. The United States did not wish to support a new state that it expected to be defeated in the 1948 War. And if Israel survived it would be even less welcome, since US diplomats anticipated either that it would become a Soviet client state or that support for Israel would drive the Arab states to become Soviet clients. The United States, consequently, imposed an arms embargo on both sides. Following the war, the United States demanded that Israel allow the return of Palestinian refugees and cede a land corridor between Egypt and Jordan but was rebuffed on both counts. The Israeli military procured its arms and equipment from the Soviet bloc in the 1948 War and from France in the Suez War of 1956. Eisenhower condemned the French-British-Israeli invasion and compelled Israel to withdraw from the Sinai. In contrast to the lukewarm US support afforded Israel, the United States landed marines in Lebanon in 1958 and twice deployed the Sixth Fleet to express its support for the Jordanian monarchy.

In the context of the Cold War, the paramount US concern was to continue maintaining proper relations with the Arab countries as part of its overall effort to contain the USSR. Thus it kept Israel only in its peripheral vision. As the failure of the Eisenhower Doctrine to shepherd the Arab countries into the Western camp became obvious, there was less fear that Israel would spoil US-Arab relations. During President Kennedy's term, the United States finally agreed to supply weapons to Israel, starting with defensive Hawk antiaircraft missiles. Still, before the outbreak of the 1967 War, the United States remained cautious. Even as Egypt expelled the UN forces (stationed since the Suez War to separate the two sides), hastily moved its troops into the Sinai, and closed the international waterway of the Red Sea to Israeli shipping, the United States would not intercede to break the closure. It remained ambivalent with regard to the Israeli decision to launch the 1967 War. President Johnson stated that if Israel went to war alone it would remain alone, though it is believed that Johnson's CIA director let his Israeli counterpart know that the United States had no objection to Israel going to war to lift the closure.

Israel's initial fears that the United States would force it to withdraw again from the Sinai as it had done in 1957 were not borne out. In fact, the United States and the other Western countries stood solidly against the Arab demand, represented by the USSR in the Security Council, to condemn Israel for aggression and to demand its one-sided withdrawal without any diplomatic recompense. A hard-fought diplomatic struggle that lasted almost six months was concluded with Security Council Resolution 242, which affirmed the political independence and territorial inviolability of every state in the region. The resolution, in effect, recognized the Green Line as

Israel's border for the first time. The rest of the resolution was more ambiguous. While the preamble emphasized the inadmissibility of the acquisition of territory by war, the text itself called for the withdrawal of Israeli armed forces only "from territories occupied in the recent conflict"—a wording that evades withdrawal from *all* the occupied territories. Moreover, the resolution introduced a new, third consideration by affirming the right of the regions' states to "live in peace within secure and recognized orders." Both Lord Caradon, the British representative who drafted the final version, and Arthur Goldberg, the US ambassador to the UN, explained later that they had wished to leave the door open to the redrawing of borders through minor territorial adjustments.[65] Such ambiguity—the assertion of the principle of territorial integrity combined with practical loopholes—was the consequence of Cold War rivalries. A country in "our" camp should be able to get away with what another country in the rival camp should not. Israel waited until May 1968 before assenting, and Syria rejected the resolution. Egypt accepted the resolution, and the peace treaty it ultimately reached with Israel is based on the principle of territorial integrity, thus requiring full Israeli withdrawal from the Sinai (but not from Gaza). Resolution 242 was adopted with a narrow focus on the conflict between Israel and its Arab neighbors; it still viewed the Palestinian question as a nonpolitical refugee issue. The PLO rejected Resolution 242 resoundingly.

The United States was determined to take advantage of Israel's defeat of Egypt and Syria, since by the late 1950s and early 1960s those countries had signed up with the Soviet bloc. Following the 1967 War, regional and global interests became deeply intertwined, and from then on the Israeli-Arab conflict played out within the framework of the Cold War. President Johnson was keen to ensure Israeli air superiority by furnishing Israel with Skyhawk planes and, later, with Phantom jets. Israel was welcomed into the American Cold War bloc. Under the Nixon Doctrine, the United States began viewing Israel as a strategic partner in countering Soviet influence in the Middle East.

The proof of Israel's value as a pro-American Cold War warrior was established during the September 1970 Jordanian crisis. As King Hussein was fighting to put down a Palestinian attempt to topple his regime, a Syrian tank unit invaded Jordan. Following speedy three-way negotiations, Israel threatened to use its air force against Syria if it were to deploy planes against the Jordanian ground forces. Meanwhile, the United States promised to protect Israel from possible Soviet intervention. The Jordanian forces were now able to prevail, and the Syrian tanks withdrew. The US-Jordan-Israel bloc had acquired the upper hand over the USSR-Syrian-PLO partnership, and a strong perception of common interests was established between the United States and Israel.

The clearest demonstration of the new strategic alignment came during the 1973 War, in which the Israeli forces were surprised by a coordinated Egyptian-Syrian attack into the territories Israel had conquered from them in 1967. The United States not only undertook a massive airlift to resupply the Israeli forces fighting on two fronts but also raised the US military's state of readiness when the USSR appeared ready to dispatch combat units.[66] After the war, the United States was able to move Egypt into its own column of supporters. Egypt became one of the rare defectors of the Cold War, and the United States played a key role in bringing Egypt and Israel together to reach their peace treaty in 1979, in the process pressuring the Begin government to agree to full withdrawal from the Sinai. Since then, Israel (like Egypt) has been the recipient of advanced US military weaponry and foreign aid equaling approximately $3 billion per annum. In 2016 a new ten-year agreement was signed to provide Israel with about $4 billion a year. During the Reagan presidency, the United States and Israel also signed a free trade agreement and a Memorandum of Agreement on US-Israeli strategic cooperation.[67]

The convergence of the national interests of the United States and Israel helped elevate their relationship to a symbolic level. The United States has two circles of special relations: the first includes the United Kingdom and the countries of the Anglosphere, with which the United States shares a historical trajectory as settler colonies, cultural similarities, and language; the second, a looser circle of countries, deemed "special" because they serve as "model nations," includes Israel. The claimed specialness commonly reflects the sway of US domestic religious and ethnic groups to give the relationship with their country of origin or affiliation a political and cultural salience. The rise of Israel's importance and the growing influence of the Jewish community in the United States are closely related.

At the core of the American Jewish community's support for Israel have been two factors: that community's extraordinarily centralized and nondemocratic structure and the internalization of Israel as a core component of modern Jewish identity. Israel was nowhere near as important to American Jews prior to the 1967 War as it became afterwards. A cautious US Jewry played only a small role even in seeking the assistance of the US government to save the Jews of Europe during the Second World War. Though laboring under the prevalent anti-Semitism in American society and government, the frantic campaign of the Emergency Committee to Save the Jewish People of Europe was established by a small Revisionist group outside the American Jewish leadership. Henry Morgenthau Jr., then secretary of the Treasury, played an important role in setting up the War Refugee Board to assist European Jews, but this was done as late as January 1944. Only the US shift from the ambivalence of the Eisenhower years to the Nixon-Kissinger administration's explicit support in the 1970s removed the stigma of dual loyalty and created the space for American Jews to find Israel.

The contemporary public unanimity of American Jewish voices and the harsh rejection of public criticism of Israeli policies are contingent on a unique set of organizational structures. There is a plethora of Jewish community organizations, running the gamut from social service bodies such as B'nei B'rith and Hadassah, through the organizations of synagogues of the major denominations, to legal associations such as the Anti-Defamation

League. These are brought together under the aegis of a single body—the Conference of Presidents of Major American Jewish Organizations—making "official" Jewry an organization of organizations. There is little democracy in the community. As this body's presidents have recognized, they represent not all Jews but those who are willing to be involved, often by providing financial support. This hierarchical and oligarchical structure is situated to the right of the majority of US Jews. Though Prime Minister Rabin had harsh words for the American Israel Public Affairs Committee (AIPAC)—the main Jewish body lobbying the US government—it has been singularly effective in enlisting bipartisan congressional support for the proposition that strong US-Israeli relations serve the interests of the United States. Until 2016, measures supported by AIPAC were opposed by less than a few dozen members of Congress.

According to Dov Waxman's recent study, there have been and still are cracks within the Jewish community, but this dissent is not well known. As he points out, the rise of the Likud to power in Israel in June 1977, and events such as the massacre of Palestinians in the Sabra and Shatila refugee camps by Israeli-backed Maronite Falange militias in September 1982, have sown discord between Israel and American Jewry. This contention finds its expression, as Waxman demonstrates, in the relations between different portions of American Jewry. Arrayed against each other are two relatively small groups—the "peace camp" versus the donors, activists, and bureaucrats who make up the establishment and enjoy the unconditional support of a large segment of Orthodox Jews.

In between is the "silent majority" that does not feel itself represented by either camp; it supports negotiations leading to a two-state solution but does not trust the Palestinian leadership. Since fewer than one in three non-Orthodox Jews feel that "caring about Israel is essential to being Jewish," they do not challenge the Jewish oligarchy and, under the current circumstances, remain apolitical when it comes to the Israeli-Palestinian conflict and the occupation. The younger generation of American Jews, as pointed out by the American journalist Peter Beinart, have lost interest in an Israel that no longer corresponds to their liberal values. Most of the Orthodox Jewish community is closely aligned with Israel's nationalist and religious Zionist communities.[68] The growing gap between the American Jewish establishment and the liberal Jewish community, as well as with a more multicultural American society, are likely to reduce AIPAC's effectiveness in presenting the Likud version of Israel's interests as coinciding with the US national interest.[69]

Israel has enjoyed consistent US diplomatic support in the UN's Security Council for a long time. John Mearsheimer and Stephen Walt have calculated that between 1982 and 2006 the United States vetoed thirty-two Security Council resolutions critical of Israel—more than the total number of vetoes cast by all other Security Council members.[70] But a "veto-proof" Security Council was not always available to Israel. Lara Freidman, the director of policy and government relations for Americans for Peace Now, quantified the record of previous presidents, and reports that during the Johnson administration, the Security Council passed seven resolutions critical of Israel; under Nixon, at least fifteen; under Ford, two; and under Carter, fourteen. The number peaked at twenty-one under Reagan, then declined to nine under Bush senior, fell to three during the hopeful Clinton years that coincided with the Oslo process, and rose back to six under Bush junior, to reach zero after 2011. During President Obama's years in office, the Security Council has passed a single resolution that specifically censors Israel. In 2011 Obama even instructed the US delegation to the UN to veto a draft resolution critical of Israeli settlements that explicitly used the language of the official US policy. The rationale given by Ambassador Susan Rice was that such a resolution might undermine peace efforts by making Israel appear vulnerable and thus give the Palestinian side an advantage in future talks.[71]

This "antiveto" protection has been one of the most significant Israeli "force multipliers," but it is equally clear that instead of being available at all

times it fluctuates with domestic considerations and the changing circumstances of the Israeli-Arab conflict. Israel's special relationship with the
United States has benefited from the role of the upwardly mobile and self-
confident liberal Jewish community, but unlike other special relationships,
Israel's elevation to this status is supported more broadly. US exceptionalism
and foreign policy habitually carry a religious stamp, and the self-same religious half turn that we saw in Israel and among Palestinians has played an
important role in the United States as well. American Protestants fall roughly
into three categories: mainline Christian churches, Evangelical Christians,
and Dispensationalists, and significant portions of the latter two are very
supportive of Israel. Mainline churches in general wish Israel to be viewed
through the same frame (for example, of human rights) as the United States'
other foreign partners. Evangelicals hold that helping "Israel" will bring
divine support. Dispensationalists reject the replacement theology of Christianity (the view that the New Covenant has replaced the Mosaic Covenant
and that the Christian Church has replaced the Israelites as God's people)
and hold that the fulfillment of God's promises to restore the Kingdom of
Israel—the old and separate covenant—is a precondition for the Second Com-
ing. The politicization and rise of Evangelical and Dispensationalist Protes-
tantism, which combine as part of their global vision anticommunism and
opposition to the UN with support for Israel, have greatly enhanced the
influence of the Jewish establishment in creating a domestic American "fire-
wall" against criticism of Israel. Initially the Moral Majority, then the Christian Coalition, and most recently the more narrowly focused Christians
United for Israel have lobbied for unqualified support of right-wing Israeli
policies. The strong support of Evangelicals for Israel and its colonization at a
time when they were building megachurches and confidently observing the
shrinking of the mainline churches is especially striking. Ironically, from a
theological viewpoint, Evangelicals and Dispensationalists expect Jews to
convert to Christianity or be destroyed at the end of time, but "in the short

run" these views do not get in the way of cooperation between Christian Zionists and Likud leaders.

For its articulation and growth, the special US-Israeli relationship has required its own institutional underpinning: first the American Jewish community, joined later by the Christian Evangelicals and for a period after 9/11, by the foreign policy neoconservatives (i.e., "neocons"). In response to the 9/11 terror attacks on US soil, the neoconservative coterie, formed around the belief that the United States should take full advantage of the collapse of the USSR and the end of the Cold War to recreate the world in its own image, were given a chance to put their ideological vision into effect. The loose grouping of the American Jewish community, Christian evangelicals, and neocons is viewed as the "Israel Lobby," though they operate as much in parallel as in coordination with each other.

The unwavering support Israel received from the Evangelical community, however, is likely to fall as the share of white Evangelical Protestants is declining. Twenty-seven percent of Americans over 65 are white mainline Protestants, but only 10 percent of millennials are, and the hold of religion on American society itself is weakening. The influence of neocons has been waning, and the falling out between AIPAC and the Obama administration over the Iranian nuclear deal increased friction between the United States and Israel. A generational change in the leadership of US Jewry, anticipated for example in the breaking away of "Open Hillel" student organizations from the official and conservative Hillel, portends a Jewish community more critical of Israeli governmental policies. At the same time, the new Republican administration and Congress are likely to remain among Israel's strongest supporters in the United States.

The diplomatic protection of the United States is a key direct enabler of Israel's continued colonization and limited willingness to compromise with the PNA, but it is important not to take for granted uncritical U.S support for Israel. A general evaluation of the relative weight of national interests and of the special relationship reveals crises in which the special relationship did not suffice to protect Israel's policy preferences, since the United States was not willing to absorb painful losses to its national interest. Both the start and the end of the 1973 War provided such test cases. On October 6, 1973, when Israel belatedly discovered that the massing Egyptian and Syrian armies on its borders were not engaged in military exercises but were on the brink of attacking the Israeli forces, it sought to engage in a preemptive aerial strike. President Nixon and Foreign Secretary Kissinger, viewing the pending war in the context of the larger frame of the Cold War, warned Israel against preemption. At its most desperate hour, Israel conceded to the US request. Being reduced to a defensive posture, it absorbed the full brunt of its enemies' attacks and suffered heavy losses. Even with the reversal of its military fortunes, Israel yet again conceded to the US request not to press its advantage against the Third Egyptian Army that it had successfully encircled. Instead, Israel allowed the United States to come to Egypt's aid and raise the siege. In the wake of the war, the United States pressured the right-wing Begin government to reach a peace accord with Egypt in spite of an Israeli reluctance to remove its Sinai settlement and return all of the peninsula to Egyptian sovereignty. Fast-forward to 2016, and the inability of a fully mobilized AIPAC to scuttle the nuclear deal with Iran, or even receive the support of the majority of Democratic senators, is a further and more recent demonstration that US interests trump Israeli wishes. These crucial incidents demonstrate that national interests outweigh special relations and give the lie to "The tail wags the dog" as an interpretation of the two countries' relationship.

There are also international divisions within the US government with regard to its Israeli policy. The US State Department publishes periodic condemnations of Israeli colonization in the OPT. On July 27, 2016, it expressed opposition to the publication of new housing tenders in the East Jerusalem settlements, which, as the statement concluded, are part of an ongoing process of land seizures, settlement expansion, legalizations of outposts, and denial of Palestinian development that risk entrenching a one-state reality of perpetual occupation and conflict. We remain troubled that Israel continues this pattern of provocative and counterproductive action, which raises serious questions about Israel's ultimate commitment to a peaceful, negotiated settlement with the Palestinians.[72]

The gap between the State Department's repeated sober assessment and the White House's acquiescence to Israel's policies in the OPT is striking and highlights the extent to which the United States enables Israel's "provocative and counterproductive action." As long as the United States continues veto-proofing the Security Council, Israel is unlikely to keep its promises to US administrations to uproot the settlement outposts that are illegal even under Israeli planning law, and its colonization is likely to continue into the indefinite future.

In March 2010, General David Petraeus questioned the view that US national interests coincide with Israeli interests. He stated to the Senate's Armed Services Committee that insufficient progress toward Israeli-Palestinian peace was one of the most prominent "cross-cutting issues that serve as major drivers of instability, inter-state tensions, and conflict. These factors can serve as root causes of instability or as obstacles to security" in the Middle East.[73] In 2013, retired General James Mattis stated, "I paid a military security price every day as the commander of Central Command because the Americans were seen as biased in support of Israel, and all the moderate Arabs who want to be with us . . . cannot come out publicly in support of people [i.e. the United States] who don't show respect for the Arab Palestinians." He further expressed opposition to the continued Israeli settlement, which he said would lead to an Israeli apartheid regime in the West Bank, and he called for the resolution of the Israeli-Palestinian conflict on the basis of a two-state solution.[74] There has been considerable pushback against these sharp departures from US policy toward Israel, and while the breakdown of large parts of the Middle Eastern state system following the Arab Spring have tempered the impact of such statements, they offer an influential alternative view.

International humanitarian law (IHL) is the key indirect enabler of Israeli occupation. The central role played by the Shamgar Doctrine's interpretation of IHL in immobilizing the occupation is tragic and ironical in equal measure. In the first essay I discussed the two fundamental legal dimensions of belligerent occupation: first, that military control does not give a country sovereignty over that territory, and, second, that an occupying power is entrusted with the management of the occupied population's everyday life. The former principle limits the powers bestowed on the belligerent occupier by the latter principle and prohibits it from dispossessing the population whose public order and civil life it regulates or from colonizing its land. A third principle emerges directly from the previous two: a belligerent occupation is perforce *temporary* and cannot be turned into a permanent conquest, since that would violate the conquering nation's duties toward the occupied population and would change the sovereignty status of the territory in question. The centrality of this principle for IHL leads me to ask a series of questions that, on their face, make little sense and should not even be asked: How long may a situation of temporariness last while still remaining temporary? What is the expiration date of belligerent occupation? What happens under IHL if such occupation lasts indefinitely? And, finally, is it possible for the requirement of temporariness itself to perpetuate the Israeli occupation?

The Israeli HCJ explicitly bases many of its decisions on the premise that Israeli occupation is temporary. It justified its consent to the construction of settlements by recalling that belligerent occupation under IHL is temporary and that since settlements cannot continue past the end of the occupation, they, by extension must also remain temporary. The elasticity of the concept of time, however, is already on display in the 1979 Bet-El ruling in which Justice Miriam Ben-Porath suggested that "permanent community" was, in fact, a "purely relative concept." [75] Her observation was based on the precedent of the removal of Israeli settlements from the Sinai as part of the Camp David peace accord that had been signed two years earlier. The Israeli withdrawal from Gaza in 2005 is a more recent example the courts may cite in the future, and there are additional illustrations of temporariness in Israeli legal documents. The property title deeds of houses built in settlements include a clause that specifies that they remain in effect only as long as the Israeli military remains in control of the area. Taking refuge in the Geneva Convention, the HCJ feels free to focus on this narrow set of facts and ignores the massive outlay of funds needed for the project of settlement construction. The movement of 405,158 Jewish settlers into the West Bank, the incursion of another 207,100 settlers into East Jerusalem (by mid-2016) and, finally, the construction of the Separation Wall running mostly through the OPT all indicate long-term plans but are ignored by the court.

A circular logic is in play here: Israel is able to use the stipulation of the temporary character of occupation to make long-term changes in the name of extended security risks, many of which are the result of the violations of the law of occupation. As long as peace talks go on, or there is an expectation of their renewal, and as long as Israeli authorities describe their colonization as temporary, IHL does not become an obstacle to colonization. Under IHL a new legal category is born, creating what Eyal Weizman calls "permanent temporariness." [76] Israeli occupation is temporary and will always remain temporary.

In 1982, Shamgar further developed his doctrine in order to explain away the potential problems associated with the longevity of a belligerent occupation by arguing that, "pending an alternative political or military solution, this system of government could, from a legal point of view, continue indefinitely." But Orna Ben-Naftali rejects the attempt to seamlessly substitute "indefinite" for "temporary" by pointing out that time is not accidental to legal thinking. Demarcated time as a limited and contested resource is embodied in both foundational legal presumption and the very principle of legality itself. If prison sentences could be set without an upper time limit they would render freedom meaningless. Similarly, an indefinite occupation does not leave room for the reinstatement of sovereignty, a time when the occupied population can determine its own destiny. The casual disregard of the constituent principle of an occupation's temporariness reinforces the denial of the occupied population's human rights and citizenship rights in both the short and the long term. And, as Ben-Naftali sums up the consequences of the Shamgar Doctrine's preference for a rulebook conception of law over a rights conception, "In making the very rule of law a casualty of an indefinite occupation, it corrupts the law." John Dugard, special rapporteur of the UN's Commission on Human Rights, concluded that "the rule of law is one casualty of the conflict in the OPT, but the main casualties are the people of Palestine and Israel."[77]

The illusion of the occupation's temporariness, and its incorporation into Shamgar's interpretation of IHL, constitute the hard, legal dimension of denialism and in so doing play an important role in its perpetuation. As long as the occupation remains "temporary," it can be viewed as a historical incident and the OPT can be viewed as lying outside of the boundaries of Israel. The Palestinians of Gaza and the West Bank, consequently, are still invisible to most Israelis, even after a half century of occupation, and even to those, such as members of the security forces and settlers, who come into daily contact with them in the OPT. They resemble the Palestinian "present absentees" of Israel after the 1948 War within the Green Line. As Ariella Azoulay and Adi Ophir insightfully point out, "The false temporariness of 'the occupation' generates perpetual blindness that is at one and the same time caused by the ruling apparatus in the territories and is one of its active mechanisms." The externalization of space through the bifurcation of time—permanent on one side of the Green Line, temporary on the other—removes the need, indeed the very possibility, of feeling responsible for the circumstances under which occupied Palestinians live. Temporariness at once constitutes Palestinians as the subjects of Israeli colonial rule and denies their colonial subjugation. Temporariness is also a potent Israeli mechanism of separation and exclusion, of averting one's gaze from that which is plainly visible. It clears the conscience of Israelis by bracketing their participation in the occupation's maintenance and permits the continued domestic and widespread international acceptance of Israel as a democratic state.[78]

The shortcomings of the framework of IHL that make it ripe for misuse are hardly accidental. They are rooted in the European origins and Europocentric nature of the laws that regulate warfare. Medieval and even modern European states' fluctuating fortunes and frequent warfare commonly led to an agreed-upon redrawing of the boundaries in favor of the stronger parties. The expectation that wars end with peace accords reflects the European historical experience, even if such accords were regularly discarded when the defeated party felt strong enough to challenge them in a new round of hostilities. Under circumstances of repeated exchanges of territory, without regard to the wishes of their inhabitants, military occupations were indeed temporary and lapsed when prior sovereignty was restored. This is the historical experience that was codified in the major treaties of IHL, but it does not necessarily fit the colonial world, where violent struggles took place between European great powers and movements of national liberations that were not state actors. Though two Additional Protocols for improving the protection of civilians in asymmetrical civil and anticolonial wars were added to the Geneva Convention in 1977, they focus on regulating the hostilities and do not address the postoccupation situation. The new protocols did not revisit the nature and temporal aspect of occupations or the expectation that such occupations will end in a peace accord. The Additional Protocols have been ratified by the vast majority of countries but not by the United States, Israel, Turkey, Iran, Pakistan, or India and consequently are not understood as customary law binding upon all countries.

Belligerent occupations continue to be regulated by the Hague Regulation and the Fourth Geneva Convention—the bulk of the IHL, which does not recognize a category of "illegal occupation" but only the violations of an occupying military's obligations toward the occupied population. When UN secretary general Kofi Annan in March 2002, during the Second Intifada, called on Israel to "end the illegal occupation of Palestinian territories," rather than to stop violating IHL, his spokesman had to admit that he should not have described the occupation as illegal.[79]

Nor is permanent temporariness merely an oversight or the unthinking extension of the European experience to the postcolonial world. Temporariness has both deeper roots and more far-reaching goals. It has been a part of European colonial policies since at least the end of the First World War, when it was used to reconcile two essentially contradictory principles, as analyzed in a masterful study of the Mandatory system by Susan Pedersen. On the one hand, each of the victorious Allied powers wanted to be compensated for its wartime hardships by being allowed to annex its conquests. On the other hand, the wave of internationalist and anti-imperialist sentiment that swept the globe—and the concrete promises of self-determination given during the war to local allies—favored granting independence to colonies. The bargain worked out was that, as part of the League of Nations system of Mandates, peoples not deemed "able to stand by themselves under the strenuous conditions of the modern world" were not granted sovereignty. Instead, colonies of the defeated Imperial Germany and portions of the Ottoman Empire were placed under the tutelage of the "advanced nations," the victorious Allied powers, who undertook to assist their development—but under oversight to keep imperial rule more humane. "Class A" Mandates, including Palestine, Syria, and Iraq, were to be given administrative advice and assistance by their Mandatory power "until such time as they are able to stand alone." It was, in short, left up to the Mandatory authorities to drive themselves out of business by certifying the maturity of the people they ruled over.[80] The Palestine Mandate negated even this purpose by the incorporation into the Mandate's Charter of the Balfour Declaration's promise to assist in the creation of a Jewish commonwealth on the land of Mandatory Palestine.

With the rejection of the Versailles Treaty by the US Senate and the end of Woodrow's Wilson presidency, the Mandatory compromise collapsed. According to Pedersen, "Mandated territories were no better governed than colonies across the board and in some cases were governed more oppressively,"[81] and as early as 1922 it became clear that the Mandatory authorities were no longer committed to the eventual implementation of the right of national self-determination. Not surprisingly, Britain did not formally conclude a single Mandate in Iraq until 1932, all the while keeping its military bases in Iraq and suppressing rebellions against figurehead rulers.

For historian Beshara Doumani, the Mandatory and subsequent Palestinian experiences reveal the "Iron Law" of the conflict over Palestine: a refusal "either to recognize or to make room for the existence of Palestinians as a political community." Denying for Palestine the conventional fit between land and identity that obtains elsewhere produces a set of deep ironies by putting Palestine and Palestinians "out of phase" with each other. In fact, the very Mandate that created the state of Palestine only assigns the land's inhabitants civil and religious rights and never mentions the word *Arab*. Palestinian-ness as an identity was, consequently, born out of the collective trauma of displacement of the Nakba just when Palestine itself was lost to Palestinians. Palestinians who were treated as a humanitarian refugee problem rather than a political community for the longest time, are still not a sovereign political community.[82]

Mandates were an attempt to extend the European colonial system, while the Fourth Geneva Convention of 1949 sought to universalize and humanize the experience of warfare and occupation that obtained between European states, which always ended with a cease-fire and peace treaty. In spite of their difference, both remained in the service of European colonial aspirations. The Mandate, with its denial of Palestine national rights, is long gone, but its legacy survives, not least, through the IHL's suspension of Palestinian sovereignty through its notion of temporary occupation. Delayed sovereignty and the open-ended nature of the Mandatory arrangement and IHL's definition of occupation as a temporary stage suspiciously resemble each other, while leaving to the discretion of the foreign authority in charge both the role of attending to the needs of the occupying people and that of deciding when to bring their presence to an end. The two legal frameworks share a central characteristic: they take place in a *sovereignty vacuum*. This vacuum, as explained by Yehouda Shenhav, allows the formation of an anomalous patchwork of legal frameworks in which extraterritorial rights of settlers, the use of military orders, the maintenance of states of exception, partial annexations, and violent suppression are common practice.[83] The Shamgar Doctrine is, for all practical purposes, the redefinition of IHL as a virtual British Mandate under which the Yishuv was built into a Jewish state-in-the-making, down to the extension of citizenship rights to Israeli settlers under the British Defense Emergency Regulations of 1945.

The legal feature that allowed Shamgar to perform this sleight of hand was that both the Mandate and occupation by international law are expected to remain *temporary* but their termination is at the discretion of the Mandatory authority or the occupier. An expectation of temporariness, however, has an opposite consequence as well. A common feature of settler-colonial projects, especially of their latter instances, is the dread experienced by the settlers that they might be reversible. In the case of Palestine, this Israeli fear is rooted in the peculiar way land was transferred from Palestinian to Jewish hands during the primitive accumulation era of the Yishuv. Since land in Palestine, as observed by the late Baruch Kimmerling, was never "free," as it appeared to be on other colonial frontiers, but had to be acquired on a nascent land market, the Jewish side had to take several steps to attain its full possession. Kimmerling distinguished between three levels of control over territory—presence, ownership, and sovereignty—with the former two serving as placeholders until the latter could be asserted. But even after Israel's establishment, the Zionist fear of decolonization persisted—the apprehension that even when territory had come under formal Jewish sovereignty it might effectively revert to Arab hands unless it was buttressed by Jewish ownership and presence.[84] Mere Arab presence or ownership in a settler-colonial society posed a threat to Jewish sovereignty, as can be discerned from the two main Judaization projects—the establishment of the towns of Upper Nazareth and Karmiel in the 1950s and 1960s and the construction of the Misgav Regional Council's hilltop outlooks starting in 1979 in the Galilee, the only region of Israel with an Arab majority. The fear that Zionism's "territorial advent is tentative and fragile," in the words of the anthropologist Dan Rabinowitz, "is crucial for a fuller understanding of the Israeli attitude to land."[85] The fear of reversal, namely the replacement of the Jewish population with a returning Palestinian population, is commonly used to justify Israeli toughness and unwillingness to compromise, but as long as Israel's borders remain indefinite and the Israeli-Palestinian conflict is ongoing such a reversal remains a possibility.

As long as temporariness remains an Israeli subterfuge for creating permanent facts on the ground, it is also available as an essential component of Palestinian resistance. The temporariness of Israel's boundaries plays an important role in the Palestinian understanding of the nature of the conflict. Palestinians, on their part, insist on rolling back some aspects of what Israel considers *faits accomplis*, namely that any accord be based on the pre-occupation boundaries and that the rights of the refugees of the 1948 Nakba be recognized. Palestinian refugee camps have also maintained a sense of temporariness by keeping to a minimum such infrastructural improvements as the planting of trees, the widening of roads, and the upgrading of housing. The West Bank remains an "open frontier" and, therefore, potentially the object of decolonization. Temporariness serves both the supporters and the opponents of the occupation, though the former use it actively while the latter do so mostly by their steadfast refusal to budge.

A survey of the "Law of Occupation," leads Lisa Hajjar to the conclusion that "occupation law is not merely an inadequate tool for analyzing this [phenomenon]; it can also help legitimize the very . . . arrangements upon which it depends." [86] In the simplest terms, the law of occupation presumes that the occupier, without any external supervision, can serve as a trustee to the occupied population—a questionable assumption. To make it even simpler, if you ask the wolf to guard the sheep you should not be surprised that by morning there will be fewer sheep than there were in the evening.

There have been three sets of recommendations on how to rectify this lacuna within the framework of IHL. Eyal Benvenisti points to several mechanisms now available to partially compensate for the asymmetry in the occupier-occupied relationship. Among these, he lists the exercise of judicial review not only by domestic courts but also by third countries and international tribunals; civil suits for compensation; UN standing committees; and special representatives, as well as missions and commissions, that invoke human rights standards. There is also the practice of tying international trade and foreign investment between countries to their standards of human rights.[87] He recognizes that "while these . . . modalities are important, they still leave much to be desired." Orna Ben-Naftali, Keren Michaeli, and Aeyal Gross have suggested the creation of a new category of illegal occupation for indefinite occupations, which would trigger a range of consequences. These could include sanctions up to and including the invocation of Chapter Seven of the UN's Charter, which authorizes the Security Council to take either military or nonmilitary action to remove a threat to peace. Such revision of the Geneva Convention, however, appears impractical under the current structure of the UN.[88] Finally, another radical reform has been proposed by Asli Bâli as part of a symposium in *Jadaliyya* on law and occupation. She argues that a "separate and higher standard of obligations [should] be imposed on belligerents that deliberately prolong their occupation of territories seized in war." With every added year of occupation, the balance between the occupier's security needs and the occupied population's human rights would shift further and further in the direction of the latter. Taking this argument to its logical conclusion, she and anthropologist Darryl Li claim that "the full human rights of the population under occupation in the long-run will require their full enfranchisement" [89]—in short, the creation of one state with equal rights for all of its inhabitants.

Legal reform, as desirable as it is, cannot replace political and international incentives to bring Israeli occupation to an end. The longevity of the Israeli occupation of the West Bank, East Jerusalem, and Gaza, and the absence of signs for its termination, are the result of a confluence of factors. Among these is Israel's desire to take advantage of the conquests of the 1967 War to extend its boundaries into the religious geography of Jewish antiquity not only around its edges but through the settlement of Israel's religious Zionists among the dense Palestinian population at the heartland of the West Bank. This practice is at variance with Israel's colonization strategy prior to 1948, which sought to keep Jews and Palestinians apart as much as possible. As a result, Palestinian methods of resistance and legitimation became radicalized, giving prominence to Hamas which rejects the Oslo process's central tenets. The vanguardist role of both Gush Emunim and Hamas in their respective societies has provided them with support, resources, and prestige. Hamas won the 2006 elections to the Palestinian Council, while religious Zionists have been able to gain influence in the military, media, and national politics. At the same time, each is hampered by considerable opposition. The religious Zionist community is internally divided along several fault lines. Hamas has shown signs of interest in a modus vivendi, though not in a peace accord, with Israel. Both organizations will remain important actors in influencing their societies and through them the contours of the occupation, but they will not necessarily write the next chapter of the Israeli-Palestinian conflict.

The role of the external actors, the enablers, is particularly important at this juncture. The ineffectiveness, dereliction, and European bias of IHL and the formation of a "special relationship" between the United States and Israel during the Cold War (that is manifested in feeble US verbal objections without corresponding actions) have perpetuated the longevity of the occupation. The contrast between contemporary and earlier US policy could not be sharper. Following the 1956 Suez War, in which Israel, France, and the United Kingdom wrested the Sinai Peninsula from Egypt after President Gamal Abdel Nasser's nationalization of the Suez Canal, the United States sought to distance itself from the war's colonial designs. The United States voted for a Security Council resolution that condemned the invasion and demanded that the United Kingdom, France, and Israel withdraw their forces from the Sinai. By March 1957, all Israeli troops were withdrawn. For the United States to take either a legal or a political route to withdraw its blanket foreign policy protection for Israel would require the continued decline of both the Evangelicals' and the neocons' influence, the politicization of the American Jewish community's silent majority, the rise of a new and more liberal Jewish leadership, and a redefinition of the United States' broader interests in the Middle East, as well as a new administration that would revive an emphasis on the US national interest at the expense of special interests.

How Has the Occupation Transformed the Israeli–Palestinian Conflict?

Israel had already assumed control of all of Palestine, had ramped up colonization under the Likud governments of prime ministers Begin and Shamir, and had become locked in the "hurting stalemate" with the occupied Palestinians by the almost six-year-long First Intifada when something new emerged: Israel and the Palestinian Liberation Organization (PLO) entered into diplomatic negotiations for the first time. This was a new beginning. I focus this essay on the slow, hesitant, inconclusive, and currently broken diplomatic process between Israel and the Palestinian National Authority (PNA). Furthermore, I consider just how significantly this turn toward diplomacy has affected the larger conflict between Israelis and Palestinians, which began in the late Ottoman era.

A long and tortuous route led to this opening. The PLO's position toward Israel's existence tracked the fortunes of the Israeli-Arab conflict. The Palestinian National Charter of 1964 declared that establishing Israel was contrary to the will of the Palestinian people and, consequently, was illegal. Further, because Jews are adherents of a religion—one without historical or religious ties to Palestine—rather than a nation, they are devoid of any national rights. Following the setbacks of the 1967 War, the PLO began an internal, though inconclusive, conversation about the feasibility of a secular-democratic Palestine for Muslims, Christians, and Jews. In the wake of the accomplishments of Palestine and its Arab allies during the 1973 War, the PLO reverted to its hard line. By the late 1980s, however, recognizing that it was impossible to defeat Israel, the PLO started down the path to territorial partition. Israel, on its part, viewed the PLO and its many constituent bodies as a terrorist organization well into the First Intifada and treated all Palestinian resistance acts, whether violent or nonviolent, as terrorism to be suppressed.

The Oslo Declaration of Principles (DOP) and its follow-up agreements were the opening efforts of two secular national movements in pursuit of compromise, on terms to be negotiated. The asymmetrical power relation between the state of Israel and stateless Palestinians—in the absence of clear international incentives or pressures on Israel, and coupled with the contradictions and weaknesses of international humanitarian law (IHL)—permitted only a limited, repeatedly stalemated, and drawn-out "peace process." In late 2016 (as I am writing this essay), the diplomatic process is at an impasse. Many question the potential for reversing the occupation through a territorial partition. Observers of the conflict debate whether the chance of an Israeli withdrawal and the formation of two states is on its deathbed, in the morgue, or already in the cemetery.

In this essay, I will offer several *feasibility analyses*, given currently prevailing circumstances, of the promised political products of a diplomatic or nonviolent solution. The first option is the establishment of two states—a Palestinian state on evacuated occupied land, side by side with Israel. The second option is the one-state solution in either of two main versions—(1) a binational state or (2) the civic polity of one person, one vote. Mine is not a philosophical discussion of the merits and demerits of these political resolutions but a much more modestly conceived feasibility study from the perspective of the social sciences.

I will pay equally close attention to the potent Palestinian civil society movement, which seeks to replicate the success of the antiapartheid movement that brought down the white supremacist government of South Africa by mobilizing a global network of activists and supporters. Since its inception in July 2005, a call for the nonviolent boycott of Israeli companies and universities, divestment by foreign companies, and sanctions by international bodies and governments from Israel and its institutions (Boycott, Divestment, Sanctions—BDS) is gaining ground. I will examine the BDS movement's analysis and offer another feasibility study of its tactics and the implications of those tactics for alternative political options.

I

Though peace talks between Israel and the PLO (and subsequently the PNA) went on more or less continuously from January 1993 until April 29, 2014, only three rounds contributed significantly to the potential architecture of a future agreement. First, the original Oslo negotiations led to the mutual recognition of Israel and the PLO, arranged for the formation of an interim Palestinian government—the PNA—and committed Israel to sequential but partial territorial withdrawals. Second, the 2000 Camp David talks made it clear for the first time that the talks' final outcome would be the establishment of a Palestinian state side by side with Israel and that the control over Jerusalem would be divided between the two countries. Finally, the 2007-8 Annapolis talks saw the virtual abandonment of the Palestinian refugees' right of return and established that the 1967 borders would be the basis of territorial partition between the two states and, consequently, that any territorial exchange between the parties would be of roughly equal size. Since no final peace accord has been reached, these terms themselves are subject to renegotiation.

My starting point in analyzing the course of diplomacy will be its end point—the last round of Israeli-Palestinian peace negotiations between

Prime Minister Ehud Olmert and President Mahmoud Abbas that were set in motion by the Annapolis Conference in November 2007. True, from July 2013 to April 2014 Secretary of State John Kerry conducted shuttle diplomacy between Olmert's successor, Benjamin Netanyahu, and Mahmoud Abbas, but it led nowhere. Furthermore, Kerry failed to follow up on the negotiations' collapse with the next logical step—the publication of parameters for a future peace accord—as President Bill Clinton had done with the "Clinton Parameters" in December 2000. This last round of diplomacy, consequently, will play no role in this survey.

Israeli-Palestinian diplomacy has had an unusual run of reversals. A series of tragic, violent, and unforeseen dramatic breaks and breakdowns have marred attempts at diplomacy: the political assassination of Yitzhak Rabin; Barak's loss in the Israeli elections shortly after the Camp David talks of 2000 in the wake of Hamas suicide attacks; Sharon's stroke and irreversible coma; Hamas's victory in the elections to the second Palestinian Council and the brief Hamas-Fatah battle that ejected Fatah from Gaza; and Olmert's indictment and eventual imprisonment for corruption. These and other misfortunes are almost enough to make one believe that fate is set against all Israeli-Palestinian diplomatic initiatives, and even peace itself. Subsequent statements by the parties after each inconclusive round of talks, asserting that they would have needed only a bit more time—just a few more weeks or months—to reach an agreement only add to the sense of despondency. In contrast, Netanyahu, who never undertook a diplomatic initiative of his own and did what he could to place spokes in the peace process's wheel, sits in the prime minister's office and is being reelected repeatedly. Certainly, Israeli-Palestinian peacemaking had its share of tragedies, but Rabin's assassination, the waves of violence, and Hamas's electoral triumph are not separate from the peace process but rather part of the way it has unfolded.

The repetition of dead-end negotiating patterns points to even deeper roots of the impasse. Each of the Israeli prime ministers who eventually made compromises in talks with the Palestinians—Rabin, Barak, and Olmert—chose first to negotiate with the Syrians and only after the failure of those talks turned to the Palestinians as second best. All the Israelis were halfhearted peacemakers with the Palestinians, as Arafat was about entering talks with Israelis and as Abbas was in bringing them to a conclusion. Consequently, there was always a great deal of hesitation, if not unwillingness, to follow up on promises and meet deadlines. Israeli and Palestinian leaders also proved reluctant to fulfill important offers made verbally during the talks. On occasion, maps were shown but not shared, points that had already been agreed upon were subsequently reopened, and the principle of "Nothing is agreed on until everything is agreed upon" meant that negotiations frequently had to be restarted from scratch.

These tactics yielded multiple versions of each side's positions. In each stage of Israeli-Palestinian peace talks, the terms (as well as the intentions and overall vision of each side) were shrouded in secrecy and confusion, leading to considerable finger pointing after the fact. In large part, this veil of mystery emerged from the unwillingness or inability of leaders—who faced strong opposition from their respective extremist wings—to engage in broad public education campaigns to reinterpret the past and analyze the failures of the present so that they could break new ground. All leaders kept their own counsel; hid information even from political partners; and proceeded through alternative, uncoordinated, and sometimes even conflicting negotiating channels. The Olmert-Abbas talks were no exception. They were conducted in three tracks: one between foreign ministers Tzipi Livni and Ahmed Qurei (Abu Alaa), another between Olmert and Abbas; and, still another through technical committees tasked with working out the details. Secretary of State Condoleezza Rice sometimes joined the political tracks.[1]

Olmert was the first Israeli prime minister to agree, in principle, to base the future border separating Israel and Palestine on the June 5, 1967, boundaries (namely, on the Green Line). He shared this intention with Rice in May

2008 and on September 16 he made an offer to Abbas to give up 5.8 percent of Israel's land within the Green Line to compensate the Palestinian side for 6.3 percent (or possibly 6.5 percent) of the territory encompassing the settlement blocs and Jerusalem ring towns that Israel would annex (see map 5). Abbas agreed to a swap that would offer Israel only 1.9 percent of the West Bank, the actual built-up area of the colonies. By May 2010, after the talks with Olmert were over, Abbas informed US mediator Senator George Mitchell that he would consent to a 3.8 percent territorial exchange allowing Israel to annex most of the settlement blocs' expanse. The same terms were repeated in talks between Abbas and Yitzhak Herzog, the leader of the Zionist Camp Party (successor to the Labor Party). Herzog and Abbas agreed in April 2014 to an Israeli withdrawal to the 1967 borders to be accompanied by a 4 percent territorial exchange. Because Herzog's party came in second in the 2015 elections, this agreement never got off the ground.

Throughout the talks, Abbas rejected the inclusion of two key settlements in Olmert's blocs to be annexed by Israel: Ariel—the sole large settlement town that does not lie along the Green Line but is in the heart of the northern West Bank (Samaria)—and Har Homa—the penultimate seal closing the bottleneck of the ring towns around East Jerusalem and thus cutting it off the West Bank (leaving only area E1 unbuilt) (see map 3). Under Olmert's plan, about forty-five thousand settlers (15 percent of the settler population) would have needed to be evacuated to Israel; under Abbas's plan, this figure would be some seventy-four thousand settlers (about 25 percent of the settler population at the time). The difference in these numbers stemmed from Abbas's insistence on Palestinian territorial contiguity and Olmert's preference for minimizing the number of Israeli colonists needing to be evacuated.

The two sides were much closer in their discussion of what are frequently considered the most divisive issues: (1) East Jerusalem, which Olmert and Abbas agreed to partition; and (2) the return to Israel of only very small numbers of Palestinian refugees who had been displaced in the Nakba. In these respects, both leaders were at odds with the vast majority of their constituents, some of whom would view the proposed compromises as the betrayal of their core aspirations. The leaders' divisive proposals indicate their serious desire to reach an agreement. At the same time, the unpopularity of their stances signaled the potential limits of compromise between Israelis and Palestinians, hinting at the reasons for the inconclusiveness of the talks.

The likely reason for Olmert's willingness to partition East Jerusalem was his knowledge, as Jerusalem's former mayor, that united Jerusalem had been merely a catchphrase and never a reality. Additionally, he was unwilling to work toward unifying the city by raising the standard of living and social services in Arab Jerusalem to the level of Jewish Jerusalem. The two men agreed to partition the city on the basis of its demographic reality. Olmert acceded to the territorial partition of Jerusalem by (1) handing over to the Palestinian state the twenty-eight Palestinian neighborhoods and villages that had been included in Greater Jerusalem's municipal boundaries while (2) keeping the seam and ring towns built across the Green Line in East Jerusalem. Partition gave both sides a capital in Jerusalem, though the Palestinian capital would be on the city's periphery. Abbas and Olmert were able to bypass historical and religious concerns by offering to form a joint trusteeship over the Old City and its Holy Basin to include trustees from five states—Israel, Palestine, Jordan, Saudi Arabia, and the United States. Olmert and Abbas agreed to leave the administration of the Islamic sites, including the Temple Mont/Haram as-Sharif, under the current waqf (Islamic endowment).

Though these proposals were based on the 2000 Clinton Parameters, they also resurrected a weaker and somewhat ambiguous version of the 1948 UN Partition Resolution's old designation of Jerusalem as a *corpus separatum*, though they reduced it to just the Holy Basin in East Jerusalem. They also revitalized the eighteenth-century Ottoman sultan's "status quo" *firman* (edict) reaffirming the division of ownership over the most important holy sites among their respective Muslim, Christian, and Jewish holders in the Holy Land.

With regard to refugees, it was Abbas who took a radically conciliatory position. He repeatedly made it clear to Olmert, including in December 2006, when he stated, "I know how sensitive you are to the refugees. I can tell you one thing: We are not aspiring to change the nature of your country." Israel agreed to let in between five thousand and fifteen thousand, while the upper number Abbas seems to have demanded in his negotiations with the United States was sixty thousand—a far cry from the millions of Palestinian refugees and their descendants for whom the right of return had been originally proclaimed.

Finally, Olmert's acceptance of the Palestinian demand to withdraw the Israeli military from the Jordan River paved the way for consensus on security measures. This would allow the demilitarization of the Palestinian state and the patrolling of the border along the Jordan River by an international force. The talks, however, fizzled out because of Olmert's impending indictment and Livni's apparent request for Abbas to wait until she had replaced Olmert. The talks were never resumed because of the December 2007 Gaza war that inflicted massive casualties on its residents and pushed the two sides apart and, possibly, because Abbas was reluctant to continue.

The Annapolis talks' terms and tenor stand in sharp contrast to the previous major round of talks, which took place between Barak and Arafat in President Bill Clinton's presence in Camp David in 2000. Participants and observers of the Camp David talks highlighted one or two major obstacles to the conclusion of an Israeli-Palestinian peace accord. The first one was the refugee question, a topic of immense significance, since it epitomizes the conflict for Palestinians and had been the lived experience of Palestinians most adversely affected by the conflict. In a sweeping overview of Israeli-Arab negotiations, the historian Shelly Fried concluded that "the common denominator in all the conferences from Lausanne [1949] to Taba [2001] was that the refugee problem was the main obstacle to reaching an agreement."[2] Elie Podeh, in an even more sweeping vista of missed opportunities—from the 1919 Faysal-Weizmann Agreement to the Olmert-Abbas talks—asserted that "the Jerusalem issue was undoubtedly the most contentious at Camp David." In particular, Israelis and Palestinians could not compromise on sovereignty over Temple Mount/Haram as-Sharif.[3] Shelly and Podeh's conclusions are widely shared. The explanation of Ilan Pappé is that unlike territory, where the formula of "land for peace" offers a credible trade-off, Jerusalem and the refugee issue cannot be treated merely as business matters: they fall in the realm of the conflict's intangible aspects, since they require the assumption of historical responsibility and, as such, are associated with fairness, guilt, restitution, and, ultimately, justice.[4]

Yet the last round of meaningful Israeli-Palestinian negotiations shows, contrary to Fried, Podeh, and Pappé, that the major stumbling block between the parties was neither Jerusalem nor the refugees but the Israeli colonies and the new borders required to accommodate the settlers. We learn from Olmert and Abbas's inability to reach an agreement on the future borders of Israel and Palestine that an essentially 1:1 ratio of exchange—a consistent Palestinian demand to match the terms of the peace agreement reached between Egypt and Israel—was insufficient. Any territorial exchange—even Olmert's "generous offer"—required not only the removal of a sufficient portion of the colonies and the evacuation of their settlers but also the assurance of the contiguity and viability of the state of Palestine. Short of such accommodation, Palestine would have only truncated sovereignty. If the borders separating the two states were not properly delineated, the occupation would continue afflicting the everyday lives, livelihoods, and freedom of movement of Palestinians in the West Bank and East Jerusalem.

Since the end of the 2008 talks, there has been one significant change in Israel's negotiating terms, and it has turned into the main stumbling block.

Already in 1988, in response to a long-standing demand by Israel and the United States, the PLO had recognized the state of Israel. As part of the Oslo DOP, the PLO had also recognized "the right of the State of Israel to live in peace and security." But during the preparatory talks for the Annapolis Conference, Foreign Minister Livni raised one new demand: she asked that the future agreement recognize "Israel [as] the state of the Jewish people . . . and Palestine for the Palestinian people." Prime Minister Netanyahu made the first part of her request—the recognition of Israel as a Jewish state by the PNA—into a full-fledged *sine qua non* in a speech he gave to the US Congress in May 2010.

If a Palestinian leadership recognized Israel as the state of the Jewish people, as Netanyahu now requires, it would, in one fell swoop, accept that Israel's Palestinian citizens—some 21 percent of its population in 2015—would live in a state with two-tiered citizenship, in which what was defined as "good for Jews" would be the public good while Palestinians would remain second-class citizens. Even more significantly, such an "admission" would make Palestinians strangers to Palestine, strangers in their own land; it would negate their identity as a people and throw out the legitimacy of their historical narrative. Such a declaration by the PNA is a "poison pill" that no Palestinian leaders could accept, since it would require their denial of the existence of the very nation they lead.

Unwillingness to declare Israel as a Jewish state does not, however, mean that the Palestinian leadership also denies the right of self-determination of Israeli Jews. PNA officials have suggested a way of getting around Israel's demand by agreeing to recognize Israel by any name it wishes to use to designate itself in the UN, such as the "Jewish Republic of Israel." Alternatively, the original November 1948 UN General Assembly partition resolution, which resolved that "independent Arab and Jewish States" be established in Palestine, could be invoked to bypass the new demand. The reason for the use of the generic names at the time was that neither state had chosen its name. Yet a reference to the language of this old resolution in a future Israeli-Palestinian accord could serve as a way of accepting the Israeli demand to be recognized as a Jewish state without carrying the exclusionary significance demanded by Prime Minister Netanyahu and without invalidating the equal Palestinian claim. Of course, such a choice of words could follow only on the heels of an Israeli acceptance of the partition of Palestine into two states.

Now that we have examined the recent attempt to present the Israeli-Palestinian conflict as between the Jewish people and the Palestinian people, it behooves us to turn to its other, broader framing as an Arab-Israeli conflict. Israel's demand to be recognized as the state of the Jewish people, which has been a spoke in the wheel of diplomacy, contrasts with the Arab world's significant turn toward a diplomatic outcome to the conflict. In 2002, the Arab League in its meeting in Beirut unanimously endorsed a Saudi proposal that came to be known as the Arab Peace Initiative (API). The API offers to normalize the relations between the Arab countries and Israel following the diplomatic resolution of the Israeli-Palestinian conflict. The initiative requires full Israeli withdrawal from the occupied territories, including the Golan Heights, and the establishment of an independent Palestinian state with East Jerusalem as its capital on the Palestinian territories evacuated by Israel. These requirements, even the absence of defined boundaries for East Jerusalem, leave room for a full withdrawal that includes territorial exchange. The API also raises a modest demand for a "just settlement" of the refugee problem based on UN Resolution 194. The new formulation allows for negotiations over refugees' rights instead of their wholesale implementation, as was the custom in previous formulations. In return the Arab states promise to do the following: "(a) Consider the Arab-Israeli conflict over, sign a peace agreement with Israel, and achieve peace for all states in the region; (b) Establish normal relations with Israel within the framework of this comprehensive peace." The novelty of the API is striking. In effect, the 2002 Beirut initiative fully reversed the Arab League's Khartoum summit's "three no's" that were adopted in the wake of the 1967 War (no peace with Israel, no recognition of Israel, no negotiation with Israel) and pledged to the "three yes's" of peace, recognition, and negotiation.[5]

The Saudi-proposed API was adopted not long after 9/11 and "served to solidify the Saudi image as a loyal American ally."[6] It is customary, consequently, to downplay its sincerity. At the same time, the Arab League endorsed it again in 2007, and Saudi leaders have repeatedly reaffirmed their commitment to its terms. Even more significantly, the Saudi-inspired proposal doesn't stand alone but fits into the larger diplomatic process of Israeli-Arab peacemaking that began with the peace accord Egypt signed with Israel in 1977. The API would fulfill Israel's longest-held wish: its recognition as a legitimate state by its Middle Eastern Arab neighbors. The Sharon government, in the midst of Second Intifada, rejected the API from the start, but Israel's subsequent leaders have not given it a hearing either or offered to use it as a jumping-off point for comprehensive talks; indeed, within Israel, there has been practically no public discussion of its merits and shortcomings. The ignoring of the API, combined with the demand that the Palestinians recognize Israel as a "Jewish state," casts doubt on the Israeli claim that it has no partner to make peace with.

II

Close to a decade has passed since the end of the Annapolis talks, and Israeli colonization has continued apace under Prime Minister Netanyahu. It is time to examine the feasibility of territorial partition against the background of the inroads into the West Bank and East Jerusalem made during the half-century-long Israeli colonization project. Has the ongoing and increased colonization of Palestinian territories closed off the path to creating a contiguous and viable state of Palestine? Is territorial partition still possible? I will investigate how much territorial exchange, how many settlers, and what kind of territorial configuration would be necessary to allow for the formation of such a Palestinian state.

The Palestine Royal Commission (known as the Peel Commission) and UN General Assembly Resolution 181 both favored the partition of Palestine between the Mediterranean Sea and the Jordan River into two nation-states, one majority Jewish, the other majority Arab. The two-state solution is so widely affirmed because it is based on the principle of sovereignty, which is the foundation of our international order. The logic of sovereignty promises stable and governable states, separated by recognized international borders. It is, consequently, the default option. But this outcome might no longer be possible. Already in the late 1980s, the then deputy mayor of Jerusalem and director of the West Bank Data Base Project Meron Benvenisti declared that the occupation had become irreversible: Israeli colonization had penetrated too far and wide into the West Bank to allow for the kind of territorial partition required for a two-state solution to the conflict.[7] Where Benvenisti was the pioneer, many followed. Indeed, "irreversibility" has become the consensus view of most observers today.

To be sure, there are holdouts to this view. To mention just one, Israeli journalist Ari Shavit, the author of *My Promised Land*, suggests we have another decade before colonization makes partition irreversible.[8] But such assessments remain at the gut level. Moreover, they give full credence to the hyperbole of Israeli settlers who wish to reassure themselves by convincing others that they have been successful in planting themselves in the West Bank (even as they clamor for more housing permits and subsidies). But just how accurate is the irreversibility thesis?

Nobody has examined whether the terms discussed by Olmert and Abbas are still applicable—whether it is still possible to separate Israeli settlers and Palestinians—more carefully than Shaul Arieli, who is a retired colonel, a board member of the Council for Peace and Security, the author of *amicus curiae* briefs to the High Court of Justice [HCJ] against the military's proposed delineation of the Separation Wall, and a hands-on expert on Israeli borders and settlements.[9] He inquires whether the price to be paid for separation is reasonable from the two parties' national perspectives. Among the 2,935,000 Palestinians residing in the West Bank in mid-2016 live 405,158 Jewish settlers (according to the Civilian Administration), making up 13.8 percent of the West Bank's population. (I will discuss later in this section East Jerusalem and its compact Jewish ring settlements.) As these numbers indicate, within the West Bank, Palestinians outnumber Israelis 26 to 1, thus maintaining a crushing demographic dominance. Nor has the number of officially recognized settlements budged, rising from 124 in 1993 to only 126 in 2015.

No less important is the fact that 73.9 percent of the Jewish settlers are concentrated in towns built close to Israeli population centers, hugging the eastern side of the Green Line—that is, as close to Israel as possible. In the 1990s, the number of Israeli settlers in the West Bank grew annually between 8 and 10 percent. During Prime Minister Netanyahu's second and third governments from 2009 to 2015, the settler population's growth rate declined from the already low 5.3 percent to 4.1 percent (see figure 1), adding about 98,500 individuals over seven years (see figure 2). Their settlement pattern replicates the general colonization pattern, with roughly 75 percent of new settlers choosing to live near the Green Line. Of all the West Bank colonists, only 105,660 live in the heart of the West Bank, and their numbers grew in 2015 by only 3,880. The size of an average Israeli Jewish family is 3.54 persons, but in the West Bank in 2015 it was 4.75 persons.[10] For these settlements—inhabited almost exclusively by religious Zionist families, many of them young—an estimate of 4.75 persons is probably too low, but it yields an estimated 22,244 households.

Another consequential indicator of the changing character of colonization is that almost 90 percent of the settler population's growth in 2015 was due to natural growth since the past twenty years have seen a dramatic reduction in the relocation of Israeli citizens across the Green Line (see

How Has the Occupation Transformed the Conflict?

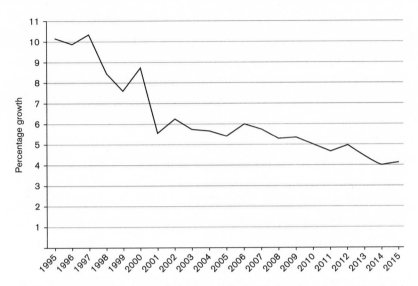

Figure 1. Percentage of settler population growth in the West Bank, 1995–2015. Reprinted by permission of Shaul Arieli from www.shaularieli.com/?lat=he.

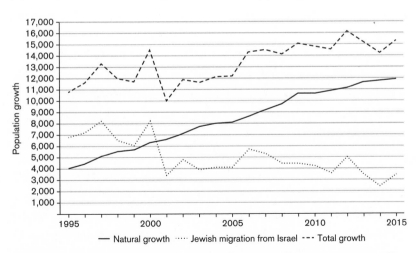

Figure 2. Sources of settler population growth in the West Bank, 1995–2015. Reprinted by permission of Shaul Arieli from www.shaularieli.com/?lat=he.

figure 2). While in 1996, six thousand Israelis moved to West Bank settlements, fewer than two thousand did so in 2014. In the past, the colonization
project mobilized practically all parts of Israel's population, but by now it
has become almost exclusively the project of only two sectors. Mostly large
and poor *haredi* families, self-identifying as "settlers against their will,"
supply 45 percent of the colonists and the largest share of the growth in the
settler population. Most move into Modi'in Illit and Beitar Illit, two megas-
ettlements just to the east of the Green Line. The few remaining *haredi* settlements in the heart of the West Bank, such as Immanuel, grew by only
twenty-seven residents in 2015. Besides *haredi* settlement, colonization
remains an undertaking of the religious Zionist camp, but their settlements
have grown unevenly: some have expanded, others have stagnated, and still
others have shrunk. This group contributes less than a fifth of the annual
settler population growth, scattered across dozens of small colonies. The
secular settlements of the Allon Plan in the Jordan Valley added only 216 settlers during the five years of Netanyahu's second term. The growth of the
ring towns of Eastern Jerusalem has also remained anemic, adding about five
thousand new residents, many of whom are Palestinian citizens of Israel.
Just as significant is the fact that the total built-up area of Israeli settlements
occupies no more than 2 percent of the West Bank's land mass and that the
colonies themselves are spread out over just 4–5 percent of it, with the small
religious Zionist settlement in the center of the West Bank constituting only
0.4 percent of the land mass of West Bank Israeli settlements in general.

Nor can we ignore Israeli planning's sleight of hand. Though the colonies
take up 2 percent of the West Bank, their jurisdiction encompasses as much
as half of it.[11] Whole colonies have the character of Potemkin villages: a single core of houses whose municipal boundaries lie far away and have been
marked since 2011 as a "Blue Line," determined not by planning logic but by
the widest property line that can be drawn around state land. The settlement
cores are, consequently, lumped together with small clusters of houses or

even outposts in outlying areas. These lie usually at great distances and even across wide highways or riverbeds and retain within their municipal boundaries dozens of illegal homes. The settlements also contain commercial and public buildings and enclaves of private Palestinian land that, in principle, their owners are allowed to cultivate but not build on. Regional council boundaries are equally capacious: as much as 35 percent of the West Bank falls under the jurisdiction of the regional councils of Har Hebron, Gush Etzion, Mate Benyamin, Megilot, Shomron, and Bik'at Hayarden. This includes large swaths of land empty of settlements, some portions of which are designated as firing ranges or natural reserves, but all together they serve as land reserves for future colonization.[12]

The Israeli colonization project—notwithstanding the massive outlay of capital, institutional support, and military protection—has been unable to alter the demographic balance of the West Bank and has failed to provide either effective Israeli control or possession of land and ownership over it. "In view of these numbers," Shaul Arieli concludes, "Jewish settlement had failed in achieving its aim [since] it had not created the conditions for the annexation of the West Bank to Israel." The concentration of settlers and the tapering off of the settler population leave open the possibility of a territorial swap that would allow for the political separation of the majority of Jews and Palestinians, since, in practice, most of them are already separated.

Arieli has provided us with a count of the number of settlers who reside in the settlements in the heart of the West Bank, namely outside the settlement blocs. I would like to offer an additional method of calculation that will allow us to measure their political preferences as well—their political will, so to speak (see table 1). Tabulating the votes received by the Jewish Home, the religious Zionist Party led by Naftali Bennett, in the March 2015 elections to the Knesset will give us the strongest indication of the number of settlers who live where they do for religious, in some cases messianic, reasons and who therefore are likely to place religious obligation above democratic rules and, consequently, be the most likely to oppose any evacuation as part of a potential peace accord with the PNA. In addition, the table provides us with the number of Likud voters, among whom we are likely to find the highest percentage of those who support the settlements for ideological nationalist reasons, though people vote for Likud for many additional reasons as well. In general, Likud voters are more likely to operate within the rules of democracy and *mamlachtiyut* and, consequently, are less likely than religious Zionist settlers to heed a call by religious Zionist rabbis to oppose settlement evacuation. Finally, the number of votes given to all other parties will allow us to gauge the support given to parties that are either opposed or indifferent to settlement and, in general, draw support for ethnic, socioeconomic, or other reasons.

I have broken down the settlements into four different categories: (1) religious Zionist settlements, many of which were set up by Gush Emunim and belong now to Amana, the logistics branch of settlement enterprise that helped construct a small number of non-religious Zionist settlements as well; (2) mixed colonies, a portion of whose residents are secular and religious Zionists, and in some cases *haredi;* (3) secular settlements established either for the sake of an improved quality of life or for ideological nationalist reasons, and in some cases for both; and, finally, (4) *haredi* settlements.

Table 1 breaks down the result of the elections by parties. There is a surprisingly small number of Jewish Home voters outside settlement blocs (see discussion of blocs later in this section) or even within religious Zionist Amana settlements. Of religious Zionist settler voters, 26.5 percent lived in the four settlement blocs—the largest number in the Gush Etzion Bloc—that lay adjacent to the Green Line; they were unlikely to be affected by territorial exchange that would be part of a diplomatic solution. Nor did all members of the religious Zionist settlements outside the blocs vote for the Jewish Home Party, the party that purported to best represent them; indeed, only 53 percent did so. The rest of their vote was split: the Likud received another 15 percent—possibly as part

TABLE 1

Votes cast for the Knesset by political party, settlement category, and location, March 2015

(number and percentage of votes)

	Political party			Totals by settlement category (100%)
	JEWISH HOME	LIKUD	ALL OTHER PARTIES	
All settlements				
Religious Zionist (Amana or Gush Emunim)	21,303 (55.5%)	6,985 (17%)	10,756 (27.5%)	39,044
Mixed (secular and religious)	10,231 (24%)	16,009 (37.6%)	16,381 (38.4%)	42,621
Secular	6,453 (14.9%)	15,738 (36.1%)	21,366 (49%)	43,557
Haredi (ultra–Orthodox)	1,410 (3.6%)	1,090 (2.7%)	37,263 (93.7%)	39,763
Totals in all settlements by party	39,397 (23.9%)	39,822 (24.1%)	85,766 (52%)	164,985
Settlements outside settlement blocs				
Religious Zionist (Amana or Gush Emunim)	15,211 (53%)	4,323 (15%)	9,166 (32%)	28,700
Mixed (secular and religious)	6,455 (31.5%)	5,734 (28%)	8,285 (40.5%)	20,474
Secular	5,252 (17.4%)	11,607 (38.4%)	13,381 (44.3%)	30,240
Haredi (ultra–Orthodox)	173 (8.8%)	106 (5.4%)	1,688 (85.8%)	1,967
Totals outside settlement blocs by party	27,091 (33.3%)	21,770 (26.7%)	32,520 (40%)	81,381

SOURCE: calculated from http://votes20.gov.il/.

of "strategic voting" to enhance its overall size in the Knesset, a decision that itself indicates a certain measure of flexibility on the part of religious Zionist voters, and another 32 percent went to other parties, in particular to a splinter religious mizrachi party (Yachad).

The Jewish Home, however, also received some votes in mixed and secular settlements though only a tiny number in *haredi* settlements. Not surprisingly, it had supporters in mixed settlements, where they received an additional 10,231 votes; of these, 6,455, or 31.5 percent of the total votes cast in mixed settlements, were from settlements outside the settlement blocs. Even secular settlements provided voters to the Jewish Home, mostly the ideological nationalist ones. Close to 16 percent of voters in secular colonies gave it their vote, but these numbers added to the Jewish Home's tally only 6,453 in all settlements and 5,252 in settlements outside the blocs. The Jewish Home received 39,397 votes in all 126 settlements of the West Bank, 27,091 votes in all colonies that lay outside the settlement blocs, namely the ones that would need to be evacuated, and only 15,211 in settlements that were exclusively religious Zionist (i.e., that belonged to Amana and its precursor, Gush Emunim). Even if we add to the Jewish Home's tally the 39,822 votes given to the Likud in all settlements, the combined total comes to only 79,219 votes, and the sum total of Jewish Home and Likud votes outside the blocs falls to 48,861—a tiny number, and only 1.15 percent, of the 4,210,884 Israelis who cast a valid ballot. A combined Jewish Home and Likud vote in all settlements amounts to less than half of all votes cast. The settlers in the West Bank make up 4.7 percent of Israel's population, and the total number of their ballots, 164,985, amounts to 3.9 percent of Israeli voters. Outside the settlement blocs, that number falls to 1.9 percent of all Israeli voters in the March 2015 elections. The electoral power of the settlers outside the settlement blocs is tiny, so their future remains vulnerable to political shifts.

Arieli also casts doubts on the claim that colonization advances Israeli security. Asking just how secure transportation would be in a mixed ethnic region—a classic consideration in the long history of the Israeli-Palestinian conflict (and civil wars in general)—he insists that many of the small Israeli settlements scattered amid the bulk of the Palestinian population do not possess safe access to roads. Special bypass roads had to be constructed to these settlements or closed off to Palestinian vehicles, but these roads only increase the friction between Palestinian residents and settlers. They also require the deployment of yet additional security forces. From a military viewpoint, then, Israeli colonies in the middle of the West Bank provide no security for Israel.

Another military consideration touches on the effect of the layout of future borders between the two states. Any annexation would lengthen, potentially double or triple, the 313-kilometer-long Green Line. But the smaller and less twisted the future border is, the easier and cheaper it would be to guard. Equally importantly, a less intrusive border would enhance the territorial contiguity of a Palestinian state, inflicting less damage to the fabric of life in Palestinian villages. Withdrawing from the land while leaving in place features of the occupation that adversely affect the Palestinian residents' everyday life experiences—such as intrusive borders—would defeat the purpose of territorial partition.

It has been argued that counting only the colonies and their population underestimates Israeli presence in the West Bank. Jeff Halper, founder of the Israeli Committee against House Demolitions, also includes in his analysis of the Israeli "matrix of control" "the maze of laws, military orders, planning procedures, Kafkaesque bureaucracy, settlements and infrastructure," all designed to immobilize Palestinian residents by controlling key junctures. In particular, he emphasizes the role of the highway system and bypass roads in generating formidable obstacles to Palestinian movement.[13] Of course, the Separation Wall, built in response to the suicide bombings within the Green Line during the Second Intifada, does the same on a massive scale. Though this infrastructure is an important part of the matrix buttressing Israeli control, its components have not come up in peace talks, for a simple reason: they play only a subsidiary role and are less of an obstacle to negotiations than the colonists who reside in the OPT. These features of the occupation—such as the legal apparatus of the occupation and the Separation Wall—would be dismantled or moved with the end of occupation or, in the case of highways and roads, would be left in place.

Arieli also points out that, though the difference between the Israeli and Palestinian proposals for the resettlement of Palestinian refugees into Israel within the Green Line appears significant, in fact it is hardly so. Israel expressed a willingness to repatriate only five thousand refugees, while the Palestinian side insisted during the Annapolis talks on upwards of sixty thousand returnees, but both numbers are negligible. They would not significantly alter Israel's ethnic composition, especially when considered in relation to the subtraction of approximately three hundred thousand of East Jerusalem's Palestinian residents from Israel's population. Both Israel and Palestinian numbers are small, and very likely much too small, not only from the Palestinian perspective but also from the Israeli one—after all, during the 1949 Lausanne Conference following the 1948 War an Israeli "goodwill offer" would have allowed the return of one hundred thousand refugees into a country with a much smaller Jewish population and would have compensated the others.

Arieli's data-driven, thorough, and dispassionate analysis asserts the continued viability of territorial partition and of keeping the door open to its continued consideration. Even so, he poses two serious challenges to the Olmert proposal, each of which could undermine territorial partition altogether.

The first reservation concerns the settlements' layout. Arieli questions whether the geographical placement of the colonies allows, even under conditions of equal exchange of territories, for the creation of a continuous and viable Palestinian state. To address this concern we need to examine the issue of settlement blocs, the very category used by Israel to define the areas it wishes to annex under a peace agreement. The logic is that clustering settlements in blocs makes it possible to annex the smallest areas of compact settlement to Israel and to evacuate the remaining scattered settlements. These blocs have never been defined officially, so the term is used loosely and may encompass areas of varying sizes. We do have, however, one useful list. On the eve of the 2006 elections, Olmert's platform for the new centrist party, Kadima, promised unilateral Israeli withdrawal from the West Bank with the exception of the Etzion and Ariel blocs and the three additional blocs of the Jerusalem wraparound (*otef*) area. In total, five blocs would be annexed to Israel. Using Olmert's document and the route of the Separation Wall as the closest proxy for a future border allows us to discern five distinct blocs, moving from south to north (see map 5).

1. Gush Etzion bloc: includes a compact cluster of ten religious Zionist settlements located east of Bethlehem and south of Jerusalem, as well as the large *haredi* city of Beitar Illit to its north and Efrat further east.

2. Ma'aleh Adumim bloc: consists of the eponymous city plus four additional settlements. It is separated from Jerusalem, which lies directly to its west, by zone E1 (East—1), the last unbuilt area adjacent to East Jerusalem.

3. Givat Ze'ev bloc: includes the eponymous city and four additional settlements southwest of Ramallah and northwest of Jerusalem.

4. Modi'in Illit bloc: is anchored by the eponymous *haredi* city that lies northwest of Jerusalem and includes three additional settlements.

5. Ariel bloc: this bloc, instead of hugging the Green Line, is thrust into the West Bank in the shape of an elongated finger that includes the eponymous city and twelve additional settlements scattered south east of Qalqilya.

It has been suggested that there is also a sixth bloc, the Karnei Shomron bloc, which begins near Qalqilya and runs eastward from Alfei Menashe through Karnei Shomron, to Kedumim, near Nablus. This bloc would constitute another deep-reaching finger into the heart of the West Bank, but since the Separation Wall ends east of Alfei Menashe—leaving both Karnei Shomron and seven more settlements on its west side—this string of colonies cannot be viewed as a bloc that is comparable to the others on our list.

While the Gush Etzion, Givat Ze'ev, and Modi'in Illit blocs lie adjacent to the Green Line and their annexation to Israel would not severely affect Palestinian lives, the same cannot be said about the two remaining settlement blocs. The annexation of the entire Ma'aleh Adumim bloc would leave in its wake two serious problems. The first is that area E1 is the only remaining land bridge between the West Bank and Jerusalem. The inclusion of parts of East Jerusalem in the state of Palestine would require Palestinian sovereignty over E1 and, possibly, Har Homa. The second is that Israeli negotiations have also sought to include in this bloc an additional territorial expanse east of the city of Ma'aleh Adumim that stretches almost to Jericho, in order to provide it with land reserves for development. Though this bloc, as currently constituted, is much smaller and shorter than that of the two fingers mentioned above, its location at the narrow waist of the West Bank, east of Jerusalem, effectively divides the West Bank into southern and northern portions, making its territorial contiguity impossible. Without such contiguity a future Palestine would not be a viable state. To allow for the delineation of nonintrusive borders, the Ma'aleh Adumim would have to give up its hinterland and the Mishor Adumim industrial zone. Since E1 is unbuilt and most of the Ma'aleh Adumim land reserves are empty, the redrawing of this bloc's boundaries is feasible.

The remaining finger stuck into the heartland of the West Bank—the Ariel bloc—poses the most serious obstacle to an Israeli withdrawal. The construction of Ariel was proposed in the 1973 electoral platform of the Labor

How Has the Occupation Transformed the Conflict?

Party on the basis of the Galili Document. Actual construction commenced in 1978 by the Begin government, and the bloc now reaches a full thirteen miles into the West Bank, which is only about thirty miles wide. Ariel, a mostly secular city, with a population of 19,299 at the end of 2015, is the fourth-largest settlement town in the West Bank, and half of its population consists of immigrants from the former Soviet Union. The city, however, is not an employment center of nearby settlements. Its main employer is Ariel University, with an enrollment of about fifteen thousand students who commute from all over Israel rather than from just from the West Bank settlements. Ariel has no Jewish settlements within a radius of three miles. The largest nearby settlement is the *haredi* town of Immanuel with a population of 3,197 (in 2014), and the sum total of the nearby nine colonies that either have their own independent municipal councils or belong to the Shomron Regional Council is around 1,000. These settlements do not form a discernible bloc but are strung along the Trans-Samaria Highway (Route 5). The Ariel finger bisects the West Bank, and the very existence of Ariel and its assorted settlements constitutes an insurmountable obstacle to territorial partition. Without the bloc's evacuation, there can be no diplomatic resolution to the Israeli-Palestinian conflict.

The second reservation concerns the exchange of territory. Arieli questions whether Israel has enough real estate to exchange for the settlement blocs without harming its own rural communities and economy. Though Olmert offered the equivalent of 5.8 percent of Israeli territory within the Green Line, some of it adjacent to Gaza, and the rest to the southern Hebron region, in return for 6.3 percent of the West Bank, an examination of this and other proposals of territorial exchange convinced Arieli that "it is not possible [for Israel] to carry out a territorial exchange exceeding 4 percent. The addition of more territory would significantly damage tens of Israeli villages within the Green Line, as well as the national infrastructure." [14] Not surprisingly, Arieli calls for the reconsideration of the very concept of "settlement blocs," in particular the imaginary Ariel bloc, because over the years they have taken hold of the Israeli imagination and become a stumbling block. It is necessary to think of each settlement separately and consider annexing only the "first line" of settlements—the ones that hug the Green Line and are not separated from it by Palestinian towns and villages.[15] This idea was at the heart of the December 2003 Geneva Initiative (reissued in September 2009), which was agreed upon privately between Yossi Beilin (former Israeli deputy foreign minister and minister of justice), and Yasser Abed Raboo (former culture and arts minister in the PNA). This approach, according to Ariel's painstaking analysis, would make a 4 percent exchange feasible.

Arieli's two objections are interconnected: the annexation of the Ariel bloc to Israel would require a territorial exchange of roughly an additional 2 percent of the West Bank, an area that is too large for Israel to be able to afford. What would it take to remove this obstacle? Let me recall a helpful historical precedent. When the Arab Legion in the 1948 War surrounded Mt. Scopus, site of the historical campus of the Hebrew University, and transformed it into an enclave within Jordanian-controlled territory, Israel both built a new campus in Givat Ram in western Jerusalem and sent monthly convoys to the old campus to maintain its control. After the 1967 War, the Mt. Scopus site was rebuilt, and it is now the main campus of the Hebrew University. Instead of being evacuated, Ariel University could potentially remain an Israeli enclave within the state of Palestine. After all, universities attract diverse student bodies and create multicultural spaces; Ariel University, which already has a small percentage of Palestinian students from Israel, could open its doors to Palestinians from nearby towns and villages. Another possibility is equally worth considering: Israel has offered to rectify the adverse effects of annexing area E1 to Israel by building tunnels and overpasses that would allow Palestinians to bypass Israeli built-up areas. This arrangement would provide connection but not territorial contiguity. However, if Israel believes that this is a viable option for Palestinians, it can do the same for Israelis in Ariel by transforming Ariel from a bloc into an enclave connected to the Green Line through a similar bypass road.

Short of either of these arrangements, Ariel would have to be evacuated with the other religiously motived settlements in the northern part of the West Bank. Since Ariel is a overwhelmingly secular city, proposed by the Labor Party and built by Likud, its residents do not have the same religious reasons for living in the West Bank as do their religious Zionist counterparts and should be more amenable to moving back to Israel in return for proper compensation.

What would be the cost of evacuating a sufficient number of settlers into Israel to allow for an equivalent territorial exchange? If we added to the 22,244 settler households that reside outside the settlement blocs the 4,400 settler households in the town of Ariel and another 250 in nine of the settlements linking Ariel to the Green Line, Israel would have roughly 27,000 households to evacuate. These make up slightly more than 30 percent of the colonies' households. No more than four hundred Jewish households work the land—or rather, employ Palestinian agricultural workers who cultivate it—making up about 1.5 percent of the West Bank. In other words, West Bank Jewish settlers have not sunk the kind of roots that their predecessors did from the times of the Yishuv and the years of mass migration after independence. These farms, furthermore, are located in the Jordan Valley, the most sparsely colonized area. Only 7 percent of construction undertaken in the colonies is directed toward industry and agriculture; the rest is for private homes and public buildings. The settlements themselves provide mostly movable service jobs, such as K-12 teachers and security guards and personnel. There are only two significant industrial parks in the West Bank, Mishor Adumim and Barkan, and these employ Palestinian laborers almost exclusively. Instead of working in or near their settlements, as much as 60 percent of the Israeli labor force in the West Bank commutes daily to jobs within the Green Line.

Keeping in mind that Israel absorbed close to a million immigrants between 1989 and 2006 from the former Soviet Union, resettling about twenty-seven thousand households of Hebrew-speaking Israeli citizens should not be a particularly daunting task. A country that has created roughly eighty thousand new jobs per year in the past decade would not find it difficult to add approximately six thousand new jobs annually for each of the, say, five years of the peace agreement's implementation. About six thousand new housing units per annum for the five years would also be required, a number far exceeded by Israel's annual demand. In Arieli's calculation, a mere 2 percent increase in the national budget would cover the creation of new employment and housing necessary to accommodate the evacuated families. Since roughly the same amount is spent directly per year on West Bank settlement, the financial result would be a wash.

Arieli's numbers and assessment demystify the irreversibility thesis and provide us with concrete evidence to work with. Though his analysis keeps alive the possibility, and attendant hope, of a solution to the Israeli-Palestinian conflict through the traditional route of creating a new sovereign state of Palestine, his two caveats can be seized upon as precisely the reasons that it is no longer feasible. We are left with the question: Does the state of Israel have the ability and will to give up the absurdly expansive territorial reserves of Ma'aleh Adumim; evacuate the obstructionist religious Zionists, as well as the more pliant secular settlers of Ariel; and trade 4 percent of its territory in return for being allowed to annex the settlement blocs?

Notwithstanding the detailed blueprint and Arieli's favorable evaluation of the workability of territorial partition, his two reservations still leave serious doubt about the feasibility of territorial partition in 2017. I propose to test the feasibility of territorial partition through the forceful evacuation of settlers by consulting the two precedents of earlier Israeli territorial withdrawal. Subsequently, I will ponder the will, or level of political commitment, of religious Zionists to oppose such evacuations and of the secular left-of-center Israeli middle class to make them happen.

Israel has twice evacuated settlers voluntarily. On both occasions Ariel Sharon, as head of the Southern Command and later as prime minister, played a crucial role. As part of the peace accord between Egypt and Israel, the secular town of Yamit and its surroundings were evacuated. Most of the 625 families left of their own accord, and the rest, jointly with newly arrived Gush Emunim members, barricaded themselves on their buildings' roofs; they were eventually dragged away by soldiers in an operation that was all but complete in half a day on April 23, 1982. Some of the resisters included supporters of Rabbi Meir Kahane who vowed to take their own lives rather than being evacuated, but these were idle threats, and no lives were lost during the process. Michael Feige, who spent several weeks in Yamit before the evacuation, observed that, notwithstanding the attempts of Gush Emunim members to produce difficult images and a painful legacy, the evacuation from the Sinai was a personal but not a national trauma and was soon forgotten.

The second—and by far more significant—evacuation of settlers from twenty-two colonies in the Gaza Strip and four in the northern West Bank accompanied Israel's decision to unilaterally "disengage" from the Gaza Strip in response to the Second Intifada with the intention of forestalling more far-reaching Israeli concessions. The majority of these settlements were religious Zionist, and, jointly with activists once part of Gush Emunim, they organized the Movement to Stop the Withdrawal (from the Katif Bloc of settlements in Gaza). They led demonstrations, prayers, the flying of orange ribbons. Nissim Leon observed that in light of this planned all-out mobilization of religious Zionism and the expectations of a bitter, violent, and protracted struggle, "the restrained protest of the religious Zionist communities was . . . striking." In fact, as reported by the Israeli TV correspondents Yedidya Meir and Sivan Rahav-Meir, "Most religious Zionists did not go to

Gush [Bloc] Katif when it was about to be dismantled. Most did not block roads, did not refuse [army] orders (in fact they played key roles in the disengagement operations), did not clash with the eviction forces and, except for attending one or two demonstrations, did not change their lives." [16] A well-organized military operation easily subdued the settlers and their supporters' passive resistance, and the evacuation of Gush Katif settlements in the Gaza Strip took place in less than ten days; evacuations in the West Bank took no more than two days. There were images of scuffling and tears, but neither evacuees nor the soldiers and police who evacuated them suffered serious physical harm.

One of the explanations given for such limited engagement, if not apathy, on the part of religious Zionist settlers in the West Bank and within the Green Line is their respect for the value of *mamlachtiyut*. This term, sometimes translated as "statism" but better understood as "state-centrism," was coined with Israel's establishment in 1948 to express and demand adherence to the state over sectoral identities—whether *haredi*, religious Zionist, Labor, or Revisionist. *Mamlachtiyut* was introduced as part of Ben Gurion's efforts to unify these distinct sectors' disparate institutions and bring them under state authority. While the *haredi* opposed this approach—their goal was to keep separate from the secular state—religious Zionists, as well as the other sectors, were part of the Zionist movement and were amenable. Today, religious Zionists are divided into two factions: (1) the "yeshivas that follow the line," who hold *mamlachtiyut* as a central value, attributing to the state itself religious significance, and (2) a faction that places religious commandments above secular ones. The former are less likely to object to the dismantling of certain settlements.

Leon offers another, potentially complementary explanation for the hesitant response of the religious Zionists to the call for resistance, which places them within the context of broader social changes of embourgeoisement experienced by Israeli society. The messianic radicalism of Gush

Emunim, in Leon's view, has been balanced, and indeed overpowered, by the entry of the university-educated graduates of religious Zionist high schools and yeshivas into the new Israeli middle class. Though the new professions, in which religious Zionists are overrepresented in comparison to their share in the population, provide higher incomes, they are also vulnerable to job insecurity. Thus religious Zionists prize pragmatism. Their middle-class lifestyle choices have brought accusations of insufficient piety from prominent religious Zionist rabbis. In another study, the anthropologist Joyce Dalsheim, who studied the evacuation of the Katif bloc settlers from Gaza, highlights one group of evacuees who, instead of blaming the Israeli government, question their own culpability in the process that led to the evacuation of the Katif bloc and inquire as to God's larger purpose in allowing it to happen. In doing so, she challenges the idea that religious Zionist settlers are united in their views. The once messianic settlers are neither socioeconomically monolithic nor motivated solely by religious considerations, and their religious rationales vary. While settlement in Gaza does not carry the same religious imprimatur as it does in the Jewish "homeland of antiquity" in the West Bank, it is telling that the vast majority of the settlers from the same religious and socioeconomic background were unwilling and a minority among them unable to disrupt these evacuations.[17]

This feasibility analysis leads me to conclude that the term *irreversible* is best rejected but that the remaining obstacles to territorial partition, though not insurmountable, are formidable. The obstacles to the evacuation of settlers are political, not geographical.

Relatively few Israeli political and social forces clearly support the kind of compromise with the PNA outlined in the Olmert-Abbas negotiations, which would require the removal of some 27,000 settler households from the Occupied Palestinian Territories (OPT). Israel no longer possesses a powerful peace movement. The Israeli-Egyptian and subsequent Oslo Accords were catalyzed by and generated massive support from the Peace Now movement, which was a true match to Gush Emunim. The 1982 Lebanon War and the Sabra and Shatila refugee camp massacres by the Lebanese Maronite Falange units allied with Israel led to an outpouring of opposition, including the largest demonstration in Israel's history. The demonstration, some four hundred thousand strong according to the police estimate, led to the formation of the Kahan Commission of Inquiry and, upon the publication of its report, to Ariel Sharon's resignation as minister of defense. Today, Peace Now is a pale imitation of its old self. Its destruction is due in large part to the wave of suicide bombings that were not confined to the OPT but carried out within the Green Line as well, indiscriminately targeting both settlers and the residents of Israel. The place of the mass Israeli peace movement was taken by an assortment of nongovernmental organizations (NGOs) who carry on their struggle through the mobilization of public opinion and legal action. The best known among them are B'Tselem and Yesh Din (both of which conduct research, collect evidence, and litigate human rights violations in the OPT), the Public Committee Against Torture in Israel, Ir Amim (which works for an equitable and stable Jerusalem with an agreed-upon political future), and Breaking the Silence (which collects testimonies of soldiers about the violations of the laws of war). These organizations, and many others like them, are small, speak the universal language of human rights and liberalism, and depend on funding from abroad, mostly from the European Union and its member states, and thus cannot fill the gap left by a mass peace movement with clear political goals.

The much-reduced strength of the peace camp is accompanied by an overwhelming sense among professionals, the middle class, and the kibbutz movement legatees, many of whom are concentrated in the coastal zone (derogatorily called "the Tel Aviv State" or described as a detached liberal elite by their opponents), that the settlers have "succeeded" in imposing their will on the rest of Israeli society. The "State of Judea," as some left-of-center activists suggest, has defeated the state of Israel. Having seen the loss of the political predominance of the Labor Settlement Movement (LSM) and a severe reduction in the power of the political parties associated with it (the Zionist Camp, the Labor Party's most recent iteration), left-of-center activists now struggle for the right to remain different, for more personal, less public goals: not having to betray principles for the sake of employment and income and being able to safeguard their children from religious nationalist indoctrination at school. In this weakened position, the supporters of the two-state solution seek to hold back the tide of right-wing politics and culture but no longer view themselves as capable of reversing through electoral means the historical trend that promotes ongoing colonization.

The Zionist Camp has turned into a pale version of Rabin's Labor Party, and Israeli NGOs are focusing not so much on the political resolution of the conflict as on recording and struggling against specific violations of occupied Palestinians' human rights. But there is still considerable support for territorial partition and a two-state solution within Israel, despite the many years of rule by the right-of-center Likud government and its religious Zionist allies. The same is true for Palestinians. In 2012, 67 percent of Israeli citizens expressed support for a future agreement reached by any Israeli prime minister to establish a Palestinian state side by side with Israel. By 2014, that number had fallen to 60 percent, but it has remained steady since then, despite the *habbah al-sha'biyya* knife attacks that started in September 2015. A joint survey of the Israel Democracy Institute and the Palestinian Center for Policy and Survey Research from August 2016 found that 51 percent of Palestinians and 59 percent of Israelis (though only 53 percent of Jewish Israelis) back a two-state solution to the Israeli-Palestinian conflict. When presented with a "package deal" based on terms similar to those of the Olmert-Abbas negotiations from 2008, the number drops to 39 percent of both Palestinians and Israeli Jews and 46 percent of all Israeli citizens. To break down these results further: among Israelis, 84 percent of left and moderate left, 59 percent of center, and 18 percent of right and moderate right citizens support a two-state solution; among Palestinians, 57 percent of Fatah voters, 25 percent of Hamas voters, and 46 percent of voters for other factions support the agreement package. The findings fluctuate according the questions' wording, and the reliability of answers to hypothetical questions has low confidence intervals, but these results still provide a valuable rough assessment of the general populace's positions.[18] These survey results clearly demonstrate that the two-state solution continues to be an important option.

Mouin Rabbani, who is a senior fellow at the Institute for Palestine Studies and coeditor of *Jadaliyya*, warns his readers against extending disillusionment with the Oslo process to its objective. There is no evidence, he suggests, that territorial partition has been seriously attempted in the context of the Oslo agreements. Settlers and settlements, he says, "are matters of politics, not of physics." And in politics, existing dynamics can be transformed and reversed by the mustering of sufficient political will and resources. There is, ultimately, also "no evidence it cannot be done." [19] It would require the evacuation of some twenty-seven thousand households of settlers, about twenty-two thousand of them religious Zionists. The resistance of these legacy settlers might be less than commonly thought, both because their social positions reflect the state-centered ideological and institutional *mamlachtiyut* and because such opposition would endanger their social status and mobility. At the same time, the weakness of the active supporters of territorial partition diminishes the political will to carry out partition. Against this background, the role of the BDS network, the topic to be addressed in section V, appears to be crucial for moving Israel and the Israeli-Palestinian conflict toward resolution.

III

The alternative to territorial partition is the one-state solution. It has two main versions, and I will now examine their feasibility. The first is binationalism. For about two decades (between 1925 and Israel's establishment in 1948), and in contrast to all Zionist approaches, which have acknowledged only Jewish national rights, binationalists postulated the equality of Jews and Palestinians. But it was binationalism with a singular twist: by claiming that being a majority—whether Arab or Jewish—was not to be viewed as a precondition for possessing national rights, they sought to overturn the classical tenet of modern democratic politics that accords the power of decision making to majorities. Instead, they championed a binational state in which the Jewish and Arab communities, regardless of their demographic ratio, were to share political sovereignty while remaining autonomous in managing their internal affairs. In contemporary political theory, their proposals would fall under consociationalism, a framework developed by the political scientist Arendt Lijphart on the basis of the Dutch experience with four nonterritorial political groupings: Calvinist, Catholic, socialist, and liberal. Its major features are mutual veto power regarding fundamental issues, internal autonomy for the management of each group's own affairs, and proportional representation (sometimes skewed to boost the smaller groups).[20]

All champions of a single Palestinian-Jewish state remind us that binationalism was originally a "Jewish program." The many versions of Jewish binationalism—liberal, socialist, capitalist—however, have received only perfunctory consideration, although the disappearance of advocacy for it among Jews and its reappearance among Palestinians requires an explanation. Israelis' dismissive attitude toward binationalism as a solution these days is especially surprising because one would imagine that Jewish authorship of binationalism would render it more acceptable to Israeli Jews. Acknowledging that a binationalist solution has been discussed for close to a century allows us to examine the causes of its defeat in the past and to learn from its failure.

There were two prominent efforts on the part of Jewish organizations to settle the Jewish-Palestinian conflict in a binationalist fashion.[21] The first, by

Brith Shalom (Alliance for Peace), was formed in 1925, faded by 1933, and was rekindled between 1942 and 1948 under the name Ichud (Unity). Brit Shalom was a coterie of liberal humanist intellectuals, primarily from Germany, and also included like-minded intellectuals from the former Austro-Hungarian Empire, especially Prague. The second well-known binationalist effort was led by the League for Jewish-Arab Rapprochement and Cooperation, which began operating in 1939 and disintegrated around 1945. The League was an alliance of political parties with a mass base led by the parties of the Left, in particular Hashomer Hatzair and Poalei Zion Left, and also included individual members of other parties. There was also a third, short-lived, capitalist-inspired, ad hoc binationalist effort, identified in the historical record simply as the undertaking of "the Group of Five" (Gad Frumkin, Moshe Smilansky, Pinḥas Rutenberg, Moshe Novomeysky, and Judah L. Magnes) at the beginning of the Arab Revolt in 1936.

Jewish binationalists, then, had many constituencies and multiple configurations; they were liberals, capitalists, and socialists in turn and were organized as small groups and as a mass movement. Many of the prominent leaders of the Labor Settlement Movement (LSM) and the General Zionists (the secular middle-class wing of Zionism) also espoused binationalist goals at one time or another. Offering a political doctrine that would have obviated the need for imperialist support and the use of antidemocratic measures to create a Jewish majority in Palestine gave binationalists a unique ethical grounding. For this reason, binationalists became an intellectual and moral force to reckon with, but they never acquired real political influence among the Jewish community during Mandatory times.

The Ichud and the League's blueprints for a binationalist state fluctuated between expressing political parity in either a Legislative Council or Jewish and Arab canton-based elections, but they mostly focused on the use of education to close the gaps between the two national movements. Nor did its proponents wish for binationalism to be implemented right away or for

Britain to leave the contending parties to themselves and depart Palestine. Neither body produced a social or economic binationalist program or sought to create mixed labor markets, since these would have challenged the LSM's separatist state-building policies. Even so, Hashomer Hatzair's submission to the Anglo-American Commission in 1946 came to the fateful but unavoidable admission: "The road of economic separation lead[s] to political calamity." Capitalist binationalism alone sought some measure of labor market mixing, but when the Jewish Agency's leadership debated its propositions it considered binationalism to be not a permanent resolution of the national conflict but rather a lull in it—a "cease-fire" or a "phase," rather than the architecture of future Jewish-Arab relations.

Albert Hourani, a representative of the Arab Office to the Anglo-American Commission, highlighted this problem in his March 1946 testimony: "A binational state of the kind that Dr. Magnes suggests can only work if a certain spirit of cooperation and trust exists and if there is an underlying sense of unity to neutralize communal differences. But that spirit does not exist in Palestine." [22] Binationalism was haunted by a paradox that manifested itself in the havoc its two-stage program would wreak on the potential for building trust between the contending communities. In the first stage, the majority was asked to treat the minority as its equal, in return for which, in the second stage, the erstwhile minority's truest promise would be not to exploit its newly created demographic majority and instead to continue to treat the once-majority (but now-minority) equally. But the ongoing attempt of the Jewish minority to transform itself into the majority within the binationalist framework it proposed generated understandable anxiety in the Arab majority, as large-scale Jewish immigration after Hitler's rise to power did among Palestinian Arabs. Binationalism, born out of the economic separation in Mandatory Palestine and the profound mistrust it bred, could not foster the integration and the ensuing trust that should have been present as the prerequisites for its flourishing.

There was little, if any, binationalist sentiment among the Arabs of Palestine at the time. The reason for their indifference to binationalism, simply put, was that during the Mandatory era Palestinian Arabs were favored by their majority status. Under democratic political doctrine, they were the legitimate claimants to sovereignty as the majority, and seeking to hold onto majority status is what territorial nations perforce do. This was well recognized by the Zionist side, as cogently expressed by Berl Katznelson, one of the prominent LSM leaders: "An average young Arab will not follow the path to a binational state, as long as he has a one-national one." The obverse is true today: Jews don't "need" a binational state since they have a one-national one.

Ali Abunimah, a well-known Palestinian American journalist and cofounder of the Electronic Intifada, offers a Palestinian historical perspective on binationalism. He suggests in his *One Country: A Bold Proposal to End the Israeli-Palestinian Impasse*, from 2006, that not just Jewish but also Palestinian organizations have advocated for a one-state solution. Following the 1967 War, the Palestinian national movement took its first steps in the direction of cooperation between Arabs and Jews. The January 1969 meeting of Fatah's Central Committee described its final objective as "the restoration of the independent democratic State of Palestine, all of whose citizens will enjoy equal rights regardless of their religion." What was left unclear was whether Fatah sought to overturn the PLO Charter's narrow criteria allowing only "Jews who had normally resided in Palestine until the beginning of the Zionist invasion," presumably before the Balfour Declaration, "[to] be considered Palestinians." At another time, Arafat suggested that the state proposed by the PLO would contain 1.25 million "Arabs of the Jewish faith," raising questions about the future of ashkenazi Jews, the majority of Israel's population at the time. By February 1970, Arafat stated that "every Jew who will give up . . . Zionist ideology" would be welcome in a secular democratic Palestinian state. Significantly, defining Jews as a religious group would have stripped them of their own rights to define themselves as a political community.[23] This would, in effect, reverse the Balfour Declaration, which allotted national rights to Jews and civil and religious rights to the existing non-Jewish communities in Palestine.

The Fatah and PLO statements in the half decade after 1967 remained vague (and sometimes contradictory), and can hardly be described as binationalist. The lack of specificity makes it difficult to view the "secular democratic state" formula—which would feature a Palestinian Arab state with a yet undefined percentage or number of Jews—as the equivalent of the Jewish binationalist propositions. Soon thereafter, in the wake of the 1973 War, the PLO shifted away from its one-state objective, going back to the goal of reconquering Palestine and then, in the late 1980s, to the goal of territorial partition. The short-lived and vague plan for a "secular democratic" state for religious groups was not the mirror image of Jewish binationalism.

Binationalism is the credo of the minority—the politically weaker but not necessarily less numerous party. Hence, it started as a Jewish program and turned into a Palestinian one only recently. This conclusion removes much of the appeal of binationalism, leaving it as a political strategy for hard times for the weaker party but not for both parties or for the long run. Nor can two national communities be stably connected solely at their political apex; socioeconomic integration needs to be part of their members' everyday lives, giving each national community a stake in the prosperity and further development of both by forming spheres of overlapping interests and aspirations. These conditions do not exist in Israel and the OPT.

I V

No feasibility examination of the other version of the one-state solution—the civic polity of one person, one vote—has been put forward by those who view it as the only possible outcome. Very likely it is this conviction that gets in the way of studying its workability: there is little need to prove that a one-state is feasible if nothing else is possible.

How to conduct a feasibility study of a Palestinian/Israeli shared-state or one-state solution, namely a one-person, one-vote scenario based on civic citizenship without regard to national background? Given the importance attached by many to this optional future, I am required to give it particularly serious consideration. Since the one-state solution is a counterfactual, a subjunctive conditional, an answer to the question "what if," I propose to take the following course in my analysis. I will start by assessing it within the broad context of social scientists' and philosophers' analyses of the institutional and cultural factors that promote social stability in multinational states. In addition, the proposed one-state solution must pass comparison with historical precedents of nation building and trends, both outside and inside the Middle East, as well as with contemporary cases. Finally, I will collect the rare remarks, unsystematic and abstract as these are, that have been made on the setting up of a future unitary state and its character. I will subject the one-person, one-vote state's features to two types of logical analysis to gauge (1) whether the means proposed match up with the ends and (2) whether the arguments presented follow a logical order or are circular. An indirect feasibility study, the kind I am proposing here, is not the equivalent of the one I conducted earlier in this essay for the two-state and binationalist outcomes and therefore cannot yield the same level of confidence; nonetheless, it is a necessary and unavoidable exercise if we are to have a serious discussion of this option.

What can the discipline of political science, which studies political institutions, states, and political behavior, teach us about multinational states? A first, sobering conclusion is that political scientists who study the possibility of transition from a conflictual to a stable multinational (or multiethnic) state do not contemplate straightforward one-person, one-vote states but only their more modest federal versions. One of the most careful students of federalism is Brandan O'Leary, who studied federal power sharing in Northern Ireland and Iraq's Kurdish region. O'Leary concluded that, where the territorial layout of the relevant minority communities can be made to correspond with internal borders, federalization may become a harmonizing device. In other words, federalism can work in countries that are equally amenable to territorial partition. Conversely, where there is insufficient ethnic clustering, the proposition "To each nation let a province be given" cannot be met. In our case there are several small, fairly homogeneous clusters: Palestinians in Areas A and B, and just possibly in parts of the Galilee, and Israeli Jews in the coastal valley. But there are no clearly delineated ethno-regional clusters; in fact, this is the very reason for doubting the possibility of partition without territorial exchange.

O'Leary also observes that in liberal democracies the share of a given ethno-national group stands as a proxy for its potential electoral power. Consequently, "a *Staatsvolk*—a people who own the state" has the ability to dominate other ethno-national groups through its sheer numbers and need not fear its rivals. A *Staatsvolk* is thus a prime candidate to lead a federation, and its demographic preponderance should allow it to be generous toward smaller groups, especially when the resulting federation will have multiple minorities. Conversely, "If there is no *Staatsvolk*, then majoritarian federalism, of whatever internal territorial configuration, will not be enough to sustain stability" and it is not likely to survive.[24] The precondition of a stable ethno-national majority does not exist in Israel/Palestine. As of 2012, Jews are a small minority in the land between the Mediterranean Sea (including Gaza) and the Jordan River. The rate of natural increase of Palestinians in the OPT is higher than that of Israeli Jews (the gap is much smaller among Jewish and Palestinian citizens in Israel). According to population studies scholar Sergio DellaPergola, the share of Jews by 2020—including non-Jewish members of their families—would be 77 percent within Israel, 56 percent of the combined population of Jews and Palestinians within the Green Line and the West Bank, and only 47 percent of the combined population of Jews and Palestinians within the Green Line, the West Bank, and Gaza.[25] Given the relatively high intermarriage rate among Jews in Western countries and the slowly declining share of their offspring who consider themselves Jewish, these ratios are not likely to change as a consequence of mass aliya (immigration) to Israel. Both the current demographic ratio and the higher birth rate among Palestinians make the kind of federalism O'Leary envisions impossible.

An alternative approach breaches the boundary between philosophy and political science and, consequently, holds that social unity depends not so much on institutions and demographics as on shared values. John Rawls, the late American philosopher of socially-conscious liberalism, put forth the proposition that divided and pluralistic liberal societies are held together when "public agreement on questions of political and social justice supports ties of civic friendship and secures the bonds of association." [26] Two Canadian philosophers, Charles Taylor and William Kymlicka, suggest that where shared notions of justice might not be possible multiculturalism might accommodate diversity. Citizens, in Taylor's view, "might find it exciting and an object of pride" to labor jointly to build a society built on deep diversity. Kymlicka, on his part, agrees that without a commitment to "deep diversity" multinational states will not stay united. He adds, however, the qualification that the citizens of a stable multinational state "must value not just 'deep diversity' in general, but also the particular ethnic groups and national cultures with whom they currently share the country." [27]

Kymlicka raises a host of profound questions about the importance of culture, values, and practices vis-à-vis social institutions, as well as intriguing questions about similarities between the central values of Jewish and Muslim societies. Abunimah, for example, invokes his mother's memories of peaceful experience between Jews and Arabs in Palestine before the creation of Israel—such as playing with a Jewish girl next door—as a source of inspiration. The political scientist Leila Farsakh suggests that the reinvigoration of "the present Arab identity with the cosmopolitan character that it once had" would be a necessary step along the path to form a Jewish-Palestinian state.

A first step would be the rehabilitation of the concept of the Arab Jew, which would allow viewing Israel as part of a broader Arab heritage rather than as the outpost of an alien Western culture." At present, she observes, "Most of the Palestinian debate on the one-state solution, while inclusive of Jews, avoids engaging with the complexity of Jewish identity and history. It clearly repudiates Zionism, but it seeks to incorporate the Jewish person as a neutral repentant entity." [28] Elsewhere in the Middle East, for example in contemporary Morocco, there are attempts by the monarchy to recall the country's Jewish population as part of its cultural festivals; but Moroccan, Palestinian, and Jewish memories of shared life harken back to a kinder, multireligious community that was erased by the rise of nationalism.

A search for values shared by Jews and Palestinians may direct us to the centrality of familial values for both Palestinians and Israelis, but the growing emphases on defining both Israeli Jews and Palestinians in not so kind Judaic or Islamic religious terms, respectively, overrides such similarities. A much more likely area of overlap may be found between those in either community who hold on to liberal values of pluralism and tolerance and would like to remove personal status law from under religious jurisdiction. I will, however, cut short this discussion by reminding us of Kymlicka's warning that mutual cultural attraction is the product of ongoing social solidarity rather than the basis for its future emergence. The circumstances for its appearance and strengthening do not exist within the current conflict and ongoing occupation.

The historical record of the formation of *Staatsvolk* federations or nation-states with shared values is not encouraging either. Civic citizenship and civility are possible and do exist, but they are more fragile than robust and need careful cultivation. Processes of national homogenization that started in the late Middle Ages in the western end of the European continent relied on bureaucratic uniformity, educational standardization, and economic integration. Even these practices were commonly complemented with the expulsion or destruction of religious communities that would not assimilate. Protestants in France, Muslims in Spain, and Jews across Europe (in particular, in England, France, and Spain) bore the burden of this religious cleansing. As homogenization spread eastward, the bloodlands of eastern Europe experienced the most horrendous homogenization, again having Jews as its most reviled victims. This process has continued its eastward creep and has seen the breakup, some of it violent, of both the Soviet Union and Yugoslavia, and even of Czechoslovakia. In the Middle East, and to a lesser extent in Africa, the great ethnic, religious, and sectarian "unmixing"—we have to use this social science term with caution because it hides the whole gamut from expulsions, to forced assimilation, to genocide behind the terminology of civil wars—continues with gruesome persistence under our eyes. The many denominations of Christians, some formed at the time the religion was consolidating its orthodoxies, and other small and ancient religious communities that survived for centuries are rapidly disappearing from the Middle East. The forced departure of Christians and the ferocious sectarian conflicts raging from Yemen to Turkey and from Syria to Afghanistan, as well as the reinventing and recharging of age-old Sunni-Shi'a divisions, serve as a cautionary tale to promises of civic one-state goals in the region. The Middle East does not appear to be hospitable these days to accommodation between ethnic and religious groups. The absence of any attempt to update the one-state vision in the wake of the multiple civil wars in the Middle East following the hopeful days of the Arab Spring is troubling. Nor has any reflection been offered on how Hamas would fit into the proposed rights-based civic political order.

The beginning of the twenty-first century has not been very hospitable to civility or civic citizenship outside the Middle East either. Countries with both a *Staatsvolk* and shared liberal, political, and cultural values are being challenged by secessionist movements: Spain by Catalans, Great Britain by Scots, Belgium by the Flemish (even though they are the country's majority).

It is further mindboggling that in the mid-2010s desperate and destitute Middle Eastern refugees to the Western heartlands of civility are viewed as threatening the stability of the European Union, the world's only supranational conglomeration. Nor does the United States seem immune to the siren calls of racism.

My next step is to examine the status of citizenship, not just within Israel, the OPT, and Europe, but in the rest of the Middle East. The director of the Norwegian Institute of Human Rights at the University of Oslo, Nils Butenschon, in his introduction to *Citizenship and State in the Middle East*, distinguishes between three types of citizenship regimes, which he terms (1) *singularism*, where a single nationality or religious group dominates the state community, as in Turkey, Iran, and Israel; (2) *pluralism*, where the elites of multiple communities share in governing the state through a power-sharing agreement, as in Lebanon; and (3) *universalism*, where citizenship status is based on individual rather than group identity, a type for which he does not provide an example from the Middle East. The rest of the book explains how both the colonial legacy and the power structures of Middle Eastern states are constructed in ways that make it difficult—if not impossible—to enshrine a legacy of liberal citizenship in the Middle East. Butenschon' s volume was published in 2000, many years before the Arab Spring and its powerful democratizing aspirations and early successes—but also before the brutal demonstration of the enduring power of military and nepotistic, authoritarian, Islamic, patriarchal, and sectarian authority, as well as the weakness of most Middle Eastern civil societies. Manuel Hassassian, writing in the same volume, distinguished Palestinians from these general tendencies and held up the democratic potential of the PNA, though he wondered whether it would come to fruition.[29] In the twelfth year of President Abbas's four-year term, with the suspension of the legislative work of the Palestinian Legislative Council for over a decade, and with the political and territorial split between Hamas in Gaza and the PNA in the West Bank, little doubt remains. At this historic moment, the Middle East, including Palestine, does not offer a path to a civil vision of citizenship in which group membership is irrelevant to individuals' rights within the state.

Finally, I will examine what little the champions of the one-state solution tell us about its expected features. Abunimah, who is commonly described as the leading American proponent of the one-state solution, claims that it could "in theory resolve the most intractable issues: the fate of Israeli settlements built since 1967, the rights of Palestinians, and the status of Jerusalem." Abunimah's book also stands out by putting forth a program of eight principles to ensure that the one state-to-be would rest on common values. The first principle is that "the power of government shall be exercised with rigorous impartiality on behalf of all the people." He anchors this demand in a full complement of human rights, freedom from discrimination, and equal treatment, thus potentially subjecting legislation to judicial review.[30] This and the other principles are drawn from the Universal Declaration of Human Rights and, as such, would be a great advance for Israel, which has only a single basic law for the protection of human dignity and relies on a judicial bill of rights, as well as for the PNA, which does not have such constitutional underpinnings.

Yet this whole visionary exercise ignores the nature of electoral politics, in which each party represents the interest of a distinct constituency, often in conflict with other parties and their constituencies. Just how does one elect a government that will ensure "rigorous impartiality"? My task, a not particularly happy one, is to point out that principles are always expressed through institutions and that, while it might be easier to reach agreement on principles, the latter require as much attention.

The question is not just whether a unitary, federal, or even confederal state would be preferable. Rather, to reduce this query to its simplest level, who will be the prime minister? The chief justice, whose court decides whether the government has been impartial? Or for that matter the commander of the military? The police commissioner? The head of the Nuclear Energy Commission? In fact, whatever the choice of electoral system—single- or multiple-member constituencies, district based, proportional with a low threshold, proportional with a high threshold, mixed majoritarian and proportional, first-past-the-post, two rounds, transferable votes—just how effectively could any institutional engineering prevent the polarization that preceded it from resurfacing? Will Israeli Jews and Palestinians vote for issue-oriented or class-based parties or, more likely, will the results of the election turn out to be nationalist plebiscites? Cross-cutting interests and loyalties are necessary for the former, but where the many forms of disadvantage overlap, the latter is unavoidable. As long as unresolved issues from the 1948 War, the Nakba, or maybe just the occupation itself remain, unresolved conflicts will hover over and shape domestic party politics and therefore the elections.

Abunimah also offers that a single state "offers the potential to deterritorialize the conflict and neutralize demography and ethnicity as a source of political power and legitimacy." He asks rhetorically, "What if an Israeli Jew who wanted to live in Hebron, or a Palestinian who chose to move to Tel Aviv or Jaffa, was simply able to do so?" But what about the Israeli Jews already living in Hebron? Is Abunimah suggesting that they would be able to stay, regardless of the ways in which they had muscled their way into Hebron's old Jewish Quarter? Would the city's Palestinians who were forced out to make room for such Israeli Jews and their families consent? Will the one-state solution accept the status quo on the day it is declared? Abunimah posits that the future state would not only foster economic opportunity, social justice, and dignified life for all of its citizens but also "establish fair and efficient mechanisms to compensate victims of conflict and redress inequalities caused by unjust practices of the past." [31] This is an apolitical formulation that, true to the author's general thrust, would treat all victims equally. It also avoids addressing the concrete and distinct features of the Israeli-Palestinian conflict.

The legal scholar Noura Erakat is much more explicit and forceful in exploring, in a series of articles, the outstanding issues between Israeli Jews and Palestinians. Though South Africa is her explicit model for the establishment of a state with equal political rights, she highlights the fundamental ways in which even the postapartheid state has fallen short. In contrast to South Africa, where the persisting poverty gap of blacks and whites demonstrates that the removal of discriminatory laws is insufficient, "transitional justice must feature rehabilitative policies" in the future Palestinian/Israeli state; otherwise Palestinians, regardless of their status as citizens, will suffer "ghettoization, systematic impoverishment, and criminalization."[32] To prevent the legacy of the occupation and discrimination from undermining the future unitary state, Erakat suggests that it address a long list of considerations, namely the "historical, contemporary, territorial, and national claims of Jewish-Israelis and Palestinians." It also

> must answer questions about return, repatriation, forced migration, past and present, among Jews and Palestinians throughout the Middle East, and questions of national homeland—of future immigration policies, the prospects of binationalism, competing claims to property, and this is to say nothing of restitution and redress for all the suffering wrought upon occupied lands and their populations.[33]

Such massive restoration and redistribution, however, negates many of the benefits Abunimah lists for shepherding Israeli Jews and Palestinians into a single state. Her single-state solution alone will not deterritorialize the conflict and neutralize demography and ethnicity as sources of political power and legitimacy; it will not freeze the status quo but will reopen it to major change. The Separation Wall, and the hardships it imposes on Palestinians who find themselves on its "wrong" side, could indeed be removed by demolishing the wall. But many legitimate Palestinian demands would be devilishly complex to address. How would the losses incurred by the 1948 refugees be addressed? Jews forced out of the Arab world after the 1948 War left considerable property behind, but who should compensate them? More fundamentally, is there any reason to tie together claims for the Jewish property, held by Arab states, with the losses suffered by Palestinian refugees? Would victims and relatives of victims of terror acts be compensated? The victims of the three Israeli wars against Gaza? What should happen to colonies built on land seized for temporary military needs that no longer exist after a diplomatic solution, or to settlements built on state land that was so seized on the basis of questionable definitions and practices? Of course, since colonization is illegal under Article 49 of the Fourth Geneva Convention, in principle all settlements may be required to be removed as part of rehabilitative practices. Doing so, however, would return us by a circuitous route to the two-state solution based on territorial exchange, whose lack of feasibility has directed Erakat to seek a single-state solution in the first place.

The same caveat applies to all versions of a one-state outcome that seek to evacuate large numbers of colonists, with or without territorial exchange. If the "one-staters" envision freezing the "facts on the ground" as they are and having all colonists stay *in situ*, then many aspects of the occupation will not end. But when the ensuing disruption is on a larger scale than that required for a two-state solution, the latter is likely to make more practical sense. How does one strike a balance between justice and practicality while also ensuring a measure of stability? In sum, to evaluate the one- and two-state solutions it is insufficient to examine each one's feasibility separately; they have to be viewed in tandem, and their trade-offs need to be calculated as well. Erakat is clear eyed about the pitfalls attendant on working out the institutional character of the one-state solution. Though she titles her article "Even One State May Not Be Enough," she ends on the warning note that once such a program is laid out, "strident supporters of the one-state solution may find it less appealing, prompting some to birth new visions altogether."[34] It would not be surprising if such visions see a U-turn back to territorial partition.

V

The BDS civil society movement broke into the public arena with its call in July 2005. Its resistance tactics are based on the double rejection of the premises of Oslo and the violent means of the Second Intifada and Hamas. BDS is a loose network of some 170 Palestinian civil society organizations, from trade and professional unions through social service and women's organizations to bodies already dedicated to specialized struggles (such as the Palestinian Grassroots Anti-apartheid Wall Campaign and the Palestinian Campaign for the Academic and Cultural Boycott of Israel). Philosopher Omar Barghouti, one of the movement's founders and major intellectual spokespersons, presents the movement's means and goals in his volume *BDS: Boycott, Divestment, Sanctions: The Global Struggle for Palestinian Rights*.[35] The movement has many spokespersons, and their emphases and preferences vary. Abunimah and Erakat offer two additional keen analyses of the issues raised by BDS. Their writings are at once supportive of BDS and critical of some of its aspects.

To start, we need to recognize just how innovative the BDS movement is. In at least three ways, BDS places the Palestinian struggle against Israel on a new footing that is transgressive compared to other approaches. First, the BDS movement is unlike the PNA, which is seeking to end the Israeli occupation of the West Bank, Gaza, and East Jerusalem through the creation of a state in part of Palestine, and is distinct from Hamas, which wishes to establish an Islamic state in all of Palestine. It struggles for equal rights—humanitarian, human rights and fully equal citizenship—rather than for a Palestinian state. This shift is revolutionary. After all, the biggest accomplishment of the Palestinian national movement in the 1970s was the redefinition of the "Palestinian Question" from a refugee problem to a legitimate struggle for national self-determination. From then on, instead of viewing Palestinian refugees as a social problem in search of humanitarian aid, the international community began focusing on the Palestinian national question seeking political resolution. Simultaneously, from its inception, the PLO was engaged in setting up the institutions of a state in exile in the refugee camps it had access to. The attainment of a Palestinian state has been held up as both the core of the Palestinian cause and its vehicle, as well as the cement holding the institutions of Palestinian life together, and all other Palestinian political parties still adhere to this goal. Thus the rejection of the state paradigm and its replacement with a rights-based framework have not achieved predominance within Palestinian political life. BDS is a thorn in the side of both the PLO, which negotiated the Oslo DOP and the subsequent agreement outside the framework of international law, and Hamas, which has no commitment to human rights. Consequently, BDS has had to bypass both the PNA and Hamas to operate and coordinate its own campaign. Its strategy consists of calling on companies, civic bodies, and institutions around the world to boycott, divest from, or impose sanctions on Israeli businesses, universities, and institutions and foreign companies that transact business with them until the movement's goals are met.

Second, unlike the PNA, which operates in the international diplomatic arena, and unlike Hamas, which views armed struggle as the main tool of its long-term goals, BDS employs nonviolent means to reach its goals. Its approach recalls the practices of the First Intifada. Unlike both the PNA and Hamas—which frequently act in an authoritarian fashion and use violence against each other—the BDS movement requires and supports a democratic order. Precisely because BDS depends on grassroots mobilization and is a participatory mass movement, this reliance reinforces the movement's nonviolent approach. It depends not only on Palestinian civil society bodies and NGOs but also on an international civic solidarity movement, rather than regional Arab or Muslim supporters such as the Rejection Front states (Syria, Libya, Algeria, etc., who refuse to consider a negotiated peace with Israel), the Arab League, and the Organization of Islamic Cooperation. It seeks to mobilize global civil society for support and publicity for Palestinian demands and protests (as epitomized by the highly sophisticated militant—but largely non-violent—resistance movements in villages such as Nabi Saleh and Bil'in against the appropriation of their land by Israel). BDS demands are represented by local support organizations that seek to act as catalysts for the adoption of BDS practices in European countries and, increasingly, the United States. The BDS network carves out a distinct terrain for a new type of Palestinian resistance that is located within, and is associated with, global civil society.

Third, the BDS movement seeks to unify the respective struggles of the three major fragments of the Palestinian people—Palestinian citizens of Israel, occupied Palestinians, and scattered Palestinian refugees—in a single political program. The rights-based approach serves as a necessary common foundation for the attempted merger of the distinct demands of each of these fragments; their attempted political merger in a common struggle is a segue to creating a state that will accommodate all of them. The BDS movement, therefore, has three demands:

1. End the occupation and colonization of all Arab lands and dismantle the Separation Wall.

2. Recognize the fundamental rights of the Arab-Palestinian citizens of Israel to full equality.

3. Respect, protect, and promote the rights of the Palestinian refugees to return to their homes and properties, as stipulated in UN General Assembly Resolution 194.[36]

The BDS's struggle, as described in its original call, is expected to continue "until Israel meets its obligation to recognize the Palestinian people's inalienable rights to self-determination and fully complies with the precepts of international law."

BDS separates its struggle from considerations of the "moment after" its potential success and is focused on the former alone. The BDS network, as Barghouti explains, has not taken a position as to whether it views the future of Israelis and Palestinians in terms of a two-state or a one-state outcome: "While individual BDS activists and advocates may support diverse political solutions, the BDS movement as such does not adopt any specific formula and steers away from the one-state-versus-two-states debate, focusing instead on universal rights and international law, which constitute the solid foundation of the Palestinian consensus around the campaign." In fact, he adds, writing as recently as 2011, "Most networks, unions, and political parties in the Boycott National Committee still advocate a two-state solution outside the realm of the BDS movement." [37] The BDS movement seems to be hedging its bets in order to carve out a narrow route for its distinct approach within the cross-pressures of Palestinian society, but most of its supporters are known to favor the one-state solutions discussed in section IV above.

V I

The bedrock of the BDS network's struggle is its identification of the Palestinian struggle with the successful South African antiapartheid struggle. Supporters of the BDS effort pinpoint its beginnings in the 2001 World Conference against Racism that was held in Durban in South Africa. The NGOs that participated in the conference equated Israeli policies vis-à-vis Palestinians—both within the Green Line and in the OPT—with the apartheid regime. In particular, they drew upon the definition of apartheid in the 1973 International Convention on the Suppression and Punishment of the Crime of Apartheid: interrelated policies adopted with the intention "to divide the population . . . by the creation of separate reserves and ghettoes for the members of racial groups, . . . [and] the expropriation of [their] landed property." By July 2005, they stated that the BDS movement was inspired by the "struggle of South Africa against apartheid" and the support it received from the international community. "Our South Africa moment has finally arrived," said Barghouti in a speech he delivered in 2010.[38] Related allusions to South Africa, such as the substitution of "the Apartheid Wall" for what

Israel terms the Separation Wall and the designation of an annual "Apartheid Week" held across campuses around the world, are further illustrations of the BDS's desire to closely associate Palestinians' and black South Africans' experiences and their respective struggles.

The antiapartheid struggle involved a network of organizations, among them the British-based Anti-Apartheid Movement, led by white liberal and communist emigrés; a broader coalition in the United States, which included African American groups, far-left organizations, and several independent bodies, such as the Committee on Africa and the Interfaith Coalition; and, of course, antiapartheid South African parties. Their combined efforts led to South Africa's international isolation and subsequent abandonment of apartheid and its replacement with a one-person, one-vote citizenship polity. In our world of deepening national, ethnic, and religious conflicts that periodically break out in unspeakable violence, there is something unexpected and attractive about an attempt to settle a potentially destructive conflict by framing it as a project of democratic nation building based on a shared civic identity. Postapartheid South Africa represents high aspirations and naturally serves as an object of emulation.

Though the antiapartheid movement consisted of many political parties, civil society associations, and umbrella organizations from the United Democratic Front to the Mass Democratic Movement, the main adversaries pitted against each other were the National Party (NP), and the African National Congress (ANC). The NP, speaking for the Afrikaner nationalist view, claimed that South Africa was a multinational state, comprising between ten to twelve nations, each of which was entitled to the right of self-determination. The multiple-nations program evolved out of the main thrust of apartheid—the doctrine of racial separation—adopted in 1948 by the NP on the basis of the crude racial ideal of *baasskap,* or white "bossship." Though the *verkrampte* (intransigent) elements of the NP remained satisfied with this version, by the 1960s the *verligte* (enlightened) wing of the NP reformulated apartheid's justification by seemingly adapting the then fashionable ideology of decolonization to South Africa. Under the new plan, the black majority population was assigned to tiny, impoverished, and noncontiguous tribal Bantustans or "homelands" (making up 13 percent of South Africa's land), where African tribes were allegedly free to pursue their own "separate development" and, eventually, to attain independence. Concurrently, black Africans were denied any vestiges of citizenship in South Africa and were treated as "immigrants." Their movement was strictly regulated through influx control and pass laws. The disparity between the modern framework of the nation for whites and the relegation of Africans to fragmented, frequently moribund tribal frameworks reflected an approach to nationhood that, in spite of its ideological veneer, remained race based.

This combined Bantustan system and movement control regime of racial separation was the target of the antiapartheid struggle spearheaded by the ANC. In retrospect, the ANC's oversized role in the antiapartheid movement is obvious, but for long stretches it was but one of the contenders for leading the movement, and at times it was eclipsed by its Africanist competitors. Expressions of separatist African nationalism can be found in the pronouncements of ANC leaders as well, but for most of its existence the party remained identified by the June 1955 Freedom Charter. This seminal document, drafted by the ANC and its political allies, was clear in speaking in the name of a unitary body, "the People of South Africa." The Charter declared that "South Africa belongs to all who live in it, black and white," and that all South Africans were "equals, countrymen, and brothers." It demanded the formation of a democratic regime with equal human rights and opportunities, including the right of every man and woman to vote and stand as candidates for all lawmaking bodies. Whites were admitted for the first time as members of the ANC only following the Morogoro Conference of 1969. Non-Africans were invited to serve on the ANC's center policy-making body—its

National Executive (which replaced the Revolutionary Council, a nonofficial ANC body, on which whites already served)—only after the Kabwe Conference of 1985. Though the ANC adopted nonracialism slowly, the organization did practice the policy it preached.[39]

Given the abundance of references to South Africa as a template for the BDS efforts, it makes good sense to assess just how closely BDS hews to the South African antiapartheid struggle. I have already highlighted many similarities: BDS, like the antiapartheid movement, is rights based and vies for the support of churches, student associations, corporations, and the international community to force the hand of its unwilling government. At the same time, there are several large gaps between the antiapartheid template and that of BDS. My questions, therefore, are: How far has the BDS network adapted the antiapartheid movement to make it fit the Palestinian circumstances? Has it twisted the model out of shape?

BDS departs from the ANC in several respects, and I will focus the remainder of this section on the three most important differences. First, BDS strictly adheres to a nonviolent tactic of boycotts, sanctions, and divestment, unlike the ANC, which, like other African and Arab national liberation movements of the time, established its armed wing, the Umkhonto we Sizwe (MK, or Spear of the Nation). The MK undertook several bombings between 1961 and 1963 and again between 1976 and 1984. The attacks between 1976 and 1984 claimed seventy-one dead, but although the MK promised to target only security personnel and repudiated attacks whose victims were civilians, the majority of casualties of attacks by operatives associated with the MK ended up being civilians. The ANC and several of its black opponents, in particular the Inkatha Party, were also involved in violent altercations in the buildup to electoral campaigns in the post-apartheid years of transition. It is, therefore, a mistake to romanticize the ANC's nonviolence. The BDS movement was born in different circumstances. Its leaders have consciously chosen a nonviolent path in response

How Has the Occupation Transformed the Conflict?

to the counterproductive nature of the Second Intifada's violent suicide bombings and the harsh Israeli repression these have evoked. This contrast between movements, however, is overshadowed by their two other differences.

The second significant difference between the ANC and the BDS lies in their respective relationships to Afrikaners and Israeli Jews. Unlike the ANC, BDS views cooperation, dialogue, and all forms of engagement between Israelis and Palestinians as "normalizing" the Israeli occupation and consequently rejects this path. Even when all parties to a potential political, economic, or educational activity aimed at promoting dialogue agree that the occupation is anything but "normal," the same antinormalization tactic is upheld. BDS guidelines require that any joint Palestinian–Israeli Jewish activity be based on addressing the root causes of the conflict and the requirements of justice—in effect, on the acceptance of the BDS analysis and strategy in full. Such cooperation, then, would constitute "co-resistance" to the exclusion of the multiple narratives of "coexistence." [40]

The antinormalization tactic cannot help but remind Israelis of intense opposition to the normalization of their state's existence from its inception and throw into doubt Israel's right of national self-determination. Boycotts, actually, were not invented by the Arab states. That "distinction" belongs to the Hebrew Labor campaign for replacing Arabs with Jewish workers that commenced at the very beginning of the Second Aliya in 1905. But as early as 1945, economic boycotts had become the main tools of the Arab League, which produced both a primary boycott—refusal to trade directly with Israeli companies, and a secondary boycott—a ban on third-party companies that did. It was, and still is, exercised, though unevenly, by governments and professional and civic associations. Old and new boycotts of normalization not only resemble each other but at times intersect. When the Campaign for the Boycott of Israel Supporters in Lebanon denounced Amin Ma'alouf, the Lebanese-French novelist and member of the Académie française, for praising the value of culture as a means of normalizing relations between Israel and the Arab world, it also called on the government of Lebanon to prosecute him under its antinormalization laws that criminalize collaboration and association with Israelis or investment in Israel.[41] BDS antinormalization tactics, therefore, not only are a throwback to the past but constitute a process of reversal—the severance of ties formed between Palestinians and Israelis since the start of the Oslo process and, in some cases, even before.

Antinormalization aimed at potential Jewish partners sets the BDS apart and even puts it in opposition to the ANC. In fact, BDS resembles and emulates the views of the ANC's nationalist opponents. African, or Azanian (an African name for South Africa) nationalists, such as those in the Azanian Peoples Organization, propounded that there were two nations in South Africa: an oppressing colonial, white nation and a colonized, oppressed black nation. They claimed that black Africans were the only true nation and were therefore entitled to rule South Africa. The white nation, in contrast, was expected to disintegrate as a result of the black nation's liberation struggle.[42] One of the most dramatic political expressions of this perspective was the breaking away of the Pan African Congress (PAC) from the ANC in 1959 under the leadership of Robert Sibukwe. The PAC opposed adopting the nonracial premises of the Freedom Charter, repudiated the possibility that whites could identify with the African cause in a racially divided society, and called on Africans to struggle by themselves for their freedom. PAC also rejected the possibility of minority guarantees and claimed that whites refusing to remain in South Africa under its new rulers would emigrate and that those who stay would come to identify with the African nation.[43]

In 1969, this Africanist approach found further political and cultural expression in the Black Consciousness Movement (BCM). Black Consciousness emerged among the black students who split from the multiracial National Union of South African Students to form their own South African

Students Association. Under Steve Biko's leadership, the BCM viewed the antiapartheid movement as equally a process of psychological liberation and of political transformation. Biko defined blackness broadly, including all groups called by the apartheid regime "nonwhites," but rejected mixing with white students and with white liberals because it was not possible to have "black souls in white skins." Whites, in his words, saw the oppression of blacks as "an eye-sore on an otherwise beautiful view," whereas blacks experienced this situation as one from which they could not escape for a single moment. Being opposed to apartheid, argued Biko, did not make one an ally of the black people, who needed to organize separately. In contrast to PAC, the South African Students Association did not restrict membership to blacks and defined Indians and Coloreds not only as oppressed but also as black to enable their integration into the antiapartheid movement. The BCM understood blackness as "a reflection of a mental attitude" and consequently treated black Africans who worked for the Bantustans and other apartheid institutions and Indian capitalists not as blacks but as "nonwhites." [44] Whites, however, could not become black in this political sense and participate in a joint struggle against apartheid.

Whereas the ANC's long-term goal of a single, nonracial, democratic society with a shared civic identity did not just allow but called for and required a joint struggle, this is not the case for the BDS network. In fact, BDS follows in the footsteps more of the Pan African Congress and the Black Consciousness Movement's struggles than of the ANC's nonracialism. What is missing from the BDS's approach is the spirit of the Freedom Charter—akin to the declaration that "South Africa belongs to all who live in it, black and white," and that they are "equals, countrymen, and brothers"—a commitment to a shared future. Without such a pledge, the adaptation of the South African experience to the struggle in Palestine by the BDS movement remains a weak and unfocused imitation. The ANC's appeal was rooted not in its tactics but in its universalist values and goals expressed through interracial cooperation. Antinormalization, in contrast, runs the gamut—from the rejection of medical training offered to Gazan medical personnel in Israeli institutions; to criticism of the West-East Divan Orchestra established jointly by Edward Said and Daniel Barenboim;[45] to the outcry that led to the resignation of Professor Mohammed Dajani of Al Quds University in East Jerusalem for taking a group of Palestinian students to visit Auschwitz as part of a joint program that also included a visit by Israeli students to the Dheisheh refugee camp;[46] to the ejection of Amira Hass—the only Israeli journalist (employed by *Haaretz)* to have relocated to Ramallah to report on the everyday experiences of the occupation—from a conference at Birzeit University.[47] Antinormalization imitates the Separation Wall.

Leila Farsakh, in one of the most thorough and thoughtful analyses of the issues raised by the changing tactics of Palestinian resistance, concludes that, "historically, the Palestinian national movement has never seriously considered how to cooperate with Israeli Jews to bring about a single state." "Few Palestinians" she adds, ". . . are now interested in reaching out to Israelis, let alone addressing their fears, the way the ANC did in South Africa when it worked with white activists to dismantle the apartheid regime." [48] Yet where can the experience of a shared society emerge, if not in the struggle that seeks to bring it about? Utopia is not just a book or a place but also, as suggested by Eric Hobsbawm, an experience of the society to come. If revolutionaries need proof that human nature can be changed, they will discover it within the brotherhood and sacrifices of their movement. Put evocatively by Hobsbawm, theirs is "a miniature version of the ideal society . . . If this is possible within their movement, why not everywhere?" [49] The movement for liberation is where mutual trust is experienced and the kernel of future society is formed. Conversely, without such transformative experiences, how can the possibility of freedom, justice, and equality for all (which has never yet been experienced) be believed? Though left-of-center Israeli Jews view themselves as a minority unable to stop the colonization process or end the occupation, their role in keeping up a vocal opposition is important. The ANC's white supporters during the long years of the antiapartheid struggle were never numerous either, but the interracial cooperation they engaged in was a model for the future.

BDS supporters would be able to offer a potential demonstration of the feasibility of large-scale Jewish-Palestinian cooperation, and thus to dissipate the deep-seated mistrust between the two nationalities, in Jerusalem. Though about 90 percent of the city's 300,200 Palestinians have no citizenship rights and cannot participate in the elections to the Knesset, all are residents of Jerusalem and, as such, may vote in municipal elections. The vast majority of these Palestinians choose to refrain from voting in order not to legitimize Israel's annexation of East Jerusalem. Yet these residents hold tremendous power in their hands and, in the context of a rights-based program, could decide that it is both in their own interest and an illustration of their acceptance of a shared Jewish/Palestinian political future to vote for both Jerusalem's mayor and members of the municipal council. Given the deep divisions within the Jewish electorate, especially between secular and *haredi* voters, it is reasonably likely that if they voted en masse the next mayor of Jerusalem, or maybe deputy mayor, will be Palestinian. This would not be the first time that Jerusalem's mixed population had a mayor not of the majority religion. Between 1937 and 1945 Daniel Auster and Mustafa al-Khalidi alternated in the position, though they were not universally liked. Another mixed city, Haifa commemorated in 2010 the seventieth anniversary of the death of Hasan Bey Shukry, who was the first mayor of the modern city and is remembered as "everyone's mayor." He served between 1914 and 1940, opened city tenders to both Jewish and Arab contractors, and issued Haifa city documents in both Arabic and Hebrew. The possibility of a Jerusalem city council with roughly equal numbers of Jewish and Palestinian members and a Palestinian mayor would require a level of compromise and mutual accommodation that would have a demonstration effect for the rest of the country.

The third difference between the antiapartheid movement and the BDS network concerns the appropriateness of labeling the Israeli-Palestinian conflict in its entirety as an antiapartheid struggle. It has been suggested, for example by Erakat, that the antiapartheid model is only one of the components of the BDS movement, added on top of a prior preference for nonviolent resistance, and therefore that it is not "a requisite element of BDS strategy" but merely a useful instrument and symbol. Most other supporters of BDS, however, view the association of its struggle with the antiapartheid movement as its greatest asset. The ANC's target was clear—the apartheid regime. The BDS movement, in contrast, fights for three distinct objectives: to simultaneously end occupation in the West Bank, East Jerusalem, and Gaza, the second-class citizenship of Palestinians in Israel, and long-term denationalization and refugee status for dispersed Palestinians. There exist clear and persistent expressions of solidarity between what I call the *three fragments* of Palestinian society, all of which struggle against the same adversary, but as of today they share no unified framework or common struggle. I turn now to the circumstances, and distinct forms of discrimination, under which each of the main Palestinian fragments labors. As part of my feasibility study I will inquire how likely it is for the three fragments to reunite and to combine their separate grievances into a single struggle, some seventy years after the Nakba.

As we have seen in my first essay, occupied Palestinians enjoy no citizenship rights in a recognized state, and their human rights are subordinated to IHL. The ongoing expropriation of their land—both public and private—for the benefit of the Jewish settler population, as well as the neglect and indifference of the Israeli police and military to abuses and attacks on Palestinians by settlers, highlight the duality of the legal and practical circumstances under which Palestinians live in the OPT. A 2014 report by the Israeli Association for Civil Rights, titled *One Rule, Two Legal Systems*, lists the following areas in which Palestinians' legal rights differ within the West Bank from Israeli settlers: they go to different courts; they fall under different rules of detention, search, and interrogation; they reach majority two years earlier than Israelis; their freedoms of expression, protest, and movement are constrained; they have no control over their planning institutions; and so on.[50] It may be appropriately pointed out that it is the occupation that places Palestinians under a military regime and, therefore, under military law; however, it is not the occupation but colonization that creates a dual legal system for the West Bank, an apartheid regime. There are two laws for two peoples in the OPT. *Apartheid*—racial in South Africa and national in Israel—is the best term we have for describing the coexistence of two legal systems in one territory that allocates legal rights and adjudicates disputes on the basis of different identities. What matters is not what is done but who did it.

This term, however, is unsuitable for describing the legal circumstances of either Palestinian refugees or Israel's citizen Palestinians. John Dugard, the renowned South African legal scholar, antiapartheid activist, and special rapporteur on the OPT to the UN's Commission on Human Rights, pointed out that continued land seizure for colonization, the construction of the Separation Wall, and the territorial fragmentation in the West Bank are clear indications of the existence of an apartheid regime in the OPT, but he questioned the application of this designation to Israel itself and did not raise it with regard to the status of the Palestinian refugees.[51] The BDS movement's attempt to employ the South African antiapartheid model in order to unify the respective struggles of all Palestinians is effective in the symbolic realm, but this symbolic aspect obscures the institutional, legal, and sociological dimensions of their plight.

Palestinian refugees fell—or, rather, were pushed—into a gap between two legal regimes that was constructed just for them. When the UN Conciliation Commission for Palestine (UNCCP), established in December 1948 to provide protection and negotiate durable solutions for the plight of refugees of the Nakba, fell into disuse, only the UN Refugee Welfare Agency for

Palestine (UNRWA), a welfare agency for needy refugees established in December 1949, remained. The refugees of the Nakba were left a humanitarian concern. Nor were Palestinian refugees godfathered in under the new legal framework: the subsequent 1951 Refugee Convention and the 1967 Refugee Protocol, which established universal criteria for refugee protection and the institution designed to implement them—the UN High Commission for Refugees (UNHCR). Instead, the Arab states demanded the addition of a clause to the new convention and protocol to exclude Palestinian refugees from the purview of the UNHCR because they objected to its individualized definition of refugees, to its emphasis on *non-refoulement* instead of return, to the internationalization of the refugee problem, and to the principle of giving refugees the choice between repatriation, resettlement, or host-country absorption (combined with compensation). The PLO argued equally vociferously against treating the Palestinian refugees as individual cases.

The potential conflict between the refugees' individual interests and collective rights thus led to the creation of what legal scholar Susan Akram pointedly calls a "protection gap," one from which Palestinian refugees suffer to this day.[52] Devoid of the protections of refugee law, the same Arab states that ensured their exclusion did not provide the refugees of the Nakba with human and civil rights but extended to them only temporary privileges revocable by administrative fiat. With the exception of Jordan, which made them citizens upon the conquest and subsequent annexation of the West Bank and East Jerusalem, other Arab states never formalized the refugees' legal status. Palestinian refugees, consequently, constitute as many legal fragments as the number of countries in which they reside—to mention just a few, from those in Lebanon, who are banned from many professions; to those who arrived in Jordan as refugees in the wake of the 1967 War but were not given national identity cards; to those who experienced multiple expulsions, such as those who were forced out of Kuwait following its liberation during the First Gulf War, and those who fled from Palestine to Syria, then fled Syria during its still ongoing civil war to seek refuge in Jordan; to those who long ago left the Middle East and made lives for themselves elsewhere.

This protection gap was exploited by Israel, as well, during the Oslo process. During the negotiations, Israel insisted that any agreement reached with the PNA on collective Palestinian rights would of itself extinguish individual claims.

The BDS movement misuses this self-same protection gap. UN General Assembly Resolution 194 of December 1948 stipulates that "refugees wishing to return to their homes and live at peace with their neighbors should be permitted to do so at the earliest practicable date, and that compensation should be paid for the property of those choosing not to return and for loss of and damage to property." BDS's own demand, in contrast, calls for "respecting, protecting, and promoting the rights of Palestinian refugees to return to their homes and properties as stipulated in UN Resolution 194." The BDS call alters the UN resolution by ignoring the refugees' right to choose between return and compensation. Almost seventy years after the 1948 War, living under the most varied legal authorities, and belonging to different generations, most refugees might not wish to return. BDS, however, does not give them the option of host-country absorption or compensation customarily combined with resettlement. It also ignores the clear shift toward a human rights-based approach to refugees evidenced in the 1951 Refugee Convention, which relies on an individualized, rather than group-based, definition of the refugee, and adopts the pivotal principle of the refugees' voluntary decision. The Palestinian refugee diaspora, living under many jurisdictions, fits the least into an apartheid model but is the aspect of the Palestinian situation that BDS tries hardest to force into the mold.

Akram suggests that, side by side with the PNA, a newly mandated UN body should speak for individual refugees in future negotiations with Israel to rectify this gap.[53] Her sensible suggestion recognizes the distinct interest of refugees and the need to represent it apart from the interests of the Arab states and of the other Palestinian fragments. The point is not to replace access to collective, that is national, refugee rights with individual ones but to provide some of the protections Palestinian refugees have had to live without for three generations. Abbas Shiblak concluded recently that, by the time of the refugees' third and fourth generations it makes no sense to keep them in a legal limbo without simultaneously bringing their plight closer to resolution. Among the range of demands raised by refugees are (1) the granting of citizenship rights by host Arab states side by side with (2) the preservation of part of their rights to compensation and the possibility of return, though in many cases the two sets of rights might prove to be contradictory. Additional demands mentioned include the sustainable development of refugee camps' infrastructure complemented by socioeconomic rehabilitation programs. None of these programs can serve as substitutes for Israel's recognition of the refugees' right of return as a matter of principle and negotiations over the modalities of its implementation, since that recognition would affirm their history and identity and reunify Palestinians with Palestine.[54]

Israel has always rejected this demand because of its potential legal implications and an apprehension over the return of very large numbers of refugees. Yoav Peled and Nadim Rouhana suggest that as long as the right of return is separated from concrete plans for and negotiations over the means of actual return of refugees (as well as their numbers), this fear is exaggerated.[55] After all, sovereign states exercise control over migration into their territory. A 2003 study conducted by the Palestine Center for Policy and Survey Research found that only about 10 percent of the Palestinian respondents expressed a desire to relocate and live in Israel.[56] It is equally important that no political accord be used to extinguish individual rights of compensation.

A single-minded focus on return to the refugees' homes, though their environs have been thoroughly obliterated and transformed, overlooks the passage of time and the different benefits a large range of options for redress may provide. Shahira Samy holds up the Japanese American reparations program as a possible model because its success was due to its multiple dimensions, combining reparations with official apologies and educational initiatives.[57] Palestinian refugees have memorialized their history before, during, and after the Nakba in village books and other physical memorials in their villages; continuing these traditions would provide another form of redress. Palestinian refugees would benefit from having a wider range of options.

Farsakh asks whether the time may have arrived for the Palestinian national movement's leadership—arising first out of the refugee population, and currently out of the residents of the OPT—to be assumed by the Palestinian citizens in Israel.[58] They are the constituency best placed to lead the BDS movement, since they already frame their struggle in terms of equal rights (rather than statehood) and enjoy civil and political rights within Israel. These rights are less secure and numerous than the citizenship rights of Israeli Jews. Adalah, the Legal Center for Arab Minority Rights, lists close to fifty laws that discriminate against Israel's Palestinian Arab citizens, rendering them second- or even third-class citizens. Even when it comes to political rights, political parties representing Palestinian Arab citizens were never part of a ruling coalition (though they were part of a tacit coalition supporting Prime Minister Rabin). At the same, among the Palestinian fragments they (as well as 1948 refugees in Jordan) are alone in being citizens.

Since Palestinian citizens in Israel do not have uniform political preferences, it is not very likely that they could assume the leadership of all fragments of the Palestinian people. Until the 2015 elections, they divided their vote between at least four Arab parties: the National Democratic Alliance (at-Tajamu or Balad); the Arab Movement for Renewal (Ta'al, which also incorporates a faction of Islamic Movement); the United Arab List (Ra'am); and the Democratic Front for Peace and Equality (Hadash), a joint Arab-Jewish Party (as well as two Zionist parties and a *haredi* party). All four parties support the creation of a Palestinian state in the OPT and the return or compensation of Palestinian refugees. Their programs on the status of citizen Palestinians within Israel run the full gamut—from seeking to recast Israel as the state of all of its citizens through its transformation into a binational state and the recognition of Palestinian citizens as a national minority, to the equality of Jewish and Palestinian citizens. The Haifa Declaration of May 2007—which sets forth citizen-Palestinians' collective vision—advocates creating a "democratic state founded on equality between two national groups" but simultaneously suggests that reaching a historic reconciliation "requires us, Palestinians and Arabs, to recognize the right of the Israeli Jewish people to self-determination and to life in peace, dignity, and security with the Palestinian and the other peoples of the region." Furthermore, the Declaration adds that the "democratic citizenship that we seek is the only arrangement that guarantees individual and collective equality for the Palestinians in Israel." [59] In other words, the Palestinian citizens of Israel are putting to the best use they can the rights they enjoy within Israel to overturn the discriminatory limits on those rights. Several political leaders advocate connecting Israel's Palestinian citizens to the Palestinian people outside Israel's borders, via both government institutions and NGOs, as well as boycotting elections to the Knesset. But most Palestinian citizens in Israel, probably feeling too weak and vulnerable, have not fully taken up the BDS cause. Such vulnerability, however, can also produce unanticipated strength: in 2015 the four Arab parties, despite their differences, joined forces to counter a transparent attempt to exclude them from the Knesset by raising the electoral threshold: they formed the Joint List (al-Qaimah al-Mushtarakah) and ran on a single ticket, receiving 13 seats of the Knesset's 120 and becoming the third-largest Israeli party, and chose Ayman Odeh, the leader of Hadash (the Arab-Jewish Party), as their head.

Palestinian citizens of Israel rely on multiple methods to demand equal citizenship rights: they engage in both impromptu and annual demonstrations that take place on Land Day, petition the courts, and elect members of the Knesset. Voter turnout among Palestinian citizens in the Knesset election in 2013 was 56 percent and in March 2015 was 63.5 percent, in comparison with a 71.8 percent general turnout.[60] Among the third generation of citizen Palestinians, the "stand-tall generation," there has been considerable social mobility—including the rise of perhaps as many as 20 percent into the Israeli middle class—and this cohort has created a dense network of civil organizations and NGOs to articulate and advance its cause, in part with the help of the European Union and its member states. There has also been greater mixing with the Jewish population—for example, through moving into Jewish-majority towns and transforming them into mixed towns. At the same time, this greater mixing has encountered significant backlash in the forms of vigilantism, municipal exclusionary maneuvers, and Knesset legislation. In particular, the Knesset has adopted numerous laws directly aimed at curbing expressions of Palestinian national sentiment, such as those prohibiting commemorations of the Nakba on Israeli Independence Day and ostracizing Arab and Jewish-Arab NGOs for receiving financial assistance from foreign donors. For all practical purposes, Palestinian citizens of Israel do not seem to have an alternative to focusing their major political efforts on influencing Israel's institutions. In fact, since the heady days of the Arab Spring in Syria took a tragic turn in the direction of brutal government repression and sectarian bloodletting, the campaign to realize the principles of the Haifa Declaration appears to have been placed on hold.

From an institutional perspective, unification among Palestinians is hampered by the absence today of a single worldwide Palestinian representative body, something akin to the World Zionist Organization for Jewish communities on a worldwide scale. Given that the Palestinians are among the world's most divided people, both geographically and legally—some in their homeland, others in countries bordering on it, and still others farther afield—it has always been and remains a formidable task to fuse their main fragments into a single political entity. The Palestinian National Council has sought to play this role since its establishment in 1965, but it did not speak for the "1948 Palestinians," who were cut off from their brethren and the Arab world until, absurdly, the 1967 War opened access across the Green Line. Having lost touch with Israel's Palestinian citizens, the PLO spoke mostly for the various refugee populations—the ones who had lost everything and whose plight fueled the revival of Palestinian nationalism and resistance. When, as a result of the Oslo process, the PLO, based first in Gaza, then in Jericho, and then in Ramallah, was recognized as the representative of the Palestinian people, and when Ramallah became the de facto Palestinian capital where the institutions of the PNA were established, these bodies were effectively detached from much of the refugee population. Though the Palestinian Basic Law defines the Palestinian people as *all* those who have lived in the country before May 1948 and their descendants, for the purposes of the electoral law—as pointed out by Emilio Dabed—only those who are residents of the West Bank and Gaza are included.[61]

While the PNA is the body that negotiated with Israel for the recognition of the Palestinian refugees' right of return as part of the Oslo, Camp David, and Annapolis stages of the peace negotiations, its legal status is founded on the Oslo DOP, and it has primary responsibility for the welfare of the Palestinians living in Areas A and B. In 1994, Nabil Shaath, a minister of the PNA, stated that UNRWA, rather than the PNA, was responsible for the Palestinian refugees in Lebanon. As part of the Olmert-Abbas and Livni-Qurei talks, the latter had for all practical purposes, though secretly, conceded the demand of Palestinian right of return. The *Al Jazeera* journalist Clayton E. Swisher, who published a volume of the WikiLeaked reports of the Annapolis talks, concluded that the PNA eroded refugees' rights by its willingness to outsource to the United States and select Arab governments the decision concerning the number of refugees—already put in the lower thousands—that would be allowed to return to Israel. Swisher was clearly shocked to note that the reports of the talks "give abundant indication that Palestinian refugees were again about to become victimized, this time by their own people." [62] One of the unplanned consequences of Oslo was the transposition of the most important Palestinian leadership's constituency from one group of disenfranchised Palestinians to another with distinctly different grievances and goals. In the "diaspora," the PLO spoke mostly for the refugees. As power migrated from the PLO to the PNA—which was established in Gaza and the West Bank—the latter became the organization speaking for occupied Palestinians.

Populations living under different legal regimes have different political horizons and expectations. Probably the clearest demonstration of the diversity of these horizons is the fact that only a tiny fraction of Israel's Palestinian citizens have participated in the two intifadas and the violent resistance through which Palestinians in the West Bank, East Jerusalem, and Gaza have attempted to shake off the Israeli occupation regime. There was one large solidarity demonstration with the Palestinians of OPT at the beginning of the Second Intifada, but the "October Events" of 2000 were violently suppressed by the Israeli police, resulting in the killing of a dozen Palestinian citizens. Though Farsakh charted a plausible relay process in which each Palestinian fragment has handed the leadership of the national movement to another, it is equally possible to see such a process, not as one in which each fragment in turn speaks on behalf of all, but as one in which each fragment puts its claims ahead of the others' demands. The very idea of transfer of leadership, in fact, underlines the different circumstances of the major fragments.

The demise of the Oslo process—and the expectation that the 1967 borders will serve to separate Jews and the occupied Palestinians—renewed the relevance of the Palestinian experience of 1948, of the Nakba that was ground zero for the formation of the distinct Palestinian fragments. But each of these fragments falls under a different legal regime—refugee law and protection, citizenship, and IHL—and it appears unlikely that the shared memory of the Nakba can override these sociological, institutional, and legal distinctions and serve to create the kind of effective common political platform the BDS movement desires.

VII

Given the commitment of the Likud and its religious Zionist allies to colonize in Area C of the West Bank and in East Jerusalem and their continued predominance within Israel, the relative weakness of the Israeli domestic opposition to the occupation, and the absence of serious and sustained international pressure to end the occupation, BDS will continue playing a crucial role in resisting Israeli occupation. The most significant achievement of the BDS movement is the shattering of the facade of the elaborate Israeli combination of silence, secrecy, subversion, and denialism concerning the belligerent occupation of the West Bank, Gaza, East Jerusalem, and the Golan. The BDS movement's international naming and shaming tactics have achieved several notable successes and have generated considerable anxiety in the Israeli political class and public. Two choices made by the BDS movement, however, restrict its appeal and effectiveness. Until the movement addresses and rethinks these, its impact is likely to remain limited.

The first choice, as we have seen in this essay, is BDS's vehement opposition to cooperating with Jewish Israeli opponents of the occupation, individuals and groups who could be its allies and speak on its behalf among other Israelis. Antinormalization has both tactical and long-term consequences for the future of the Israeli-Palestinian conflict. It prevents any understanding of Israeli Jewish historical experiences and even of internal divisions or internal opponents of the occupation and colonization. The rejection of cooperation makes it difficult for BDS to consider the place of Jewish Israelis in a shared future and is preventing the movement from establishing its credibility among those with whom it wishes to share a state.

A clear example of the shortcomings of a rights-based antinormalization approach concerns institutions of higher learning. BDS justifies the call to boycott Israeli universities and effectively blacklist their faculty as a form of free speech, but such boycotts paradoxically curtail academic freedom. In particular, antinormalization creates a rift with faculty and students of Israeli universities, including those in the social sciences and humanities who have produced the strongest and most articulate critiques of the occupation (and whose works are cited in these pages) and who are frequently disparaged within their own society. Some of the same considerations apply to cultural boycotts. Defining normalization as the Palestinian campaign for the Academic and Cultural Boycott of Israel does—as a "'colonization of the mind,' whereby the oppressed subject comes to believe that the oppressor's reality is the only 'normal' reality that must be subscribed to, and that the oppression is a fact of life that must be coped with"—is condescending toward occupied Palestinians.[63] It leads to accusations against those Palestinian activists who find it beneficial to work with Jewish Israeli counterparts and see the shared efforts as both a stepping-stone toward and an illustration of things to come. Finally, the tactic's shortcomings become obvious when we consider not only how it currently holds back the movement's progress but how it would affect future efforts if it succeeded. What would happen if BDS successfully weakened Israel through the combination of boycotts, divestment, and sanctions, as it envisages? Antinormalization would make any transition to negotiations—which require addressing the other side's concerns, preferences, and internal dynamics—appear "abnormal" and, for the Palestinian side, potentially treacherous. It remains vitally necessary to address these shortcomings—both analytic and tactical—in order to refocus the energies of BDS on approaches that pass historical and comparative feasibility tests.

It is worth remembering that the ANC itself adopted an antinormalization policy for a period and then rejected it. The institution of apartheid in

1949 by the victorious NP saw the Youth League sweep to power within the ANC. Tambo, Sisulu, Mandela, and the League's main ideologue Anton Lembede adopted a new Programme of Action. It reflected Lembede's emphasis on "national freedom" and "self-determination" through the freeing of the African spirit from the inferiority and dependence imposed on Africans at the hands of whites, including the white paternalism of well-meaning white liberals and communists. This psychological emphasis entailed a turn toward "Africanism." In this view, Africans, rather than constituting a nation within the boundaries of South Africa, were—by right of indigenous origins and preponderant numbers—*the* nation, and the only nation, entitled to claim and to rule South Africa.[64] But even during this Africanist period, the ANC never adopted the harsh view of whites that PAC would be known for later. By the mid-1950s, the traditional nonracial position not only had regained its place in the ANC's ideology but was advocated by the very same Youth League leaders, Sisulu and Mandela, who earlier had risen to prominence on the basis of their radical Africanist nationalism. The realization by the anti-apartheid movement of the value of its alliance with liberal and communist whites, which was the foundation of the Freedom Charter's nonracialism, could well be followed by a similar turn in the BDS movement.

The second choice that has limited the BDS network's effectiveness is its attempt to offer a comprehensive program to address the grievances of the three major fragments of the Palestinian people. Mouin Rabbani examines this comprehensive program against the background of the similarities between Israel and South Africa. South African withdrawal from Namibia did not earn the country a great deal of approval because its very regime was deemed illegitimate. But while Israel's claims to the OPT have never been recognized, its international standing as an independent state is no longer challenged, and a negotiated Israeli withdrawal from the West Bank would suffice to end Israel's stigmatization. BDS spends its energy and moral capital on a direct confrontation with the state of Israel, whereas a focus on organizing opposition to Israel's half-century-long occupation is much more likely to be successful.[65]

But maybe combining the struggle of the three Palestinian fragments—citizens in Israel, residents in the OPT, and refugees scattered in the Middle East and outside—matters less than the BDS movement would make it out to be. An examination of specific BDS campaigns demonstrates that the movement's successes have, by and large, remained restricted to resisting the occupation, rather than supporting the refugees' right of return or opposing citizen Palestinians' second-class citizenship. Some typical examples are (1) SodaStream's relocation of its factory from the Mishor Adumim industrial zone and Ahava Cosmetics' relocation of its factory from the Mitzpeh Shalem settlement to within the Green Line in reaction to demonstrations in front of their stores, (2) the decision by the 2014 Presbyterian Church (USA) to divest from companies that profit from the Israeli occupation and to boycott goods produced in settlements, and (3) the June 2015 statement by RE/MAX that it will no longer receive income from the sale of properties in West Bank settlements. Though the BDS program, as a whole, has been endorsed by unions, student associations, and churches, effective boycott and divestment actions have been commonly mounted only against the injustices of the occupation. Many of those who endorse BDS appear to support that single cause rather than its three-point program. In addition, some of the most significant moves—the European Union's extraction of Israeli compliance in labeling settlement products as such, and its consent to have the UN's Human Rights Council prepare a list of companies that operate in colonies, to mention two recent ones—have been undertaken independently of BDS and have been aimed solely at the occupation. Even among the international civil society bodies that are most sympathetic to BDS, support for the movement is by and large limited to boycotting, divesting from, and sanctioning companies and economic activities connected directly and indirectly to the occupation.

The labeling and potential boycott of the economic products of the settlements, however, is unlikely to produce significant change in Israeli policy toward the OPT, since the contribution of the settlements' industrial parks is a tiny portion of Israel's economy. Most large-scale Israeli companies in the traditional branches of the economy—with the exception of high tech, chemicals, and diamonds—operate on both sides of the Green Line. Secondary boycotts—the suspension of economic ties with Israeli companies that are headquartered within the Green Line but play a role in advancing colonization through construction, provision of mortgages, products, and services, opening branches in settlements, and so on—would be of greater importance for effective economic leverage.

This is the time to recall an important feature of settler-colonial states: the limits to their abilities, if not their ambitions. In 1845, journalist John O'Sullivan coined the term *Manifest Destiny* to describe the American mindset used to justify the settler-colonial project of expansion across the North American continent. He invoked the special virtues of the American colonists and their institutions and posited continued westward movement as a duty. The doctrine was espoused mostly by the Democratic Party, and the success of the US troops against Mexico in the 1846-48 war led to a call for the annexation of all of Mexico to the United States. This expansionist program, however, also encountered considerable resistance, not only on the part of Abraham Lincoln, Ulysses Grant, and most Whigs who opposed imperialism, but also among such southern senators as John Calhoun (who was opposed for racist reasons), John Quincy Adams (who did not wish to admit additional slave states to the Union), and O'Sullivan himself (who argued that the United States should not impose its law and citizenship on people against their will). Nonetheless, private expeditions for the annexation of parts of Mexico and Central America continued for a while. Historians such as Frederick Mack concluded that only a minority of Americans supported the "All Mexico" annexation movement. Though Alaska and Hawai'i were admitted as states to the Union, the expansion of the United States through the creation of new states south of the Guadalupe Hidalgo Treaty line had been blocked.

Focusing the BDS struggle against one of its three targets, the ending of Israeli occupation and colonization—that is, checking the expansion of a settler-colonial state—is a likely step toward challenging Israel's internal settler-colonial features as well. Breaking the élan of Zionist settler colonialism is likely to have a positive effect on the status of all Palestinians. The reduction of hostility between Jews and Palestinians in the West Bank would likely also narrow the divide between Israel's Jewish and Palestinian citizens. The possibility of a more equal citizenship, combined with the kind of cultural autonomy given to national minorities in other multinational and historically settler colonies, would receive more serious attention. Palestinian refugees would have a state to speak for them, and those in conflict zones—such as Syria and Lebanon, where they are at risk of displacement or have already been displaced—would have a homeland to turn to.

The fork in the road that Israelis and Palestinians are approaching is, as commonly believed, one that will take them either toward two states or toward one. As we have seen, the two-state solution has not become irreversibly blocked but faces severe obstacles. It would involve the evacuation of about twenty-seven thousand households of settlers and would require the political will to carry it out. In contrast, the one-state solution in the current circumstances is an uplifting but pure utopia. South Africa, where a nonracial movement that welcomed interracial cooperation had a long and distinguished history of struggle, provides the single example in which civic citizenship came to encompass both blacks and whites (who were already interdependent in the economic sphere). Among neither Israelis nor Palestinians has there been any anticipation of, let alone any necessary mental preparation for, bringing the two groups together under the umbrella of a single state. BDS's one-state vision is both overambitious and undertheorized, as well as self-contradictory.

Given the impasse at which both the two- and one-state approaches have arrived, and given the failings of BDS, the two sides are most likely to stumble ahead heedlessly. Israeli leaders, whether Barak, Olmert, or Livni, or Americans like retired General Mattis, have warned that the current trajectory takes Israel in the direction of apartheid, but Israel is there already. Continuing colonization means digging an ever-deeper hole of no return. Israeli governments seek "to manage the conflict," a task at which they have repeatedly failed, and Palestinians will find encouragement or solace in their *tsumud* (steadfastness). This road will be the bloodiest. A reformed, more focused BDS movement with Jewish allies appears the best option for weakening the commitment to colonization, sparing bloodshed, reversing the occupation, and improving the circumstances of both the Palestinian refugees and Israel's Palestinian Arab citizens.

Israeli Prime Ministers, PLO Chairmen, and Palestinian National Authority Presidents and Prime Ministers

ISRAELI PRIME MINISTERS

Name	Party Affiliation	Time in Office
David Ben Gurion	Labor	March 1949–January 1954
Moshe Sharett	Labor	January 1954–November 1955
David Ben Gurion	Labor	November 1955–June 1963
Levi Eshkol	Labor	June 1963–February 1969
Golda Meir	Labor	March 1969–June 1974
Yitzhak Rabin	Labor	June 1974–June 1977
Menachem Begin	Likud	June 1977–October 1983
Yitzhak Shamir	Likud	October 1983–September 1984
Shimon Peres	Labor	Sept 1984–October 1986
Yitzhak Shamir	Likud	October 1986–July 1992
Yitzhak Rabin	Labor	July 1992–November 1995
Shimon Peres	Labor	November 1995–June 1996
Benjamin Netanyahu	Likud	June 1996–July 1999
Ehud Barak	Labor	July 1999–March 2001
Ariel Sharon	Likud/Kadima	March 2001–January 2006
Ehud Olmert	Kadima	Jan 2006–March 2009
Benjamin Netanyahu	Likud	March 2009–

PLO CHAIRMEN

Name	Party Affiliation	Time in Office
Ahmad Shukeiri	—	June 1964–December 1967
Yahya Hammuda	—	December 1967–February 1969
Yasser Arafat	Fatah	February 1969–November 2004
Mahmoud Abbas	Fatah	November 2004–

PALESTINIAN PRESIDENTS

Name	Party Affiliation	Time in Office
Yasser Arafat	Fatah	July 1994–November 2004
Mahmoud Abbas	Fatah	January 2005–

PALESTINIAN PRIME MINISTERS

Name	Party Affiliation	Time in Office
Mahmoud Abbas	Fatah	March 2003–September 2003
Ahmed Qurei	Fatah	October 2003–March 2006
Ismail Haniya	Hamas	March 2006–June 2007
Ismail Haniya	Hamas	June 2007– (Gaza only)
Salem Fayad	Fatah	June 2007–April 2013 (West Bank only)
Rami Hamdallah	Fatah	June 2013– (West Bank only)

INTRODUCTION

1. Edward Shepherd Creasy, *The Fifteen Decisive Battles of the World: From Marathon to Waterloo* (New York: Burt, 1851).

2. Ian Lustick, "To Build and Be Built By: Israel and the Hidden Logic of the Iron Wall," *Israel Studies* 1, no. 1 (Summer 1996): 207.

1. WHAT IS THE OCCUPATION?

1. Tal Kopan and Elise Labott, "Hillary Clinton's Views on Israel Win Out in DNC Platform, for Now," CNN, June 26, 2016, www.cnn.com/2016/06/24/politics /hillary-clinton-israel-dnc-platform/; Tal Kopan, "GOP Moves to the Right on Israel," CNN, July 11, 2016, www.cnn.com/2016/07/11/politics/gop-platform -republican-convention-israel/.

2. Natasha Roth, "Most Israeli Jews Think There's No Occupation: So What Is It?," +972, May 11, 2016, http://972mag.com/most-israeli-jews-think-theres-no -occupation-so-what-is-it/119245/.

3. "Deputy Defense Minister for Education: We Need to Educate Students on the Occupation" [in Hebrew], *Walla!*, June 16, 2016, http://news.walla.co.il /item/2971062.

4. Avi Raz, *The Bride and the Dowry: Israel, Jordan, and the Palestinians in the Aftermath of the June 1967 War* (New Haven, CT: Yale University Press, 2012), 39.

5. Fatma Müge Göçek, *Denial of Violence: Ottoman Past, Turkish Present, and Collective Violence against the Armenians, 1789–2009* (Oxford: Oxford University Press, 2015), 8–9.

6. Eva Illouz, "Israel Is in National Denial Regarding Its Oppression of Palestinians," *Haaretz*, November 11, 2015, www.haaretz.com/peace/1.685389#!.

7. Mark Hoofnagle, "Denialism: About," April 30, 2007, http://scienceblogs.com/denialism/about.

8. Neve Gordon, *Israel's Occupation* (Berkeley: University of California Press, 2008), 100–106.

9. Saree Makdisi, *Palestine Inside Out: An Everyday Occupation* (New York: Norton, 2008), 103–4.

10. Association for Civil Rights in Israel, "East Jerusalem 2015: Facts and Figures," May 2015, www.acri.org.il/en/wp-content/uploads/2015/05/EJ-Facts-and-Figures-2015.pdf.

11. Baruch Kimmerling, *The Israeli State and Society: Boundaries and Frontiers* (Albany, State University of New York Press, 1989), 266, 280.

12. "Judgments of the Israel Supreme Court: Fighting Terrorism within the Law," Jewish Virtual Library, January 2, 2005, www.jewishvirtuallibrary.org/jsource/Politics/terrorirm_law.pdf, 86–89.

13. David Kretzmer, *The Occupation of Justice: The Supreme Court of Israel and the Occupied Territories* (Albany, SUNY Press, 2002), 61, 188.

14. Lisa Hajjar, *Courting Conflict: The Israeli Military Court System in the West Bank and Gaza* (Berkeley: University of California Press, 2005), 3, 44, 185.

15. HCJ 7015/02, Adjuri v. the Commander of the IDF Forces in the West Bank, in High Court of Justice, *Judgments of the Supreme Court*, vol. 1, para. 16, p. 157.

16. Yoram Dinstein, *The International Law of Belligerent Occupation* (Cambridge: Cambridge University Press, 2009), 85.

17. UN General Assembly, Report of the Secretary-General Prepared Pursuant to General Assembly Resolution ES-10/13, November 24, 2003, Annex I, Summary Legal Position of the Government of Israel, para. 4, www.icj-cij.org/docket/files/131/1497.pdf.

18. International Court of Justice, "Legal Consequences of the Construction of a Wall in the Occupied Palestinian Territory," Advisory Opinion, July 9, 2004, www.icj-cij.org/docket/files/131/1671.pdf, 180.

19. Kretzmer, *Occupation of Justice*, 197.

20. Hajjar, *Courting Conflict*, 107.

21. Kretzmer, *Occupation of Justice*, 188.

22. Ibid., 23–24.

23. "Secret Documents Reveal How Israel Tried to Evade International Scrutiny of Occupation," *Haaretz*, September 20, 2016, www.haaretz.com/israel-news/.premium-1.742757.

24. Ibid.

25. Hajjar, *Courting Conflict*, 53–56.

26. Eyal Benvenisti, *The International Law of Occupation*, 2nd ed. (Princeton, NJ: Princeton University Press, 2012), 1.

27. Makdisi, *Palestine Inside Out*, 1–14.

28. Hajjar, *Courting Conflict*, 28.

29. James Ron, *Frontiers and Ghettos: State Violence in Serbia and Israel* (Berkeley, University of California Press, 2003), 8–9.

30. Kretzmer, *Occupation of Justice*, 189.

31. *Yedioth Aharanot*, September 3, 1993, 4.

32. Gershon Shafir, "Torturing Democracies: The Curious Debate over the 'Israeli Model,'" in *National Insecurity and Human Rights: Democracies Debate Counterterrorism*, ed. Alison Brysk and Gershon Shafir (Berkeley: University of California Press, 2007), 98, 114.

33. "Chief Justice Decries Politicization of Supreme Court," *Jerusalem World News*, December 2, 2011, http://jerusalemworldnews.com/2011/12/02/chief-justice-decries-politicization-of-supreme-court/; *Times of Israel*, November 3, 2016.

34. Gordon, *Israel's Occupation*, 48–69; Rema Hammami and Salim Tamari, "Towards a Second Partition: Re-thinking Forty Years of Israeli Rule," *MIT Electronic Journal of Middle East Studies*, Spring 2008, 26–31.

35. Raz, *Bride and the Dowry*.

36. Gershon Shafir and Yoav Peled, *Being Israeli: The Dynamics of Multiple Citizenship* (Cambridge: Cambridge University Press, 2002), 184–90.

37. Geoffrey Aronson, *Creating Facts: Israel, Palestinians, and the West Bank* (Washington, DC: Institute for Palestinian Studies, 1987), 24.

38. "We Called It 'Enlightened Occupation,'" June 2007, reposted 2012, *Friends of George* (blog), www.hahem.co.il/friendsofgeorge/?p=3188; Gazit

Shlomo, *Trapped Fools: Thirty Years of Israeli Policy in the Territories* (London: Frank Cass, 2003).

39. *The Gatekeepers*, dir. Dror Moreh, 2012; Asawin Suebsaeng, "In 'The Gatekeepers' Israeli Security Chiefs Say What US Leaders Can't," *Mother Jones*, February 22, 2013.

40. Ariella Azoulay and Adi Ophir, *The One-State Condition: Occupation and Democracy in Israel/Palestine* (Stanford, CA: Stanford University Press, 2013), 127–33.

41. Adi Ophir, Michal Givoni, and Sari Hanafi, *The Power of Inclusive Exclusion: Anatomy of Israeli Rule in the Occupied Palestinian Territories* (New York: Zone Books, 2009), 20.

42. Yael Berda, *The Bureaucracy of the Occupation: The Permit Regime in the West Bank, 2000–2006* [in Hebrew] (Jerusalem: Van Leer, 2012), 111–32; Gordon, *Israel's Occupation*, 33–40, 160–63.

43. B'Tselem, *Collaborators in the Occupied Territories: Human Rights Abuses and Violations*, January 1994, www.btselem.org/download/199401_collaboration_suspects_eng.doc.

44. B'Tselem, *Deportation of Palestinians from the Occupied Territories and the Mass Deportation of December 1992*, June 1993, www.btselem.org/download/199306_deportation_eng.doc.

45. B'Tselem, "House Demolitions as Punishment," January 1, 2011, updated November 26, 2014, www.btselem.org/punitive_demolitions.

46. Jeff Halper, *Obstacles to Peace*, 4th ed. (Jerusalem: ICAHD, 2009), 57–72.

47. Landau Commission, "Commission of Inquiry into the Methods of Investigation of the General Security Service Regarding Hostile Terrorist Activity: Report," October 1987, www.hamoked.org/files/2012/115020_eng.pdf, secs. 2.27, 2.30, 2.36, 3.16.

48. *B'Tselem Quarterly for Human Rights in the Occupied Territories*, no. 1, December 1998, www.btselem.org/download/199812_issue1_eng.pdf, 6.

49. Shafir, "Torturing Democracies."

50. Lisa Hajjar, "Sovereign Bodies, Sovereign States and the Problem of Torture," *Studies in Law, Politics, and Society* 21 (2000): 105.

51. Shafir, "Torturing Democracies."

52. "Israel: 'Not Enough Evidence' to Convict Duma Arsonists," *Middle East Eye*, December 15, 2015, updated December 22, 2015, www.middleeasteye.net /news/israel-not-enough-evidence-convict-douma-arsonists-47834863.

53. Gordon, *Israel's Occupation*, 107–14.

54. Shafir and Peled, *Being Israeli*, 184–210.

55. On the "hurting stalemate," see I. William Zartman, "The Timing of Peace Initiatives: Hurting Stalemates and Ripe Moments," *Global Review of Ethnopolitics* 1, no. 1 (September 2001): 8–18, http://peacemaker.un.org/sites /peacemaker.un.org/files/TimingofPeaceInitiatives_Zartman2001.pdf.

56. Marwan Darweish and Andrew Rigby, *Popular Protest in Palestine: The History and Uncertain Future of Unarmed Resistance* (London: Pluto, 2015), 65–70.

57. Bader Araj, "From Religion to Revenge: Becoming a Hamas Suicide Bomber," in *Struggle and Survival in Palestine/Israel*, ed. Mark LeVine and Gershon Shafir (Berkeley: University of California Press, 2012), 372–83.

58. Zaki Shalom and Yoaz Hendel, "The Unique Features of the Second Intifada," *Military and Strategic Affairs* 3, no. 1 (May 2011): 18–19.

59. Ariel Handel, "Where, Where to, and When in the Occupied Territories: An Introduction to Geography of Disaster," in Ophir, Givoni, and Hanafi, *Power of Inclusive Exclusion*, 106, 113.

60. B'Tselem, "The Separation Barrier," January 1, 2011, www.btselem.org /print/51724; B'Tselem, "The Separation Barrier—Statistics," January 1, 2011, updated July 16, 2012, www.btselem.org/print/51702; UN Office for the Coordination of Humanitarian Affairs, "The Humanitarian Impact of the Barrier," July 2013, https://www.ochaopt.org/documents/ocha_opt_barrier_factsheet_ july_2013_english.pdf; Halper, *Obstacles to Peace*, 51.

61. Ariel Handel, "Gated/Gating Community: The Settlement Complex in the West Bank," *Transactions of the Institute of British Geographers* 39, no. 4 (October 2014): 504.

62. Ariel Handel, "Exclusionary Surveillance and Spatial Uncertainty in the Occupied Palestinian Territories," in *Surveillance and Control in Israel/Palestine; Population, Territory and Power*, ed. Elia Zureik, David Lyon, and Yasmeen Abu-Laban (New York: Routledge, 2011), 260–61, 269.

63. Handel, "Gated/Gating Community," 268.

64. Handel, "Where, Where to," in Ophir, Givoni, and Hanafi, *Power of Inclusive Exclusion*, 193.

65. UN Secretary General, "Report of the Secretary-General's Panel of Inquiry on the 31 May 2010 Flotilla Incident," September 2011, www.un.org /News/dh/infocus/middle_east/Gaza_Flotilla_Panel_Report.pdf; UN General Assembly, "Human Rights in Palestine and Other Occupied Arab Territories," September 23, 2009, http://www2.ohchr.org/english/bodies/hrcouncil /docs/12session/A-HRC-12-48_ADVANCE1.pdf.

66. Bradley Burston, "The Occupation Makes Israelis Stupid," *Haaretz*, November 9, 2015.

67. Hammami and Tamari, "Towards a Second Partition," 38.

68. Vladimir Ze'ev Jabotinsky, "The Iron Wall" (November 4, 1923), Jewish Virtual Library, www.jewishvirtuallibrary.org/jsource/Zionism/ironwall.html.

69. Eyal Weizman, *Hollow Land: Israel's Architecture of Occupation* (London: Verso, 2007), 87.

70. Raz, *Bride and the Dowry*, 262–80.

71. Gershom Goremberg, *The Accidental Empire: Israel and the Birth of Settlements, 1967–1977* (New York: Times Books, 2006), 118, 205–7.

72. Shafir and Peled, *Being Israeli*, 161–64.

73. "In 1976 Interview, Rabin Likens Settler Ideologues to 'Cancer,' Warns of 'Apartheid,'" *Times of Israel*, September 25, 2015.

74. Shafir and Peled, *Being Israeli*, 172–39.

75. Halper, *Obstacles to Peace*, 50.

76. Moriel Ram and Mark LeVine, "The Village against the Settlement: Two Generations of Conflict in the Nablus Region," in LeVine and Shafir, *Struggle and Survival*, 321.

77. Assaf Gavron, *The Hilltop* (New York: Scribner, 2013), 24.

78. B'Tselem, *Land Grab: Israel's Settlement Policy in the West Bank*, 2002, https://www.btselem.org/download/200205_land_grab_eng.pdf, 20.

79. Halper, *Obstacles to Peace*, 55.

80. Ophir, Givoni, and Hanafi, *Power of Inclusive Exclusion*, 604.

81. B'Tselem, *By Hook and by Crook: Israeli Settlement Policy in the West Bank*, 2010, https://www.btselem.org/download/201007_by_hook_and_by_crook_eng.pdf, 25–26.

82. B'Tselem, *Land Grab*, 47.

83. Ibid., 58–59.

84. B'Tselem, *Land Grab*, 60–61; B'Tselem, *By Hook and by Crook*, 29–30.

85. B'Tselem, *Land Grab*, 48–51; B'Tselem, *By Hook and by Crook*, 22–23.

86. Daniel Kurtzer, "Behind the Settlements," *American Interest*, March 2, 2010, 9.

87. B'Tselem, *By Hook and by Crook*, 24.

88. Ibid., 25–26.

89. B'Tselem, *Land Grab*, 55–58.

90. B'Tselem, *By Hook and by Crook*, 28–29.

91. Talia Sasson, "Summary of the Opinion Concerning Unauthorized Outpost," Office of the Israeli Prime Minister, March 10, 2005, www.mfa.gov.il/mfa /aboutisrael/state/law/pages/summary%20of%20opinion%20concerning%20 unauthorized%20outposts%20-%20talya%20sason%20adv.aspx, retranslated.

92. Amos Harel, "Settlements Grow on Arab Land, Despite Promises Made to U.S.," *Haaretz*, October 24, 2006.

93. Uri Blau, "Secret Israeli Database Reveals Full Extent of Illegal Settlements," *Haaretz*, January 30, 2009, www.israeli-occupation.org/2009-01-30 /secret-israeli-database-reveals-full-extent-of-illegal-settlement/.

94. B'Tselem, *By Hook and by Crook*, 33.

95. Ibid., 31–32.

96. Lauren Benton, *A Search for Sovereignty: Law and Geography in European Empires, 1460–1900* (Cambridge: Cambridge University Press, 2010), 28–29.

97. "Stav Shaffir: Netanyahu Has Led to the Disintegration of the Zionist Dream," *Haaretz*, October 15, 2015, www.haaretz.com/israel-news/1.680527.

98. Mark W. Zacher, "The Territorial Integrity Norm: International Boundaries and the Use of Force," *International Organization* 55, no. 2 (Spring 2001): 244–46.

99. *Jerusalem Post*, June 3, 2014.

2. WHY HAS THE OCCUPATION LASTED THIS LONG?

1. Gershon Shafir and Yoav Peled, *Being Israeli: The Dynamics of Multiple Citizenship* (Cambridge: Cambridge University Press, 2002), 163–64; Gershon Shafir, "The Jarring Mission" [in Hebrew], in *Fifty to Forty-Eight: Critical Moments in the History of the State of Israel* (Jerusalem: Van Leer Institute, 1999), 205–13.

2. Martin Gilbert, *Jewish History Atlas*, 3rd ed. (London: Weidenfeld and Nicolson, 1985).

3. D. K. Fieldhouse, *The Colonial Empires from the Eighteenth Century* (New York: Weidenfeld and Nicolson, 1966); George Fredrickson, "Colonialism and Racism: The United States and South Africa in Comparative Perspective," in *The Arrogance of Race: Historical Perspectives on Slavery, Racism, and Social Inequality* (Middletown, CT: Wesleyan University Press, 1988), 216–35; Caroline Elkins and Susan Pedersen, *Settler Colonialism in the Twentieth Century: Project, Practices, Legacies* (New York: Routledge, 2005).

4. Quoted in Lorenzo Veracini, *Settler Colonialism: A Theoretical Overview* (New York: Palgrave Macmillan, 2010), 3.

5. Ibid., 14–15.

6. Chaim Weizmann, *The Letters and Papers of Chaim Weizmann*, vol. 2, series B (New Brunswick, NJ: Transaction, 1984), 102.

7. Elkins and Pedersen, *Settler Colonialism*.

8. Shafir and Peled, *Being Israeli*, 160–61.

9. David Kretzmer, *The Occupation of Justice: The Supreme Court of Israel and the Occupied Territories* (Albany: SUNY Press, 2002), 81.

10. Council for Peace and Security, "The Settlements Do Not Contribute to Security" [in Hebrew], June 2012, www.peace-security.org.il/uploads/file /%D7%9E%D7%A1%D7%9E%D7%9A%20%D7%94%D7%94%D7%AA%D7%A0% D7%97%D7%9C%D7%95%D7%99%D7%95%D7%AA-%20%D7%A1%D7%95% D7%A4%D7%99.pdf.

11. Shafir and Peled, *Being Israeli*.

12. Anita Shapira, *Futile Struggle: The Jewish Labor Controversy, 1929–1939* [in Hebrew] (Tel Aviv: Hakibbutz Hameuchad, 1977), 26.

13. Gershon Shafir, *Land, Labor and the Origins of the Israeli–Palestinian Conflict, 1882–1914* (Cambridge: Cambridge University Press, 1989), 214–20.

14. Gershom Goremberg, *The Accidental Empire: Israel and the Birth of Settlements, 1967–1977* (New York: Times Books, 2006), 281–95.

15. Yonathan Shapiro, *An Elite without Successors: Generations of Political Leaders in Israel* [in Hebrew] (Tel Aviv: Sifriyat Hapoalim, 1984).

16. Meron Benvenisti and Shlomo Khayat, *The West Bank and Gaza Atlas* (Jerusalem: West Bank Data Base Project, 1988), 33, table 3.

17. Shmuel Sandler, "The National Religious Party: Towards a New Role in Israel's Political System," in *Public Life in Israel and the Diaspora*, ed. Sam

N. Lehman-Wilzig and Bernard Susser (Jerusalem: Bar-Ilan University Press, 1981), 164.

18. Janet O'Dea, "Gush Emunim: Roots and Ambiguities," *Forum on the Jewish People, Zionism, and Israel* 2, no. 25 (1976): 40-41.

19. Howard M. Sachar, *A History of Israel*, vol. 2, *From the Aftermath of the Yom Kippur War* (New York: Oxford University Press, 1987), 17.

20. Shafir and Peled, *Being Israeli*, 168-71.

21. Ian S. Lustick, *For the Land and the Lord: The Range of Disagreement within Jewish Fundamentalism* (New York: Council on Foreign Relations, 1988), chap. 5, www.sas.upenn.edu/penncip/lustick/lustick15.html.

22. Ehud Sprintzak, *The Ascendance of Israel's Radical Right* (Oxford: Oxford University Press, 1991), 94-99.

23. Joel Bin-Nun, "Intellectuals—Including Me—Failed: We Could Not Settle in the Hearts" [in Hebrew], September 23, 2014, http://archive.is/yoWr6.

24. Nissim Leon, "The Transformation of Israel's Religious-Zionist Middle Class," *Journal of Israeli History* 29, no. 1 (March 2010): 62-65.

25. Shlomo Swirski, "1967: A Political-Economic Turning Point in Israel" [in Hebrew], in *Society and Economy in Israel*, ed. Avi Bareli (Beer Sheva: Ben Gurion University, 2005), 109.

26. Yagil Levy, *The Divine Commander: The Theocratization of the Israeli Military* [in Hebrew] (Tel Aviv: Am Oved, 2015), 94-96, 128.

27. Uri Orbach, "The Best to the Media" [in Hebrew], Channel 7, January 9, 1987, www.inn.co.il/Forum/Forum.aspx/t700790.

28. Yair Sheleg, "The Next Target: The Conquest of the Media" [in Hebrew], in *Journalists Yearbook, 1998* (Tel Aviv: Journalists Association, 1998).

29. Levy, *Divine Commander*, 357-67.

30. "IDF Commander Seeks God's Help to Fight 'Blasphemous' Gazans," *Times of Israel*, July 12, 2014.

31. Amos Harel and Gili Cohen, "In War over Israeli Hearts and Minds, Army Becomes Ideological Battlefield," *Haaretz*, August 13, 2016.

32. "The Post That Excites the Settlers of Judea and Samaria: 'Our Lives Have Been Ruined, We Can No Longer Go On,'" *Maariv*, July 7, 2016, www.maariv.co.il/news/politics/Article-548366.

33. "Amana: The Settlement Movement," n.d., accessed November 22, 2016, www.amana.co.il/?CategoryID=101&ArticleID=166.

34. Eldad Karni and Shlomo Bashan, *Yesha Is Fun: The Good Life Guide to Judea and Samaria* (Jerusalem: Carta, 2013).

35. Ron Pundak, *Secret Channel* [in Hebrew] (Tel Aviv: Aliyat Gag, 2013), 368–407.

36. Ibid., 385.

37. George M. Fredrickson, *White Supremacy: A Comparative Study of American and South African History* (Oxford: Oxford University Press, 1981), 5.

38. Gershon Shafir, "Israeli-Palestinian Peacemaking and Its Discontents," *Contexts* 6, no. 4 (Fall 2007): 46–51, http://icga.blogspot.com/2007/11/israeli-palestinian-peacemaking-and-its.html.

39. Ayelet Waldman, "The Shame of Shuhada Street," *Atlantic*, June 24, 2014.

40. Shafir, "Israeli-Palestinian Peacemaking."

41. Ian Lustick, "To Build and to Be Built By: Israel and the Hidden Logic of the Iron Wall," *Israel Studies* 1, no. 1 (Summer 1996): 203.

42. Ibid., 207–19.

43. Charles D. Smith, *Palestine and the Arab-Israeli Conflict*, 5th ed. (New York: St. Martin's, 2004), 419–24, 437–45.

44. Michael L. Gross, "Regulating Torture in a Democracy: Death Indignity in Israel," *Polity* 36, no. 3 (April 2004): 370.

45. Shafir, "Israeli-Palestinian Peacemaking," 49.

46. Smith, *Palestine*, 397–98.

47. Shafir, "Israeli-Palestinian Peacemaking," 49.

48. Smith, *Palestine*, 457.

49. Ibid., 505.

50. Nada Matta and René Rojas, "The Second Intifada: A Dual Strategy Arena," *European Journal of Sociology* 57, no. 1 (2016): 67, 75, 80–84, 94.

51. Mia Bloom, "Palestinian Suicide Bombing: Public Support, Market Share, and Outbidding," *Political Science Quarterly* 119, no. 1 (Spring 2004): 73–75.

52. Ibid., 106.

53. Rashid Khalidi, *The Iron Cage: The Story of the Palestinian Struggle for State-hood* (Boston: Beacon Press, 2006), xxiv–xxv, 178.

54. Joe Stork, *Erased in a Moment: Suicide Bombing Attacks against Israeli Civilians* (New York: Human Rights Watch, 2002), https://books.google.com/books?id=TKHJvScrNO8C&pg=PA124&dq=HRW:+%E2%80%9CErased+in+a+Moment%E2%80%9Dviolence&hl=en&sa=X&ved=0ahUKEwi4kPeSoK7QAhUNxmMKHT3

HBmwQ6AEIHTAA#v=onepage&q=HRW%3A%20%E2%80%9CErased%20in%20a%20Moment%E2%80%9Dviolence&f=false.

55. Shaul Mishal and Avraham Sela, *The Palestinian Hamas: Vision, Violence, and Coexistence* (New York: Columbia University Press, 2006), ix.

56. Sara Roy, *Hamas and Civil Society in Gaza: Engaging the Islamic Social Sector* (Princeton, NJ: Princeton University Press, 2011), 48–49.

57. Jay Solomon and Julien Barnes-Dacey, "Hamas Chief Outlines Terms for Talks on Arab-Israeli Peace," *Wall Street Journal*, July 31, 2009, www.wsj.com /articles/SB124899975954495435; "Mashal: Hamas Is No IS, Will Accept State Based on '67 Lines," *Times of Israel*, July 27, 2016.

58. Glenn E. Robinson, "Hamas as Social Movement," in *Islamic Activism: A Social Movement Approach*, ed. Quintan Wiktorowicz (Bloomington: Indiana University Press, 2004), 112–39.

59. Ibid., 117–23.

60. Ibid., 126–29; Matthew Levitt, *Hamas: Politics, Charity, and Terrorism in the Service of Jihad* (New Haven, CT: Yale University Press, 2006), 24.

61. Levitt, *Hamas*, 17.

62. Eli Berman, *Radical, Religious, and Violent: The New Economics of Terrorism* (Cambridge, MA: MIT Press, 2009).

63. Lori Allen, *The Rise and Fall of Human Rights: Cynicism and Politics in Occupied Palestine* (Stanford, CA: Stanford University Press, 2013), 12–15, 160–64.

64. Robert O. Freedman, ed., *Israel and the United States: Six Decades of US-Israeli Relations* (Boulder, CO: Westview, 2012), 2.

65. Smith, *Palestine*, 298.

66. Karen Puschel, *US-Israeli Strategic Cooperation in the Post-Cold War Era* (Boulder, CO: Westview, 1992), 2–22.

67. Ibid., 95.

68. Peter Beinart, "The Failure of the American Jewish Establishment," *New York Review of Books*, June 10, 2010.

69. Dov Waxman, *Trouble in the Tribe: The American Jewish Conflict over Israel* (Princeton, NJ: Princeton University Press, 2016).

70. John Mearsheimer and Stephen Walt, "The Israel Lobby," *London Review of Books*, March 23, 2006, www.lrb.co.uk/v28/n06/john-mearsheimer/the-israel-lobby.

71. Lara Friedman, "Israel's Unsung Protector: Obama," *New York Times*, April 10, 2016.

72. US Department of State, "Recent Israeli Settlement Announcements," press release, July 27, 2016, www.state.gov/r/pa/prs/ps/2016/07/260577.htm.

73. Gen. David Petraeus, Statement before the Senate Armed Services Committee, Washington, March 16, 2010 (Excerpts), *Journal of Palestine Studies* 39, no. 4 (Summer 2010): 175–76.

74. Eric Cortellessa, "Ex-general and Settlements Critic Mattis Named New US Defense Secretary," *Times of Israel*, December 2, 2016, www .timesofisrael.com/ex-general-and-settlements-critic-mattis-named-new-us- defense-secretary/.

75. Eyal Weizman, *Hollow Land: Israel's Architecture of Occupation* (London: Verso, 2007), 103.

76. Ibid.

77. Orna Ben-Naftali, *International Humanitarian Law and International Human Rights Law: Pas de Deux* (Oxford: Oxford University Press, 2011), 153–55.

78. Ariella Azoulay and Adi Ophir, *The One-State Condition: Occupation and Democracy in Israel/Palestine* (Stanford, CA: Stanford University Press, 2013), 14–18.

79. Orna Ben-Naftali, Aeyal M. Gross, and Keren Michaeli, "Illegal Occupation: Framing the Occupied Palestinian Territory," *Berkeley Journal of International Law* 23, no. 3 (2005): 552.

80. Susan Pedersen, *The Guardians: The League of Nations and the Crisis of Empire* (Oxford: Oxford University Press, 2015).

81. Ibid., 4.

82. Beshara Doumani, "Palestine versus the Palestinians? The Iron Laws and Ironies of a People Denied," *Journal of Palestine Studies* 36, no. 4 (Summer 2007): 49–52.

83. Yehouda Shenhav, "What Is the Color of Critical Theory: Reflections on Post-Westphalian Sovereignty" [in Hebrew], *Teoriya Vebikoret*, 2009, 24–48.

84. Baruch Kimmerling, *Zionism and Territory* (Berkeley: Institute of International Studies, 1983), 27, 134, 139, 146.

85. Dan Rabinowitz, *Overlooking Nazareth: The Ethnography of Exclusion in Galilee* (Cambridge: Cambridge University Press, 1997), 77.

86. Lisa Hajjar, "Roundtable on Occupation Law: Part II," *Jadaliyya*, September 22, 2011, www.jadaliyya.com/pages/index/2698/roundtable-on-occupation-law_part-of-the-conflict-.

87. Eyal Benvenisti, *The International Law of Occupation*, 2nd ed. (Oxford: Oxford University Press, 2012), 318–51.

88. Ben-Naftali, Gross, and Michaeli, "Illegal Occupation."

89. Aslı Ü. Bâli, "Roundtable on Occupation Law: Part IV," and Darryl Li, "Roundtable on Occupation Law: Part VI," *Jadaliyya*, September 22, 2011, www.jadaliyya.com/pages/index/7325/roundtable-on-occupation-law_part-of-the-conflict.

3. HOW HAS THE OCCUPATION TRANSFORMED THE ISRAELI–PALESTINIAN CONFLICT?

1. The following sections are based mostly on Clayton E. Swisher, *The Palestine Papers: The End of the Road?* (Chatham: Hesperus, 2011), and Elie Podeh, *Chances for Peace: Missed Opportunities in the Arab-Israeli Conflict* (Austin: University of Texas Press, 2015), 340–56.

2. Shelley Fried, "The Refugee Issue at the Peace Conference, 1949–2000," *Palestine-Israel Journal* 9, no. 2 (2002): 31.

3. Podeh, *Chances for Peace*, 285, 292–93.

4. Ilan Pappé, "The Visible and the Invisible in the Israeli-Palestinian Conflict," in *Exile and Return: Predicaments of Palestinians and Jews*, ed. Ann M. Lesch and Ian S. Lustick (Philadelphia: University of Pennsylvania Press, 2005), 279.

5. Podeh, *Chances for Peace*, 318.

6. Ibid., 305.

7. Edward Walsh, "Study Warns That Israel May Have an Irreversible Grip on West Bank," *Washington Post*, April 24, 1984.

8. Ari Shavit, "We've Entered the Final Decade to Save Israel," *Haaretz*, December 24, 2015.

9. The data below appear either on Arieli's website, www.shaularieli.com/?lat=en, in his Facebook posts, or in his *Haaretz* articles, in either Hebrew or English, frrom the following dates: October 3, 2012, July 22, 2013, March 16, 2015, November 4, 2015, and March 16, 2016. Shaul Arieli, "West Bank Settlement Blocs Blocking Israel's Progress towards Stability," *Haaretz*, March 14, 2016.

10. CBS, Labor Force Survey for 2015; *Haaretz,* January 30, 2014.

11. Shaul Arieli, "The Settlement Enterprise Has Failed," *Haaretz,* November 17, 2015.

12. B'Tselem, *Land Grab,* 70.

13. Jeff Halper, *Obstacles to Peace,* 4th ed. (Jerusalem: ICAHD, 2009), 47–57; ICAHD, "The Matrix of Control: An Introduction," n.d., http://icahd.org /resources/matrix-of-control-videos/the-matrix-of-control/.

14. *Haaretz,* November 4, 2015.

15. Arieli, "West Bank Settlement Blocs."

16. Nissim Leon, "The Transformation of Israel's Religious-Zionist Middle Class," *Journal of Israeli History* 29, no. 1 (March 2010): 69.

17. Ibid., 73–75.

18. "Palestinian-Israeli Pulse," *PSR,* August 22, 2016, www.pcpsr.org/en /node/660.

19. Institute for Palestine Studies, "Senior Fellow Mouin Rabbani: 'Ignore Palestine at Your Peril,'" *Palestine Square* (blog), May 23, 2016, http://blog.palestine-studies.org/2016/05/23/mouin-rabbani-ignore-palestine-at-your-peril/.

20. Arend Lijphart, *Democracy in Plural Societies* (New Haven, CT: Yale University Press, 1977).

21. The following discussion is based on Gershon Shafir, "Capitalist Binationalism in Mandatory Palestine," *International Journal of Middle Eastern Studies* 43 (2011): 611–33.

22. Quoted in ibid., 629.

23. Ali Abunimah, *One Country: A Bold Proposal to End the Israeli-Palestinian Impasse.* (New York: Metropolitan, 2006), 105–9; Mark Tessler, *A History of the Israeli-Palestinian Conflict,* 2nd ed. (Bloomington: Indiana University Press, 2009), 433–45.

24. Brandan O'Leary, "The Iron Law of Nationalism and Federation?," *Nations and Nationalism* 7, no. 3 (2001): 284–91.

25. Sergio DellaPergola, *Jewish Demographic Policies: Population Trends and Options in Israel and in the Diaspora* (Jerusalem: Jewish People Policy Institute, 2011), http://jppi.org.il/uploads/Jewish_Demographic_Policies.pdf.

26. John Rawls, "Justice as Fairness: Political Not Metaphysical," *Philosophy and Public Affairs* 14, no. 3 (Summer 1985): 245.

27. Charles Taylor, "Shared and Divergent Values," in *Options for a New Canada*, ed. Ronald Watts and D. Brow (Toronto: Toronto University Press, 1991), 76; Will Kymlicka, *Multicultural Citizenship: A Liberal Theory of Minority Rights* (Oxford: Clarendon, 1995), 191.

28. Leila Farsakh, "The One-State Solution and the Israeli-Palestinian Conflict: Palestinian Challenges and Prospects," *Middle East Journal* 65, no. 1 (Winter 2011): 70.

29. Manuel Hassassian, "Palestinian Political Culture, Civil Society, and the Conception of Citizenship," in *Citizenship and the State in the Middle East*, edited by Nils Butenschon, Uri Davis, and Manuel Hassassian (Syracuse, NY: Syracuse University Press, 2000), 253–62.

30. Abunimah, *One Country*, 105, 109.

31. Ibid., 105, 110–11.

32. Noura Erakat, "Rethinking Israel-Palestine: Beyond Bantustans, beyond Reservations," *Nation*, March 21, 2013, https://www.thenation.com/article/rethinking-israel-palestine-beyond-bantustans-beyond-reservations/.

33. Noura Erakat, "Even One State May Not Be Enough," *Jaddaliya*, November 12, 2013, www.jadaliyya.com/pages/index/15082/co-editors-mouin-rabbani-and-noura-erakat-and-o.i.

34. Ibid.

35. Omar Barghouti, *BDS: Boycott, Divestment, Sanctions: The Global Struggle for Palestinian Rights* (Chicago: Haymarket, 2011).

36. BDS, "What Is BDS?," n.d., accessed November 21, 2016, https://bdsmovement.net/what-is-bds.

37. Omar Barghouti, "Omar Barghouti on 'Why BDS?'," *Mondoweiss*, April 6, 2011, http://mondoweiss.net/2011/04/omar-barghouti-on-why-bds/.

38. Abraham Greenhouse, "'Hypocrisy-Seeking Missile': Omar Barghouti's 'BDS' Reviewed," Electronic Intifada, April 22, 2011, https://electronicintifada.net/content/hypocrisy-seeking-missile-omar-barghoutis-bds-reviewed/9866.

39. Shula Marks, "The Tradition of Non-racism in South Africa," paper presented at the History Workshop, University of Witwatersrand, Johannesburg, July 13–15, 1994; C. R. D. Halisi, *Black Political Thought in the Making of South African Democracy* (Bloomington: Indiana University Press, 1999), 65.

40. Omar Barghouti, "Opting for Justice: The Critical Role of Anti-colonial Israelis in the Boycott, Divestment, and Sanctions Movement," *Settler Colonial Studies* 4, no. 4 (2014): 408–9.

41. Todd Gitlin, "Against Abnormalization: BDS Targets a Major Lebanese-Born Writer," *Tablet*, June 23, 2016, www.tabletmag.com/jewish-arts-and-culture/205968/bds-targets-lebanese-born-writer.

42. Gail M. Gerhart, *Black Power in South Africa: The Evolution of an Ideology* (Berkeley: University of California Press, 1978), 67.

43. Molefe Mafole, "The Pan Africanist Congress of Azania, 1959–1990," in *South Africa: The Dynamics and Prospects of Transformation*, ed. Sipho Buthelezi (Harare: Sapens, 1995), 47–52.

44. Halisi, *Black Political Thought*, 13–14, 110–31; Mokgethi Motlhabi, "Struggle for a Birthright: The Enduring Challenge of the Black Consciousness Movement in South Africa," in Buthelezi, *South Africa*, 64–68.

45. "PACBI: West-Eastern Divan Orchestra Violates Boycott," *Electronic Intifada*, March 24, 2010, https://electronicintifada.net/content/pacbi-west-eastern-divan-orchestra-violates-boycott/1040.

46. Ian Black, "Palestinian Professor: No Regrets over Taking Students to Auschwitz," *Guardian*, June 13, 2014, https://www.theguardian.com/world/2014/jun/13/palestinian-professor-resigns-students-auschwitz.

47. Amira Hass, "When a Haaretz Journalist Was Asked to Leave a Palestinian University," *Haaretz*, September 28, 2014.

48. Farsakh, "One-State Solution," 64.

49. E. J. Hobsbawm, *Primitive Rebels* (New York: Norton, 1959), 61–62.

50. Association for Civil Rights in Israel, *One Rule, Two Legal Systems: Israel's Regime of Laws in the West Bank*, October 2014, www.acri.org.il/en/wp-content/uploads/2015/02/Two-Systems-of-Law-English-FINAL.pdf.

51. "Life, Apartheid and Palestine: Michael Brull Meets John Dugard, South Africa's 'Father of Human Rights,'" *Newmatilda.com*, November 23, 2016, https://newmatilda.com/2016/11/23/life-apartheid-and-palestine-michael-brull-meets-john-dugard-south-africas-father-of-human-rights/.

52. Susan M. Akram, "Palestinian Refugees and Their Legal Status: Rights, Politics, and Implications for a Just Solution," *Journal of Palestine Studies* 31, no. 3 (Spring 2002): 42.

53. Ibid., 47–48.

54. Abbas Shiblak, "Passport for What Price? Statelessness among Palestinian Refugees," in *Palestinian Refugees: Identity, Space and Place in the Levant*, ed. Are Knudsen and Sari Hanafi (London: Routledge, 2011), 124–27.

55. Yoav Peled and Nadim N. Rouhana, "Transitional Justice and the Right of Return of the Palestinian Refugees," *Theoretical Inquiries in Law* 5, no. 2 (July 2004): 330–31.

56. Max Abrahms, "The 'Right of Return' Debate Revisited," *Middle East Intelligence Bulletin*, August–September 2003, Washington Institute, www.washingtoninstitute.org/policy-analysis/view/the-right-of-return-debate-revisited.

57. Shahira Samy, "Reparations to Palestinian Refugees: The Politics of Saying 'Sorry,'" In Knudsen and Hanafi, *Palestinian Refugees*, 151–56, 159–60.

58. Farsakh, "One-State Solution," 64–67.

59. "The Haifa Declaration," September 2007, http://mada-research.org/en/files/2007/09/haifaenglish.pdf.

60. *Jerusalem Post*, November 19, 2016.

61. Emilio Dabed, "PA Legislation and the Disciplinary Power of Law," paper presented at Annual New Directions in Palestine Studies Conference, March 3–4, 2016, Brown University.

62. Swisher, *Palestine Papers*, 45.

63. "Israel's Exceptionalism: Normalizing the Abnormal," October 31, 2011, Palestinian Campaign for the Academic and Cultural Boycott of Israel, www.pacbi.org/etemplate.php?id=1749.

64. Gerhart, *Black Power*, 55–67.

65. Mouin Rabbani, "Strategy before Solution," *Jaddaliya*, November 12, 2013, www.jadaliyya.com/pages/index/15082/co-editors-mouin-rabbani-and-noura-erakat-and-o.i.

Abunimah, Ali. *One Country: A Bold Proposal to End the Israeli-Palestinian Impasse*. New York: Metropolitan, 2006.

Akram, Susan M. "Palestinian Refugees and Their Legal Status: Rights, Politics, and Implications for a Just Solution." *Journal of Palestine Studies* 31, no. 3 (Spring 2002): 36–51.

Allen, Lori. *The Rise and Fall of Human Rights: Cynicism and Politics in Occupied Palestine*. Stanford, CA: Stanford University Press, 2013.

Araj, Bader. "From Religion to Revenge: Becoming a Hamas Suicide Bomber." In LeVine and Shafir, *Struggle and Survival*, 370–83.

Aronson, Geoffrey. *Creating Facts: Israel, Palestine, and the West Bank*. Washington, DC: Institute for Palestine Studies, 1987.

Azoulay, Ariella, and Adi Ophir. *The One-State Condition: Occupation and Democracy in Israel/Palestine*. Stanford, CA: Stanford University Press, 2013.

Barghouti, Omar. *BDS: Boycott, Divestment, Sanctions: The Global Struggle for Palestinian Rights*. Chicago: Haymarket, 2011.

———. "Opting for Justice: The Critical Role of Anti-colonial Israelis in the Boycott, Divestment, and Sanctions Movement." *Settler Colonial Studies* 4, no. 4 (2014): 407–12.

Beinart. Peter. *The Crisis of Zionism*. New York: Henry Holt, 2012.

Ben-Naftali, Orna. *International Humanitarian Law and International Human Rights Law: Pas de Deux*. Oxford: Oxford University Press, 2011.

Ben-Naftali, Orna, Aeyal M. Gross, and Keren Michaeli. "Illegal Occupation: Framing the Occupied Palestinian Territory." *Berkeley Journal of International Law* 23, no. 3 (2005): 551–614.

Benton, Lauren. *A Search for Sovereignty: Law and Geography in European Empires, 1400–1900*. Cambridge: Cambridge University Press, 2010.

Benvenisti, Eyal. *The International Law of Occupation*. 2nd ed. Oxford: Oxford University Press, 2012.

Benvenisti, Meron, and Shlomo Khayat. *The West Bank and Gaza Atlas*. Jerusalem: West Bank Data Base Project, 1988.

Berda, Yael. *The Bureaucracy of the Occupation: The Permit Regime in the West Bank, 2000–2006*. [In Hebrew.] Jerusalem: Van Leer, 2012.

Berman, Eli. *Radical, Religious, and Violent: The New Economics of Terrorism*. Cambridge, MA: MIT Press, 2009.

Bloom, Mia. "Palestinian Suicide Bombing: Public Support, Market Share, and Outbidding." *Political Science Quarterly* 119, no. 1 (Spring 2004): 61–88.

B'Tselem. *Deportation of Palestinians from the Occupied Territories and the Mass Deportation of December 1992*. June 1993. www.btselem.org/download/199306_deportation_eng.doc.

———. *Collaborators in the Occupied Territories: Human Rights Abuses and Violations*. January 1994. www.btselem.org/download/199401_collaboration_suspects_eng.doc.

———. *Land Grab: Israel's Settlement Policy in the West Bank*. 2002. https://www.btselem.org/download/200205_land_grab_eng.pdf.

———. *By Hook and by Crook: Israeli Settlement Policy in the West Bank*. 2010. https://www.btselem.org/download/201007_by_hook_and_by_crook_eng.pdf.

Butenschon, Nils, Uri Davis, and Manuel Hassassian, eds. *Citizenship and the State in the Middle East*. Syracuse, NY: Syracuse University Press, 2000.

Buthelezi, Sipho, ed. *South Africa: The Dynamics and Prospects of Transformation*. Harare: Sapens, 1995.

Creasy, Edward Shepherd. *The Fifteen Decisive Battles of the World: From Marathon to Waterloo*. New York: Burt, 1851.

Dabed, Emilio. "PA Legislation and the Disciplinary Power of Law." Paper presented at Annual New Directions in Palestine Studies Conference, March 3–4, 2016, Brown University.

Darweish, Marwan, and Andrew Rigby. *Popular Protest in Palestine: The History and Uncertain Future of Unarmed Resistance*. London: Pluto, 2015.

Dinstein, Yoram. *The International Law of Belligerent Occupation*. Cambridge: Cambridge University Press, 2009.

Doumani, Beshara. "Palestine versus the Palestinians? The Iron Laws and Ironies of a People Denied." *Journal of Palestine Studies* 36, no. 4 (Summer 2007): 49–64.

Durkheim, Emile. *Suicide*. New York: Free Press, 1951.

Elkins, Caroline, and Susan Pedersen. *Settler Colonialism in the Twentieth Century: Project, Practices, Legacies*. New York: Routledge, 2005.

Erakat, Noura. "Rethinking Israel-Palestine: Beyond Bantustans, Beyond Reservations." *Nation*, March 21, 2013. https://www.thenation.com/article/rethinking -israel-palestine-beyond-bantustans-beyond-reservations/.

———. "Even One State May Not Be Enough." *Jaddaliya*, November 12, 2013, www. jadaliyya.com/pages/index/15082/co-editors-mouin-rabbani-and- noura-erakat-and-o.i.

Farsakh, Leila. "The One-State Solution and the Israeli-Palestinian Conflict: Palestinian Challenges and Prospects." *Middle East Journal* 65, no. 1 (Winter 2011): 55–71.

Fieldhouse, D. K. *The Colonial Empires from the Eighteenth Century*. New York: Weidenfeld and Nicolson, 1966.

Fredrickson, George. "Colonialism and Racism: The United States and South Africa in Comparative Perspective." In *The Arrogance of Race: Historical Perspectives on Slavery, Racism, and Social Inequality*, 216–35. Middletown, CT: Wesleyan University Press, 1988.

Freedman, Robert O., ed. *Israel and the United States: Six Decades of US-Israeli Relations*. Boulder, CO: Westview, 2012.

Fried, Shelley. "The Refugee Issue at the Peace Conference, 1949–2000." *Palestine-Israel Journal* 9, no. 2 (2002): 24–34.

Gavron, Assaf. *The Hilltop*. New York: Scribner, 2013.

Gazit, Shlomo. *Trapped Fools: Thirty Years of Israeli Policy in the Territories*. London: Frank Cass, 2003.

Gerhart, Gail M. *Black Power in South Africa: The Evolution of an Ideology*. Berkeley: University of California Press, 1978.

Gilbert, Martin. *Jewish History Atlas.* 3rd ed. London: Weidenfeld and Nicolson, 1985.

Göçek, Fatma Müge. *Denial of Violence: Ottoman Past, Turkish Present, and Collective Violence against the Armenians, 1789-2009.* Oxford: Oxford University Press, 2015.

Gordon, Neve. *Israel's Occupation.* Berkeley: University of California Press, 2008.

Goremberg, Gershom. *The Accidental Empire: Israel and the Birth of Settlements, 1967-1977.* New York: Times Books, 2006.

Hajjar, Lisa. "Sovereign Bodies, Sovereign States and the Problem of Torture." *Quest: An African Journal of Philosophy* 16, nos. 1-2 (2002): 108-42.

———. *Courting Conflict: The Israeli Military Court System in the West Bank and Gaza.* Berkeley: University of California Press, 2005.

Halisi, C. R. D. *Black Political Thought in the Making of South African Democracy.* Bloomington: Indiana University Press, 1999.

Halper, Jeff. *Obstacles to Peace.* 4th ed. Jerusalem: ICAHD, 2009.

Hammami, Rema, and Salim Tamari. "Towards a Second Partition: Re-thinking Forty Years of Israeli Rule." *MIT Electronic Journal of Middle East Studies,* Spring 2008, https://dome.mit.edu/bitstream/handle/1721.3/177980/MITEJMES_Vol_8_Spring2008.pdf?sequence=1.

Handel, Ariel. "Where, Where to, and When in the Occupied Territories: An Introduction to Geography of Disaster." In *The Power of Inclusive Exclusion: Anatomy of Israeli Rule in the Occupied Palestinian Territories,* edited by Adi Ophir, Michal Givoni, and Sarai Hanafi, 179-222. New York: Zone, 2009.

———. "Exclusionary Surveillance and Spatial Uncertainty in the Occupied Palestinian Territories." In *Surveillance and Control in Israel/Palestine; Population, Territory and Power,* edited by Elia Zureik, David Lyon, and Yasmeen Abu-Laban, 259-75. New York: Routledge, 2011.

———. "Gated/Gating Community: The Settlement Complex in the West Bank." *Transactions of the Institute of British Geographers,* October 2013, 504-17.

Hassassian, Manuel. "Palestinian Political Culture, Civil Society, and the Conception of Citizenship." In *Citizenship and the State in the Middle East,* edited by Nils Butenschon, Uri Davis, and Manuel Hassassian, 246-62. Syracuse, NY: Syracuse University Press, 2000.

Hobsbawm, E. J. *Primitive Rebels.* New York: Norton, 1959.

Khalidi, Rashid. *The Iron Cage: The Story of the Palestinian Struggle for Statehood.* Boston: Beacon Press, 2006.

Kimmerling, Baruch. *Zionism and Territory.* Berkeley: Institute of International Studies, 1983.

———. *The Israeli State and Society: Boundaries and Frontiers.* Albany: State University of New York Press, 1989.

Knudsen, Are, and Sari Hanafi, eds. *Palestinian Refugees: Identity, Space and Place in the Levant.* London: Routledge, 2011.

Kretzmer, David. *The Occupation of Justice: The Supreme Court of Israel and the Occupied Territories.* Albany: SUNY Press, 2002.

Kymlicka, Will. *Multicultural Citizenship: A Liberal Theory of Minority Rights.* Oxford: Clarendon, 1995.

Leon, Nissim. "The Transformation of Israel's Religious-Zionist Middle Class." *Journal of Israeli History* 29, no. 1 (March 2010): 61–78.

LeVine, Mark, and Gershon Shafir. *Struggle and Survival in Palestine/Israel.* Berkeley: University of California Press, 2012.

Levitt, Matthew. *Hamas: Politics, Charity, and Terrorism in the Service of Jihad.* New Haven, CT: Yale University Press, 2006.

Levy, Yagil. *The Divine Commander: The Theocratization of the Israeli Military.* [In Hebrew.] Tel Aviv: Am Oved, 2015.

Lijphart, Arend. *Democracy in Plural Societies.* New Haven, CT: Yale University Press, 1977.

Lustick, Ian. *For the Land and the Lord: The Range of Disagreement within Jewish Fundamentalism.* New York: Council on Foreign Relations, 1988.

———. "To Build and to Be Built By: Israel and the Hidden Logic of the Iron Wall." *Israel Studies* 1, no. 1 (Summer 1996): 196–223.

Mafole, Molefe. "The Pan Africanist Congress of Azania, 1959–1990." In Buthelezi, *South Africa,* 42–61.

Makdisi, Saree. *Palestine Inside Out: An Everyday Occupation.* New York: Norton, 2008.

Marks, Shula. "The Tradition of Non-racism in South Africa." Paper presented at the History Workshop, University of Witwatersrand, Johannesburg, July 13–15, 1994.

Matta, Nada, and René Rojas. "The Second Intifada: A Dual Strategy Arena." *European Journal of Sociology* 57, no. 1 (2016): 65–113.

Mishal, Shaul, and Avraham Sela. *The Palestinian Hamas: Vision, Violence, and Coexistence*. New York: Columbia University Press, 2006.

Motlhabi, Mokgethi. "Struggle for a Birthright: The Enduring Challenge of the Black Consciousness Movement in South Africa." In Buthelezi, *South Africa*, 62–92.

O'Dea, Janet. "Gush Emunim: Roots and Ambiguities." *Forum on the Jewish People, Zionism, and Israel* 2, no. 25 (1976): 39–50.

O'Leary, Brandan. "The Iron Law of Nationalism and Federation?" *Nations and Nationalism* 7, no. 3 (2001): 273–96.

Ophir, Adi, Michal Givoni, and Sarai Hanafi, eds. *The Power of Inclusive Exclusion: Anatomy of Israeli Rule in the Occupied Palestinian Territories*. New York: Zone, 2009.

Pappé, Ilan. "The Visible and the Invisible in the Israeli-Palestinian Conflict." In *Exile and Return: Predicaments of Palestinians and Jews*, edited by Ann M. Lesch and Ian S. Lustick, 279–96. Philadelphia, University of Pennsylvania Press, 2005.

Pedersen, Susan. *The Guardians: The League of Nations and the Crisis of Empire*. Oxford: Oxford University Press, 2015.

Peled, Yoav, and Nadim N. Rouhana. "Transitional Justice and the Right of Return of the Palestinian Refugees." *Theoretical Inquiries in Law* 5, no. 2 (July 2004): 317–32.

Podeh, Elie. *Chances for Peace: Missed Opportunities in the Arab-Israeli Conflict*. Austin: University of Texas Press, 2015.

Pundak, Ron. *Secret Channel*. [In Hebrew.] Tel Aviv: Aliyat Gag, 2013.

Puschel, Karen. *US-Israeli Strategic Cooperation in the Post-Cold War Era*. Boulder, CO: Westview, 1992.

Rabbani, Mouin. "Strategy before Solution." *Jaddaliya*, November 12, 2013, www.jadaliyya.com/pages/index/15082/co-editors-mouin-rabbani-and-noura-erakat-and-o.i.

Rabinowitz, Dan. *Overlooking Nazareth: The Ethnography of Exclusion in Galilee*. Cambridge: Cambridge University Press, 1997.

Ram, Moriel, and Mark LeVine. "The Village against the Settlement: Two Generations of Conflict in the Nablus Region." In LeVine and Shafir, *Struggle and Survival*, 318–36.

Rawls, John. "Justice as Fairness: Political Not Metaphysical." *Philosophy and Public Affairs* 14, no. 3 (Summer 1985): 223–51.

Raz, Avi. *The Bride and the Dowry: Israel, Jordan, and the Palestinians in the Aftermath of the June 1967 War.* New Haven, CT: Yale University Press, 2012.

Robinson, Glenn E. "Hamas as Social Movement." In *Islamic Activism: A Social Movement Approach*, edited by Quintan Wiktorowicz, 112–39. Bloomington: Indiana University Press, 2004.

Ron, James. *Frontiers and Ghettos: State Violence in Serbia and Israel.* Berkeley: University of California Press, 2003.

Roy, Sara. *Hamas and Civil Society in Gaza: Engaging the Islamic Social Sector.* Princeton, NJ: Princeton University Press, 2011.

Sachar, Howard M. *A History of Israel.* Vol. 2. *From the Aftermath of the Yom Kippur War.* New York: Oxford University Press, 1987.

Samy, Shahira. "Reparations to Palestinian Refugees: The Politics of Saying 'Sorry.'" In Knudsen and Hanafi, *Palestinian Refugees*, 147–61.

Sandler, Shmuel. "The National Religious Party: Towards a New Role in Israel's Political System." In *Public Life in Israel and the Diaspora*, edited by Sam N. Lehman-Wilzig and Bernard Susser, 158–70. Jerusalem: Bar-Ilan University Press, 1981.

Sasson, Talia. "Summary of the Opinion Concerning Unauthorized Outposts." Israel Ministry of Foreign Affairs, March 10, 2005. http://mfa.gov.il/MFA /AboutIsrael/State/Law/Pages/Summary%20of%20Opinion%20Concerning%20Unauthorized%20Outposts%20-%20Talya%20Sason%20Adv.aspx.

Shafir, Gershon. "Changing Nationalism and Israel's 'Open Frontier' on the West Bank." *Theory and Society* 13, no. 6 (November 1984): 803–27.

———. *Land, Labor and the Origins of the Israeli-Palestian Conflict, 1882–1914.* Cambridge: Cambridge University Press, 1989.

———. "The Jarring Mission." [In Hebrew.] In *Fifty to Forty-Eight: Critical Moments in the History of the State of Israel*, 205–13. Jerusalem: Van Leer Institute, 1999.

———. "Torturing Democracies: The Curious Debate over the 'Israeli Model.'" In *National Insecurity and Human Rights: Democracies Debate Counterterrorism*, edited by Alison Brysk and Gershon Shafir, 92–117. Berkeley: University of California Press, 2007.

———. "Israeli-Palestinian Peacemaking and Its Discontents." *Contexts* 6, no. 4 (Fall 2007): 46–51. http://icga.blogspot.com/2007/11/israeli-palestinian-peacemaking-and-its.html.

———. "Capitalist Binationalism in Mandatory Palestine." *International Journal of Middle Eastern Studies* 43 (2011): 611–33.

Shafir, Gershon, and Yoav Peled. *Being Israeli: The Dynamics of Multiple Citizenship.* Cambridge: Cambridge University Press, 2002.

Shalom, Zaki, and Yoaz Hendel. "The Unique Features of the Second Intifada." *Military and Strategic Affairs* 3, no. 1 (May 2011): 17–27.

Shamgar, Meir. "Legal Concepts and Problems of the Israeli Military Government: The Initial Stage." In *Military Government in the Territories Administered by Israel, 1967-1980: The Legal Aspects*, 13–60. Jerusalem: Harry Sacher Institute, 1982.

Shapira, Anita. *Futile Struggle: The Jewish Labor Controversy, 1929-1939.* [In Hebrew.] Tel Aviv: Hakibbutz Hameuchad, 1977.

Shapiro, Yonathan. *An Elite without Successors: Generations of Political Leaders in Israel.* [In Hebrew.] Tel Aviv: Sifriyat Hapoalim, 1984.

Sheleg, Yair. "The Next Target: The Conquest of the Media." [In Hebrew.] In *Journalists Yearbook, 1998.* Tel Aviv: Journalists Association, 1998.

Shenhav, Yehouda. "What Is the Color of Critical Theory: Reflections on Post-Westphalian Sovereignty." [In Hebrew.] *Teoriya Vebikoret*, 2009, 24–48.

Shiblak, Abbas. "Passport for What Price? Statelessness among Palestinian Refugees." In Knudsen and Hanafi, *Palestinian Refugees*, 113–28.

Smith, Charles D. *Palestine and the Arab-Israeli Conflict.* 5th ed. New York: St. Martin's, 2004.

Sprintzak, Ehud. *The Ascendance of Israel's Radical Right.* Oxford: Oxford University Press, 1991.

Swirski, Shlomo. "1967: A Political-Economic Turning Point in Israel." In *Society and Economy in Israel*, edited by Avi Bareli, 91–116. Beer Sheva: Ben Gurion University, 2005. [In Hebrew.]

Swisher, Clayton E. *The Palestine Papers: The End of the Road?* Chatham: Hesperus, 2011.

Taylor, Charles. "Shared and Divergent Values." In *Options for a New Canada*, edited by Ronald Watts and D. Brow. Toronto: Toronto University Press, 1991.

Tessler, Mark. *A History of the Israeli-Palestinian Conflict*. 2nd ed. Bloomington: Indiana University Press, 2009.

Veracini, Lorenzo. *Settler Colonialism: A Theoretical Overview*. New York: Palgrave Macmillan, 2010.

Waldman, Ayelet. "The Shame of Shuhada Street." *Atlantic*, June 24, 2014.

Waxman, Dov. *Trouble in the Tribe: The American Jewish Conflict over Israel*. Princeton, NJ: Princeton University Press, 2016.

Weizman, Eyal. *Hollow Land: Israel's Architecture of Occupation*. London: Verso, 2007.

Weizmann, Chaim. *The Letters and Papers of Chaim Weizmann*. Vol. 2, Series B. New Brunswick, NJ: Transaction, 1984.

Zacher, Mark W. "The Territorial Integrity Norm: International Boundaries and the Use of Force." *International Organization* 55, no. 2 (Spring 2001): 215-50.

Arab Revolt, 93, 103, 200
Arab Spring, 154, 208–9, 233
Arafat, Yasser, 28, 127–29, 131–33, 138, 169, 172, 202
Area A, 44, 45, 78, 79, 125
Area B, 44, 45, 78, 79
Area C, 38, 44, 45, 79, 125, 236
Ariel, 57, 170, 189, 191, 192; bloc, 119, 187–91; university in, 189, 190
Arieli, Shaul, 177, 179, 181, 185–92, 257n9
Ashrawi, Hanan, 129
Avneri, Uri, 2
Azanian Peoples Organization, 222
Azoulay, Ariella, 35, 156

Balfour Declaration, 23, 93, 159, 202–3
Bâli, Asli, 163
Barak, Aharon, 19–21, 29, 31
Barak, Ehud, 131, 132, 168, 169, 172, 242, 243
Barghouti, Omar, 214, 216–17
BDS (Boycott, Divest, Sanction) network, 7, 214–42; and antinormalization, 221–25, 236–37; campaigns of, 239; comparison with antiapartheid movement, 220–25; demands of, 216; and global civil society, 215–16; identification with antiapartheid struggle, 217–18; and nonviolence, 215–16; and rights-centeredness, 214–15; and PNA and Hamas, 215; and unification of Palestinian struggles, 216, 238–40; and one- and two-state solutions, 216–17
Begin, Menachem, 41, 59, 90, 109, 243
Beilin, Yossi, 190
Beinart, Peter, 149
Beirut, 127, 131, 175
Beitar Illit, 62, 180, 187

belligerent occupation. *See* occupation, belligerent
Ben Gurion, David, 97, 103, 243
Ben-Naftali, Orna, 156, 162
Bennett, Naftali, 115, 181
Ben-Nun, Joel, 110
Benton, Lauren, 76–78
Benvenisti, Eyal, 24, 162
Benvenisti, Meron, 177
Bethlehem, 44–45, 55, 66, 187
Biko, Steve, 223
Bil'in, 75, 216
binationalism, 7, 166, 199–203, 204, 212, 232
Birzeit University, 42, 53, 224
Black Consciousness Movement (BCM), 222–23
blockade of Gaza, 52, 80–81, 136. *See also* Gaza
Bloom, Mia, 133
British Defense Emergency Regulations, 27, 37, 160
British Mandate, 2, 23, 71, 73–74, 94, 126, 159–60, 201. *See also* mandate system
Brit Shalom, 200
B'Tselem, 28, 36, 39, 75, 196
Burston, Bradley, 53
Bush, George W., 132, 135

Camp David, 44, 99, 155, 167–68, 172–73, 234
Central Command, 113, 123, 153
checkpoints, 49–51, 79
citizenship, 13–14; absence of for Palestinians in OPT, 12, 15–16, 18, 20, 29–30, 156; and apartheid, 226–27; BDS and, 214, 235–36, 239; civic, 204, 207, 208, 241; in East Jerusalem, 17–18, 225; Fatah's view on, 202–3; imperial, 76–77; Israeli citizens as settlers, 26; Jewish, 112, 192; Middle

Eastern, 209–10; multicultural, 206; in one-state solution, 211, 212; of Palestinians of Israel, 15, 62, 97, 180, 216, 226, 231–33, 235; of Palestinian refugees, 227–30; second class, 174, 226, 239; of settlers, 92, 160; South African, 218–19, 241

Civil Administration, 42–43, 49, 64, 68–69, 74–75, 78–79, 125, 178

Clinton, Bill, 132, 168, 172

closures, 135, 144

Cold War, 42, 86, 144–46, 151–52, 164

colonialism, 25, 69, 91, 92, 58–60; British, 37; classic dilemma of, 12; colonial metropole, 91; decolonization and fear of reversibility, 160–61, 177; Gush Emunim, 105, 112; Israeli, 25, 69, 76, 91, 97–98, 157, 241; in Middle East, 209; occupation and, 76; Palestinian resistance to, 94; vs. settler colonialism, 5, 26, 76–77, 91–92, 240–41; Shamgar Doctrine as, 25, 77; in South Africa, 222

colonization. *See* settlement

compensation, 162, 191, 228–30, 232

Conference of Presidents of Major American Jewish Organizations, 148

Council of Judea, Samaria, and Gaza. *See* Yesha Council

Creasy, Sir Edward, 1

Custodian for Abandoned Property, 71–72

Custodian for Government and Abandoned Property in Judea, 69

Custodian for Government Property, 72

Dabed, Emilio, 234

Dajani, Mohammed, 224

Dalsheim, Joyce, 195

Darweish, Marwan, 46

Dayan, Moshe, 30–31, 87, 96, 103

Declaration of Principles (DOP), 19, 30, 69, 121, 124, 125, 129–31, 137, 166, 174, 176, 215, 234. *See also* Oslo peace process

decolonization, 161–62, 219

demography and population: in Area C, 79; of Ariel, 189; binationalism and, 199, 201; citizen Palestinian, 174; dispersal and concentration, 97; under Drobles Plan, 60; Druze on Golan, 16; in East Jerusalem, 18, 171; under Fatah binationalism, 202–3; in federal state, 205; Gaza population registry, 81; *haredi*, 62; Jerusalem's Jewish, 65, 155; Jerusalem's Palestinian, 16, 65, 186, 225; of Jordan Valley, 57–58, 103; in OPT, 11–12; Palestinian birth rate, 65; under UN partition plan, 101; ratio of Jews to Palestinians, 6, 18, 205–6; ratio in OPT, 178, 181; ratio to territory, 59, 101–3, 107; in settlements, 6, 55, 59, 62, 118, 170, 178–81, 184; of Yamit, 89

denialism, 13, 23, 30, 82, 120, 156, 236

Dispensationalists, 150

Doumani, Beshara, 159

Drobles Plan, 60, 102, 109

Druze, 12, 16–17, 30

Dugard, John, 156, 227

Durkheim, Emile, 47

E1, 170, 187, 188, 190

Egypt, 1–3, 23–24, 56, 80, 87–90, 99, 143–46, 152, 164, 173, 193

Eisenhower, Dwight D., 143, 147

Eizenkot, Gadi, 117

Elkins, Caroline, 91

Elon Moreh, 55, 73, 101–2

Erakat, Noura, 212–14, 226

Eshkol, Levi, 11, 12, 57

Europe, 7, 93–94, 101, 147, 208–9

Evangelicals, 150–51, 164

expulsion, 22, 27–28, 36, 91–92, 128, 208

Farsakh, Leila, 206, 224, 231, 235

Fatah, 46, 108, 121, 127–28, 132–34, 137, 202–3

Feige, Michael, 193

First Aliya, 53, 99

First Gulf War, 49, 128, 229

First Intifada, 11, 15, 19, 29, 31, 33–34, 37, 39, 42, 46, 48–49, 113, 124, 128, 133, 138, 140, 165–66, 215

Fourth Geneva Convention, 14, 20, 24, 26–27, 30, 158–59, 213; Additional Protocols, 157. *See also* international humanitarian law (IHL)

France, 1, 143, 164, 208

Fredrickson, George, 91, 122

Freedom Charter, 219, 222–23, 238

Freidman, Lara, 149

frontier, 28, 52, 56, 58, 61

Galili, Israel, 96, 103

Galili Document, 87, 189

Galili Protocol, 57

Gavron, Assaf, 63

Gaza, 2, 11, 24, 88, 119, 189, 224; absence of citizenship and curtailed human rights in, 15, 20, 141–42; as Area A, 44; blockade of, 52, 80–81, 136; colonization in, 87, 88, 195; deportation to, 19–20, 37; as enemy territory, 80; external control of, 49, 52, 84, 134; as ghetto and frontier, 28; GNP of, 33; Hamas in, 34, 36, 81, 136; Hamas and Fatah in, 52, 108, 142, 168, 209; Hamas social welfare in, 140–41; Israeli withdrawal from, 28, 52, 80, 122, 145, 155, 193–95, 234; as occupied territory, 80; population

registry, 81; resistance in, 41; Separation Wall around, 134; terror attacks, in, 87, 124, 134; UN Reports on, 52; wars in, 35, 116, 136–37, 172

Gazit, Shlomo, 33

generational analysis, 1, 9, 91, 102–4, 111, 115, 137–39, 151, 229–30, 233

Geneva Conventions, 14, 22–24, 26–27, 155, 157, 162

Geneva Initiative, 190

Gilbert, Martin, 90

Gilo, 65–66, 72

Göçek, Fatma Müge, 12

Goldstein, Baruch, 124

Gordon, Neve, 49

Gorenberg, Gershom, 57

Green Line, 10, 30, 45, 55; and BDS, 239–40; as border, 43, 49, 136, 144, 169–71, 191; and Jewish and Palestinian populations, 205–6; Palestinians employed inside, 32–33; and Seam Zone, 79; settlement blocs adjacent to, 61, 81, 102, 118, 123, 178, 180, 182; settlement blocs away from, 188–91; settlers employed outside, 191; and Separation Wall, 186; terror attacks inside, 18–19, 48, 133, 135, 196

Gross, Aeyal, 162

Gur, Motta, 113

Gush Emunim, 5, 55; and Amana, 115–16; colonization by, 58–60, 73, 101–2, 104–10; compared with Hamas, 5, 85, 108, 120–21, 124, 137–39, 163; generation of, 105, 111, 137, 138; internal division in, 109–11, 117–18, 120, 129–30, 163; messianic frontier of, 61–62; opposition to evacuation, 193–94; origins of, 58–61, 89, 104–10; and Oslo peace process, 123–24; and Peace Now, 195–96; social mobility and, 111–12, 139; and Yesha Council, 115–16

Gush Etzion, 82, 118, 181, 187–88

Hague Regulation, 14, 27, 30, 158
Haifa Declaration, 232–33
Hajjar, Lisa, 19, 162
Halper, Jeff, 185
Hamas, 5, 28, 52, 80, 85, 127–42; BDS and, 214; and collaborators, 36; compared with Gush Emunim, 5, 85, 108, 120–21, 124, 137–39; deportation of, 37; elections and, 142, 163, 168, 198; and Fatah, 52, 108, 142, 168, 209; and human rights, 141–42; opposition to Oslo peace process, 120–22, 124, 127, 129–30, 134, 142, 163; pragmatism of, 135–37, 163–64; as social movement, 137–41; strategy of, 133–34; terror attacks of, 43, 46–47, 130–31, 168; wars with, 28, 136–37; welfare network of, 140. *See also* blockade of Gaza; Gaza
Hammami, Rema, 53
Haram as-Sharif, 81, 171, 173
haredim, 61–62, 82, 105, 123, 183, 194
haredi settlements, 180, 182, 184
HCJ (High Court of Justice), 18, 20–21, 26–29, 31, 37, 39–40, 73, 75, 98, 155, 177
Hebrew Labor, 100, 221
Hebrew University, 65, 190
Hebron, 16, 37, 44–45, 50, 55, 57–58, 79, 82, 106, 124–25, 181, 211; Areas H1 and H2, 79, 125; Jewish Quarter, 57, 124; Old City, 68, 125
Histadrut, 100
Holocaust, 25, 93; deniers, 13; survivors, 94
Holy Basin, 171

Hoofnagle, Mark, 13
Hourani, Albert, 201
human rights, 13–14, 24–25, 150; BDS and, 214, 229; Hamas and, 137, 215; and IHL, 156, 162–63; and Israeli NGOs, 13, 50, 70, 80, 109, 134, 196–97; one-state solution and, 210; of Palestinians in OPT, 18–22, 30, 77, 226–27; PNA and, 141; in South Africa, 219; training in IDF, 117
Human Rights Watch, 134

Illouz, Eva, 12–13
International Committee of the Red Cross (ICRC), 14, 25, 81
International Court of Justice (ICJ), 14, 20, 25
international humanitarian law (IHL)/ law of armed conflict, 14, 24; European origin of, 164; Hamas and, 137; Israeli interpretation of, 21–27, 29–30, 31, 77, 90, 154, 156, 160; land seizure and, 72; occupation and, 76, 86, 98, 154–58, 162; and protection offers to Palestinians in OPT, 19, 22–30, 77, 80, 160, 164, 166, 226, 236; reform of, 162–63; and settlement, 82; and sovereignty, 14, 21–22, 156–60. *See also* Geneva Conventions; Hague Regulation; occupation, belligerent
intifadas, 19, 35–37, 41–44, 48, 78, 138, 235. *See also* First Intifada; Second Intifada
Iraq, 10, 47, 128, 134, 158–59, 204
Islamic Jihad, 37, 46, 133–34, 138, 141
Israeli Civil Administration, 140
Israeli Committee against House Demolitions (ICAHD), 37–38, 185
Israeli Defense Forces (IDF), 105, 114, 116–17

Ramallah, 42, 44–45, 49, 55, 66, 187, 224, 234

Rawls, John, 206

Reagan, Ronald, 131, 146, 149

Refugee Convention (1951), 228–29

refugees, 15, 92; in Arab Peace Initiative (API), 175; BDS and, 216, 227; camps, Palestinian, 17, 35, 88, 138, 148, 161–62, 196, 215, 224; compensation of and reparations for, 212–13, 227–31, 232; individual rights of, 227–30; Jewish, 92–95, 101, 147, 212; and leadership of Palestinian national movement, 231; Palestinian, 15, 68, 212, 227–31, 241; Palestinian, as humanitarian issue, 145, 159, 214; in peace talks, 170, 172–73, 186, 234–35; PLO and, 234–35; return of, 72, 143, 230, 232; right of return of, 136, 167, 216, 239; settlers as, 92, 95; UN and, 227–28

religious Zionism/Zionists, 9, 81, 197; educational institutions of, 105, 113–14; generational dynamics of, 104–5, 139; and IDF, 112–13; impact of on Israeli society, 111–16; internal divisions of, 117–18; leaders of, 57, 113, 114; limits to appeal of, 108–9, 139; and *mamlachtiyut*, 109, 117–18, 194, 198; and media, 114–15; messianic beliefs of, 59; and opposition to evacuation, 182, 193–95; and Oslo peace process, 125–26; and settlement, 57, 58, 60, 116, 127, 163, 180, 187, 236; settlers, evacuation of, 198; and social mobility, 111–12, 139, 233; and violence, 110–11, 118–19, 130; and voting, 182–184. *See also* Gush Emunim; Jewish Home Party

resistance, 12, 30, 37, 41–48; civil, 194; and diplomacy, 11, 44; impact of, 49,

78; nonviolent, 28–29, 42; to occupation, 4, 11, 35; movements, 43, 216; passive, 194; tactics, 134, 214; violent, 41–42, 235. *See also* First Intifada; Second Intifada; suicide bombings; terror attacks

Rigby, Andrew, 46

rights. *See* citizenship; human rights

Road Map (of George W. Bush), 135

roads, 50, 61, 63, 72, 79, 118, 123, 162, 181, 185, 186, 201, 241–42

Robinson, Glenn, 137

Ron, Jim, 27

Rouhana, Nadim, 230

Ruppin, Arthur, 54

Sabra and Shatila refugee camp massacres, 148, 196

Sadan, Eli, 113

Sadat, Anwar, 89–90

Saddam Hussein, 44, 128

Said, Edward, 224

Samaria, 23, 58, 60, 69, 75, 101, 104, 116, 120, 170

Sasson Report, 74–75

Saudi Arabia, 171

Second Aliya, 54, 99, 106, 221

Second Intifada (al-Aqsa Intifada), 11, 15, 19, 29, 35, 37, 46, 48, 49, 51, 62, 131–33, 140, 158, 176, 185, 193, 221, 235

Second World War, 13, 24–25, 78, 93–94, 101, 147

Security Council, 22, 162; Resolution 242, 23, 89, 144; US votes and vetoes in 149, 153, 164

self-determination, 4, 24–25, 30, 121, 158, 174, 216, 218, 232, 238

Separation Wall, 17, 45, 50, 78–80, 83, 134–35, 155, 178, 186–88, 212, 216, 218, 224, 227

Temple Mount, 46, 81, 171, 173
territorial contiguity, 46, 79, 170, 188, 190, 191
territorial exchange, 7, 119, 167, 170, 173, 175–76, 182, 189–91, 205, 213
territorial integrity norm, 78, 145
territorial partition, 2, 6–8, 59, 95, 100, 102, 107, 121–22, 166–67, 170–71, 175–77, 185, 186, 189, 192, 195, 197–98, 203, 205, 213
territorial withdrawal, 12, 56, 83, 124–25, 135, 144–46, 238; feasibility of, 176, 192; from Gaza, 28, 155; opposition to, 58, 123, 125, 135, 138, 192–93; in OPT, 122, 124–25, 167, 170, 175, 187, 188, 192, 238; from Sinai, 3, 56, 89, 138, 146. *See also* two-state solution
terror attacks, 129–30, 135; definition of, 130, 137, 166; by Hamas, 131–34, 141; Jewish, 110; and Second Intifada 48, 131, 221; suspects, 46; timing of 130–31; and torture, 29, 39–41; on US, 151. *See also* knife attacks; suicide bombings
Third Aliya, 103
Third Temple, 81, 110
torture and physical pressure, 28–29, 35, 39–41
Truman, Harry, 143
Turkey, 158, 208–9
two-state solution, 21, 148, 153, 177, 197–98, 213, 217, 241. *See also* territorial partition

United Nations Commission on Human Rights, 156, 162, 227
United Nations Conciliation Commission for Palestine (UNCCP), 227
United Nations High Commission for Refugees (UNHCR), 228

United Nations Human Rights Council, 52, 162
United Nations Refugee Welfare Agency (UNRWA0), 228, 234
United Nations Special Committee on Palestine (UNSCOP), 94
United States, 209, 216, 218; and BDS, 216, 239; Jews in, 94, 147, 149; as settler colony, 240–41; special relationship, 6, 86, 143, 150, 152, 164; US-Israeli relations, 142–54; US-mediated peace plans, 89, 128, 171–72, 234

Veracini, Lorenzo, 91–92, 95
violence, 11–12, 29, 33–41, 43–44, 46, 62, 82, 108, 109–10, 131–35, 140–42, 168, 215. *See also* resistance; terror attacks

Walt, Stephen, 149
Walter, Barbara, 131
waqf, 34, 139, 171
War Refugee Board, 147
Waxman, Dov, 148
Weizman, Eyal, 54, 155
Winter, Ofer, 116
Wolfe, Patrick, 91, 101
World Zionist Organization (WZO), 60, 69–70, 93, 96–97, 100, 233
Wye Plantation Accord, 125

Ya'alon, Moshe, 64
Yesha, 120
Yesha Council, 60, 116, 123, 125
yeshiva, 105, 111, 112–13, 116, 195; Merkaz Harav Yeshiva, 105, 113; preparatory, 113–17; *yeshivot hakav*, 117, 194
Yishuv, 23, 32, 86, 90, 92, 94, 96, 99, 107, 112, 160, 191

Zionist Camp Party. *See* Labor Party